I0008283

APPLE M4 PRO MAC MINI USER GUIDE 2025

A Step-by-Step Manual to Master macOS Sequoia: Pro Tips and Tricks, Setup, Advanced Features, Shortcuts, Troubleshooting, and Apple Intelligence for Your Desktop

STANLEY R.D TEACHINGS

Copyright Notice

© 2025 Stanley R.D Teachings. All rights reserved. This guide is copyrighted and may not be reproduced, distributed, or transmitted in any form or by any means, including photocopying, recording, or other electronic or mechanical methods, without the prior written permission of the copyright holder, except in the case of brief quotations embodied in critical reviews or articles.

Disclaimer

The information provided in this **Apple M4 Pro Mac mini User Guide** is for educational purposes only. The author and publisher have made every effort to ensure the accuracy of the content, but make no representations or warranties regarding the completeness, accuracy, or reliability of the information contained herein.

This guide is an independent publication and is not affiliated with or endorsed by Apple Inc. in any way.

The author is not responsible for any changes made to the Mac mini or macOS software after publication. Users are encouraged to consult the official Apple website or customer support for the most up-to-date information regarding the Apple M4 Pro Mac mini.

All trademarks, service marks, and product names mentioned in this guide are the property of their respective owners. Apple Inc. and macOS are trademarks of Apple Inc.

TABLE OF CONTENTS

CONFIGURING MACOS AND SYSTEM PREFERENCES

INTRODUCTION

Purpose of This Guide

Welcome to the ultimate guide for the **Apple M4 Pro Mac mini**. If you've recently purchased this powerful machine or are considering it, you're in the right place to unlock its full potential. Whether you're a first-time Mac user or an experienced professional, this guide is crafted to meet your needs at every stage, from setup to advanced usage and troubleshooting.

A Guide That Grows With You

The **Apple M4 Pro Mac mini** is a sleek, compact powerhouse, packing cutting-edge technology into a small, efficient package. With the M4 Pro chip, a 20-core GPU, and the smooth and intuitive **macOS Sequoia**, it opens up new possibilities for everything from creative workflows to business productivity. But with all that power, it can feel overwhelming at first. That's where this guide comes in.

This guide is more than just a manual—it's your personal companion in getting the most out of your Mac mini. It's here to help you understand every feature, from basic setup to the advanced tweaks that make this machine so extraordinary. You'll learn not only how to set it up and connect all your devices but also how to customize and optimize it to fit your needs perfectly.

Whether you're editing high-resolution videos, writing code, or managing a large database, we'll show you how to tailor your Mac mini to your unique workflow.

For Beginners: No Need to Be Intimidated

If you're new to the Apple ecosystem or making the leap from another operating system, this guide will be your safe, approachable starting point. We recognize that the transition to macOS can feel like a bit of a learning curve, especially when you're used to other platforms. However, we've designed this guide with that in mind.

We'll walk you through every essential step, from unboxing your Mac mini to getting familiar with macOS Sequoia's unique features. We'll cover every part of the setup process, with simple, easy-to-follow instructions. No more confusion about how to connect a monitor, how to set up Wi-Fi, or how to organize your desktop. We've broken everything down into manageable steps, using plain language, so that even if you're new to Mac, you'll feel confident navigating your way around.

This guide will give you the confidence to explore all the features that come with your Mac mini, from basic everyday use to more specialized functions. We'll explain all the essential macOS tools, shortcuts, and settings in a way that anyone can understand.

For Experienced Users: Maximize Your Efficiency

For seasoned Mac users or those who are already comfortable with other Apple products, we know you're looking for more than just the basics. You want to get straight to the advanced features, tweaks, and customizations that make the **M4 Pro Mac mini** an ideal machine for power users.

If you're using your Mac mini for professional tasks like 4K video editing, 3D modeling, or software development, this guide will help you unlock its full potential. You'll learn how to configure your system for maximum performance, manage your system resources, and take advantage of all the specialized tools macOS has to offer.

We'll dive into macOS Sequoia's hidden features, advanced multitasking tips, and how to use the GPU and CPU to handle resource-intensive tasks. You'll also find valuable advice on security settings, integrating external devices, and setting up multi-monitor configurations that will enhance your workflow.

Even if you've been using Macs for years, there are always new tips and tricks to discover, especially with the power of the **M4 Pro chip** at your fingertips. Our goal is to ensure that whether you're using your Mac mini for work, play, or creative endeavors, you have everything you need to take full advantage of this powerful machine.

A Step-by-Step Approach to Troubleshooting

One of the most important aspects of any great guide is troubleshooting, and we've got you covered here as well. Problems can arise, and it's natural to feel frustrated when things don't work the way you expect them to. However, this guide isn't just about setup; it's also about providing solutions when things go wrong.

We understand that every user's experience is unique. That's why we've included detailed troubleshooting steps for common issues, so you can quickly identify and resolve problems without having to search through long, technical manuals. Whether it's a connectivity issue, an application not performing as expected, or a system error, we provide easy-to-follow solutions designed to get your Mac mini back up and running in no time.

Plus, we'll offer advice on how to maintain your Mac mini and prevent common issues from cropping up in the first place. By the end of this guide, you'll feel empowered to handle any situation with ease.

Your Go-To Resource for Lifelong Learning

The world of technology is constantly evolving, and so is macOS. This guide will not only help you get started but will also serve as an ongoing resource. We've organized it in a way that makes it easy to return to whenever you need to reference something specific—whether that's how to perform a system update, configure a new external device, or dive deep into a specialized task like video editing or coding.

As you grow more comfortable with your Mac mini, this guide will evolve with you, offering new tips and tools to keep you at the top of your game. We'll highlight key updates as they happen and make sure you're always in the loop with new features and best practices.

Overview of the Mac mini M4 Pro

The Apple M4 Pro Mac mini is an extraordinary leap forward in compact desktop computing. Built to harness the power of Apple's advanced M4 Pro chip, this device combines raw performance with sleek, space-saving design to meet the needs of both creative professionals and power users alike. Whether you're a video editor, software developer, or someone who demands top-tier performance from a compact system, the Mac mini M4 Pro delivers.

At the heart of this Mac mini is the Apple M4 Pro chip, a system-on-a-chip (SoC) that marks a significant evolution from its predecessors. This chip features a 14-core CPU, offering 10 high-performance cores and 4 efficiency cores. The result is a balanced powerhouse, capable of handling everything from everyday tasks to complex computational workloads. Coupled with the 20-core GPU, the M4 Pro Mac mini takes graphics processing to a whole new level, delivering exceptional power for demanding applications like 3D rendering, video editing, and gaming.

But the performance doesn't end there. The Mac mini M4 Pro is powered by macOS Sequoia, Apple's latest operating system, which enhances the user experience by seamlessly integrating hardware and software. This operating system offers faster performance, better energy efficiency, and smart features that adapt to how you work. With support for AI-driven tools, advanced Siri features, and a variety of productivity enhancements, macOS Sequoia ensures that users can work smarter, not harder.

Let's break down the key features that make the Mac mini M4 Pro stand out:

1. M4 Pro Chip – Power at Your Fingertips

The M4 Pro chip is where the magic happens. It offers groundbreaking performance thanks to its 14-core CPU and 20-core GPU. The high-performance cores are perfect for tasks that require a lot of power, such as video editing, software development, or handling large datasets. Meanwhile, the efficiency cores take care of lighter tasks, ensuring that the Mac mini runs efficiently without using excessive energy.

- **For Creatives**: The M4 Pro chip's GPU can handle demanding tasks like video rendering, animation, and 3D design without breaking a sweat. Whether you're working with Final Cut Pro, Adobe Premiere, or Blender, the Mac mini M4 Pro will provide the smoothest, most efficient experience possible.

APPLE M4 PRO MAC MINI USER GUIDE

- **For Developers**: With its multi-core capabilities, the M4 Pro chip speeds up coding and running software, allowing developers to test their apps faster and work on complex projects without delay.

2. 20-Core GPU – Graphics Like Never Before

Apple's M4 Pro chip comes with a 20-core GPU, making the Mac mini M4 Pro an ideal choice for anyone working with high-resolution visuals. If you're into gaming, video editing, or graphic design, this GPU handles everything from basic tasks to the most complex graphics with ease. The power it offers is unparalleled for a machine this size, ensuring that users can enjoy a seamless experience with even the most demanding software.

- **For Creatives**: Designers and video editors will love the GPU's ability to render high-quality visuals in real-time. Whether you're creating digital art or editing 8K video, this GPU will make sure every frame is rendered with perfect precision.

- **For Professionals**: The GPU allows for smooth, lag-free experiences when running resource-heavy applications like CAD software, scientific simulations, and more. This means professionals in fields like engineering, architecture, or scientific research can get their work done without worrying about performance issues.

3. macOS Sequoia – The Heart of the Experience

The Mac mini M4 Pro runs on macOS Sequoia, which is specifically designed to unlock the full potential of Apple's hardware. This latest version of macOS brings a host of performance optimizations, better power management, and smarter AI-driven features that make multitasking a breeze. The integration between macOS and the M4 Pro chip ensures that you get the best possible performance with smooth transitions between apps, minimized delays, and optimized battery life.

- **For Creatives**: macOS Sequoia is optimized for creative professionals, with built-in features that enhance workflows, such as the improved Final Cut Pro X and enhanced support for Adobe apps. The operating system also provides better hardware acceleration for rendering tasks, meaning your creative projects come to life faster than ever before.

- **For Professionals**: Seamless integration with other Apple devices ensures that your work is always synced and available across devices. Whether you're working on a MacBook Pro at home or your Mac mini M4 Pro at the office, your projects will be easily accessible and up-to-date.

4. Ultra-Fast Storage and Memory

With support for up to 64GB of unified memory and high-speed SSD storage options, the Mac mini M4 Pro handles multitasking and large files with ease. Its unified memory allows the CPU and GPU to access the same pool of memory, improving performance and reducing bottlenecks. This is especially important for memory-intensive tasks like video editing, 3D modeling, and running virtual machines.

- **For Creatives**: The fast storage means quicker file access, allowing creative professionals to load large assets, such as video clips, images, and 3D models, almost instantaneously. Whether you're editing a large video project or working with high-resolution textures, you won't waste time waiting for files to load.

- **For Developers**: Developers who work with large codebases, databases, or virtual environments will appreciate the speed at which their projects load and run. Whether running Docker containers, virtual machines, or compiling code, the Mac mini M4 Pro's memory and storage ensure that the workflow remains smooth and responsive.

5. Connectivity and Ports – Plug and Play with Ease

The Mac mini M4 Pro comes with an array of connectivity options to ensure seamless integration with all your devices. It features multiple Thunderbolt 5 ports, USB-C, HDMI, and a 10Gb Ethernet option for ultra-fast networking. This wide range of connectivity allows users to connect external storage devices, multiple monitors, and other peripherals without any hassle.

- **For Creatives**: Connecting multiple high-resolution monitors and external storage drives is simple and efficient, thanks to the Thunderbolt 5 ports. You can easily set up a multi-display workstation for video editing or digital design, and connect fast external drives to store and edit large media files.

- **For Professionals**: Professionals can rely on the Mac mini M4 Pro's versatile ports to hook up multiple devices, whether it's for conducting virtual meetings with high-definition webcams or connecting to complex workstations in the office.

6. The Compact Powerhouse

Despite its powerful features, the Mac mini M4 Pro remains compact and sleek, making it an ideal solution for users who need high performance but have limited desk space. Its minimalistic design ensures that it can be placed easily on any desk or workstation without taking up too much room.

- **For Creatives**: The portability and compact nature of the Mac mini make it easy to take it to different workspaces, whether at home, in a studio, or on the go. Its small footprint doesn't sacrifice performance, meaning you get a powerful creative workstation without the bulky design.

- **For Professionals**: With its space-saving design, the Mac mini M4 Pro fits neatly in any professional setting. It's easy to set up a multi-screen workstation without clutter, keeping your workspace clean and organized while handling all your computing needs.

Who Can Benefit from the Mac mini M4 Pro?

The Apple M4 Pro Mac mini is ideal for a wide range of users:

- **Creative Professionals**: Whether you're editing video, designing graphics, or creating animations, the M4 Pro Mac mini delivers the power and speed necessary to tackle even the most demanding projects.

APPLE M4 PRO MAC MINI USER GUIDE

- **Software Developers**: Developers who need to run multiple virtual environments or work on large projects will find the M4 Pro's CPU and memory management to be a huge asset.

- **Business Professionals**: From seamless multitasking to smooth video conferencing, the Mac mini M4 Pro provides a reliable and efficient desktop for professionals across industries.

- **Power Users**: Whether you're into gaming, 3D rendering, or scientific computing, the Mac mini M4 Pro offers unmatched power and customization options to suit your high-performance needs.

In conclusion, the Apple M4 Pro Mac mini is a device built for those who need power, efficiency, and versatility in a compact form. From creative professionals working on high-resolution graphics to developers building complex applications, the Mac mini M4 Pro is designed to meet the needs of today's most demanding users. With its M4 Pro chip, stunning GPU, macOS Sequoia, and extensive connectivity options, it delivers an unparalleled experience that's only going to get better with each software update.

What's Included in the Box

When you unbox your Apple M4 Pro Mac mini, you're greeted with not only the powerhouse machine itself but also a carefully organized set of components designed to get you started right out of the box. Apple takes great care in packaging its products, ensuring that everything you need is included for a seamless setup experience. Here's what you'll find inside:

1. The Mac mini M4 Pro

The star of the show! Inside the box, you'll find the Mac mini M4 Pro, a sleek, compact powerhouse designed for a range of professional and personal uses. The M4 Pro chip, combined with its 20-core GPU and high-performance CPU, makes this little desktop a serious contender for anyone in need of serious computing power. It's lighter than you might expect and comes with a matte finish that feels premium to the touch. The Mac mini has been built to offer incredible performance while taking up minimal desk space, and it does just that.

- **What You'll Love**: The small footprint but big capabilities. It's surprisingly compact for the sheer power it delivers.

2. Power Cable

Alongside your Mac mini, you'll find a neatly coiled power cable. It's a straightforward component, but don't underestimate its importance. This cable is specifically designed for the Mac mini M4 Pro's power requirements, ensuring safe and reliable operation. The cable connects directly to the power port on the back of the Mac mini.

- **What You'll Love**: It's long enough to provide flexibility in positioning the Mac mini on your desk, but not so long that it gets tangled easily. A small but well-thought-out detail from Apple.

3. Apple Manual

While the Mac mini is designed to be easy to set up, Apple still includes a user manual to guide you through the basics. The manual provides quick instructions on how to connect your Mac mini to a monitor, keyboard, mouse, and other peripherals. It also highlights key setup steps, like connecting to Wi-Fi and signing into your Apple ID. While the manual doesn't go into heavy technical details, it's a helpful starting point for first-time users or anyone who needs a refresher.

- **What You'll Love**: The manual is short and sweet—easy to skim through for the basics, with clear images showing what ports to use and what goes where.

4. Warranty and Regulatory Information

Along with the user manual, you'll also receive Apple's warranty information and regulatory documents. These are important for keeping track of your product's warranty coverage and ensuring compliance with local laws regarding the device's use. If you ever need to make a warranty claim or figure out how to get your device repaired, this is the paperwork you'll refer to.

- **What You'll Love**: While these documents aren't exactly the most exciting to read, having them in the box ensures that you're aware of your rights as an Apple customer. Plus, Apple's customer support is top-notch, should you ever need it.

5. Apple Stickers

If you've ever purchased an Apple product before, you know about the iconic Apple stickers. Included in the Mac mini box are two sleek white Apple stickers. You can stick them on your laptop, water bottle, or any other place where you want to show off your love for Apple. They're a fun, little touch that adds some personality to the unboxing experience.

- **What You'll Love**: It's the small things, right? These stickers make you feel like part of the Apple family and are a fun bonus to receive with your purchase.

6. USB-C to Thunderbolt Cable

The Mac mini M4 Pro comes equipped with Thunderbolt 5 ports, and Apple includes a USB-C to Thunderbolt cable for your convenience. This cable is used for connecting external monitors, storage drives, or other peripherals that require fast data transfer. Thunderbolt 5 is lightning-fast and supports up to three 6K displays, so you're already set to create a powerhouse workstation right out of the box.

- **What You'll Love**: The cable is sturdy and flexible, with a premium feel. It's the perfect length to start connecting peripherals without having to immediately look for an extension cord.

7. Ethernet Cable (Optional, Depending on Configuration)

In some configurations, especially those with higher-end setups, Apple might include an Ethernet cable in the box. This cable is useful if you're connecting the Mac mini to a wired network, providing a faster, more reliable internet connection compared to Wi-Fi. It's an optional addition, so not all Mac mini boxes will have it, but it's certainly appreciated by those who need it.

- **What You'll Love**: Having the Ethernet cable right in the box saves you the hassle of going out to buy one if you need it for wired internet. It's the small touches like this that make setup smoother.

8. HDMI to Display Cable (Optional)

For users connecting their Mac mini to a display via HDMI, Apple might also include an HDMI cable in the box, depending on the configuration. This cable allows you to connect the Mac mini directly to your monitor or TV for a simple, hassle-free connection. It's an easy and straightforward way to get your system up and running without additional purchases.

- **What You'll Love**: If you're new to setting up a Mac mini, this cable removes the guesswork. It's just one less thing to worry about during your setup.

9. VESA Mount Adapter (Optional)

If you're planning to mount your Mac mini to the back of a monitor, the box may also include a VESA mount adapter (depending on the configuration). This accessory helps you secure the Mac mini to the VESA-compatible mount behind your display, creating a cleaner, more streamlined workspace. It's especially useful for those looking to create a minimal desk setup.

- **What You'll Love**: The adapter allows you to use your Mac mini in creative ways, freeing up desk space while keeping everything neat and tidy.

In Summary

The Apple M4 Pro Mac mini box includes everything you need to set up your device and get started with your new setup. From the Mac mini itself to essential accessories like the power cable, manual, USB-C to Thunderbolt cable, and even the fun Apple stickers, Apple ensures you're equipped to dive right into the world of macOS. With thoughtful additions like the Ethernet cable and VESA mount adapter (for certain configurations), Apple shows their commitment to providing a smooth and enjoyable user experience from the moment you open the box.

So, when you're unboxing your new Mac mini M4 Pro, take a moment to appreciate the simplicity and convenience of each included item—it's all part of the Apple experience.

System Requirements for the Apple M4 Pro Mac mini

When you bring home your new Apple M4 Pro Mac mini, it's exciting to imagine all the amazing things you'll be able to do with it. However, before diving into all the power it offers, it's important to ensure that your setup meets the necessary system requirements. This will help ensure that your Mac mini runs efficiently, providing the best possible experience from the moment you switch it on.

APPLE M4 PRO MAC MINI USER GUIDE

In this section, we'll go over everything you need to know about the system requirements for the Mac mini M4 Pro. From macOS versions to internet connectivity and compatible peripherals, let's make sure your Mac mini is ready to perform at its peak.

1. Operating System: macOS Sequoia

The Apple M4 Pro Mac mini comes pre-installed with **macOS Sequoia**, the latest version of Apple's powerful operating system. macOS Sequoia brings new features, security improvements, and optimized performance that makes the most of the M4 Pro chip's capabilities. This operating system is designed to take full advantage of the Apple M4 Pro's hardware, including its multi-core processor and advanced GPU.

- **macOS Version**: To run your Mac mini M4 Pro effectively, you must be using **macOS Sequoia**. Make sure to update your system regularly to ensure you're getting the latest performance improvements, bug fixes, and security patches.

- **Automatic Updates**: It's recommended that you enable automatic updates on your Mac mini. This ensures that your system is always up-to-date with the latest macOS features and security fixes, keeping it running smoothly and securely.

2. Internet Connection

To set up your Mac mini and get the most out of it, a stable internet connection is essential. While the Mac mini M4 Pro is a desktop computer, it heavily relies on internet connectivity for:

- **macOS Updates**: Updates to macOS, including system patches and security updates, require an active internet connection to download and install.

- **iCloud Syncing**: iCloud is Apple's cloud storage service that seamlessly syncs your files, photos, emails, and more across all your Apple devices. Having an internet connection is vital for syncing your files and ensuring that everything stays updated across your devices.

- **App Downloads from the Mac App Store**: While the Mac mini M4 Pro comes with a set of pre-installed apps, you'll likely want to download additional software. Whether it's professional tools like Final Cut Pro or productivity apps like Microsoft Office, you'll need an internet connection to download and install apps from the Mac App Store.

- **Web Browsing and Online Services**: Of course, browsing the internet and accessing online services like streaming, video conferencing, and cloud-based software requires an internet connection.

- **Wi-Fi**: The Mac mini M4 Pro comes with built-in Wi-Fi. Ensure that your home or office Wi-Fi is stable and fast enough to handle heavy usage. A **Wi-Fi 6** router is recommended for optimal performance, especially when you're transferring large files or streaming content.

- **Ethernet**: If you prefer a wired connection, the Mac mini M4 Pro also comes with a **Gigabit Ethernet port**, which supports high-speed

APPLE M4 PRO MAC MINI USER GUIDE

internet connections. If you have access to a **10Gb Ethernet** network, the Mac mini M4 Pro can be configured to take advantage of this faster connection, ideal for high-bandwidth tasks such as video editing and large file transfers.

3. Compatible Peripherals

While the Mac mini M4 Pro is an incredibly powerful machine in itself, you'll likely want to pair it with some essential peripherals for a complete setup. Let's take a look at the key peripherals and their compatibility:

- **Display**: The Mac mini M4 Pro supports up to **three 6K displays** through its Thunderbolt and HDMI ports. Whether you're using one monitor or multiple, it's important to make sure your display(s) are compatible with the Mac mini's output. For the best experience, choose a **4K or 5K** display, especially if you're into video editing, 3D modeling, or gaming.

  - **Thunderbolt 5 Ports**: These ports support fast data transfer rates, so if you're connecting high-performance monitors or external drives, you'll benefit from the speed they offer.

  - **HDMI**: The Mac mini also supports **HDMI 2.1**, which is perfect for connecting 4K monitors or TVs, providing crisp and clear visuals.

- **Keyboard and Mouse**: You'll need a **Bluetooth keyboard and mouse** to interact with your Mac mini. Apple's **Magic Keyboard** and **Magic Mouse 2** are compatible and provide seamless integration with the Mac mini M4 Pro. However, you can also use third-party Bluetooth keyboards and mice if you have preferences for other brands.

- o If you prefer a wired setup, you can also connect a **USB keyboard and mouse** to the Mac mini's available ports.

- **External Storage**: If you're dealing with large files—whether you're a creative professional working with 4K video footage or a developer dealing with big data—an external hard drive or SSD will be essential for additional storage.

  - o The Mac mini M4 Pro has multiple **USB-C** and **Thunderbolt 5** ports, making it easy to connect high-speed external storage devices. Consider investing in a **Thunderbolt SSD** for maximum data transfer speeds, especially if you're working with large files or performing tasks that demand fast read/write speeds.

- **Headphones and Audio Equipment**: The Mac mini M4 Pro has a **3.5mm headphone jack** and also supports **Bluetooth audio devices**. If you need better sound quality, you can connect high-end headphones, speakers, or audio equipment to the Mac mini. For professionals working with audio, the Mac mini is compatible with many USB or Thunderbolt-based audio interfaces, offering advanced sound capabilities.

- **Webcam and Microphone**: For video conferencing or content creation, you might need a **webcam** or **external microphone**. While the Mac mini doesn't come with a built-in camera, it supports external webcams through USB or Thunderbolt connections. There are plenty of **4K webcams** on the market that will work perfectly with your Mac mini.

- **Printers and Scanners**: If you plan to use a printer or scanner, the Mac mini M4 Pro supports many models via **USB-C** or **Wi-Fi**. You can also connect printers and scanners that support AirPrint or use third-party software for compatibility with older models.

4. Optional Accessories to Enhance Your Experience

While the basic system requirements will get your Mac mini up and running, there are several **optional accessories** that can enhance your overall experience, whether you're a creative professional, developer, or power user.

- **Apple Studio Display or Pro Display XDR**: For those looking for high-quality displays, Apple's **Studio Display** or **Pro Display XDR** is a perfect match for the Mac mini M4 Pro. These monitors deliver stunning visuals, with accurate colors and high resolutions, ideal for video editing, graphic design, and photography.

- **Magic Trackpad**: If you prefer a touch-based interface for more precision while working, the **Magic Trackpad** is a great addition. It offers multi-touch gestures, which make navigating macOS even easier and more intuitive.

- **Apple AirPods**: For wireless audio, **AirPods** or **AirPods Pro** are excellent companions for the Mac mini. With seamless integration via Bluetooth, you can easily switch between your Mac mini and other Apple devices like your iPhone or iPad without the hassle of pairing.

- **Docking Stations**: If you're connecting multiple peripherals to your Mac mini, a **Thunderbolt docking station** can make life much easier. These docks provide extra ports, including HDMI, USB, and Ethernet, helping you streamline your setup and reduce cable clutter.

- **External GPU (eGPU)**: While the Mac mini M4 Pro is already equipped with a powerful 20-core GPU, some users working with extremely demanding graphic applications, such as 3D rendering or gaming, may choose to invest in an **eGPU**. This external GPU can give you additional graphical power, particularly if you're using an ultra-high-resolution display or doing intensive creative work.

GETTING STARTED

Unboxing and Identifying Components

Unboxing a new piece of technology is always an exciting experience. Whether it's your first Mac mini or an upgrade to the powerful M4 Pro version, the unboxing process should feel like stepping into a world of endless possibilities. In this section, we'll guide you step-by-step through the unboxing of the Apple Mac mini M4 Pro, showing you everything included in the box, and offering some tips and safety precautions to ensure that everything goes smoothly as you get started.

Step 1: Preparing for Unboxing

Before you start tearing into the packaging, it's always a good idea to prepare your space. Find a flat, clean surface where you can comfortably open the box. A table or desk works best, ensuring there's plenty of room for the Mac mini and all its components.

- **Safety Tip**: Make sure the area is free from sharp objects or liquids. If you're opening the box near any other electronics, ensure there's no risk of spilling something on your new Mac mini.

- **Hand Protection**: If you have long nails or rough hands, be mindful while handling the packaging. Gently cut or remove any tape and avoid using excessive force that could damage the box or the components inside.

Step 2: Opening the Box

Now that you've got your space set up, it's time to open the box. The Mac mini comes in a sturdy, well-designed Apple box that's easy to open. Simply lift the top flap, and you'll be greeted with the sleek Apple packaging that holds everything in place.

- **Tip**: Apple uses a "no-frills" packing design, but everything is snugly placed to avoid movement during shipping. This ensures that your Mac mini is safe and secure.

- **Note**: Keep the box in case you need to return or exchange your Mac mini for any reason, as it's the best way to ensure safe transport.

Step 3: Identifying the Main Components

Once you've opened the box, you'll see the components neatly organized. Let's walk through each item you'll find inside:

1. **Apple Mac mini M4 Pro (The Star of the Show)** The Mac mini itself is the first thing you'll see. It's compact, stylish, and packed with power. Carefully lift the Mac mini out of the box. Hold it from the edges or the base to avoid leaving fingerprints on the surface. The Mac mini is surprisingly light for its performance capabilities, but it's always good to handle it with care.

o **Tip**: Apple uses a protective plastic wrap around the Mac mini to prevent scratches. Keep it on during the initial setup to protect the surface until you're ready to place it on your desk or workspace.

o **Important**: Do not lift the Mac mini by the ports or cables; always hold it from the edges or the base.

2. **Power Cable**

Next, you'll find a power cable, which is essential to power up your Mac mini. The cable is designed to be compatible with the Mac mini's power port, and it's surprisingly long, allowing for easy connections from your desk to the nearest power outlet.

o **Tip**: Inspect the power cable for any visible damage before use. The cable is durable, but it's good practice to make sure it's in pristine condition.

3. **Apple   Manual   and   Quick   Start   Guide**

Alongside the Mac mini and power cable, you'll find the Apple manual and quick start guide. Apple's documentation is clean, clear, and easy to follow. Don't expect a thick, overly technical manual – Apple prefers simplicity.

o **Important**: Take some time to glance through the Quick Start Guide. It gives you an overview of the Mac mini's key features, including how to set it up, basic troubleshooting, and important safety tips.

4. **Apple Stickers**

   As with most Apple products, you'll find a set of Apple stickers inside the box. These small but iconic stickers are a fun bonus, and many Mac users like to place them on their laptops, water bottles, or any other surface they want to show their Apple pride.

   o **Fun Tip**: If you're not sure where to stick them yet, hold on to them for a while – they might come in handy to add a personal touch to your gear.

Step 4: Removing Protective Packaging

After identifying the components, you'll want to carefully remove the protective packaging around the Mac mini. Apple uses a combination of plastic wrap and foam to keep your new device safe during shipping.

- **Tip**: Gently peel back the protective plastic from the Mac mini. Don't rush this step to avoid accidentally scratching the surface. Take care to also remove any foam or paper that might be packed around the power cable or the manual.

- **Safety Tip**: Always dispose of packing materials responsibly. The plastic wrap and foam should be recycled properly, as they can be harmful to the environment if discarded incorrectly.

Step 5: Safety Precautions and Handling Tips

While the Mac mini M4 Pro is designed to be a sturdy and reliable piece of equipment, there are some important safety precautions to take during the unboxing and initial handling phase:

APPLE M4 PRO MAC MINI USER GUIDE

1. **Avoid Static Damage**

   Although the Mac mini is built to withstand regular handling, always be cautious about static electricity, which can damage the internal components. Try to touch a metal object or use an anti-static wristband before handling the device. This minimizes the chance of damaging sensitive components inside the Mac mini.

2. **Be Gentle with Cables**

   When handling the power cable or any peripheral cables, ensure you're not tugging or pulling on them too forcefully. Doing so can damage the connectors over time. If you need to move the cables, gently guide them into place.

3. **Avoid Direct Sunlight and Humidity**

   After unboxing, don't leave your Mac mini exposed to direct sunlight or places with high humidity. These conditions can cause long-term damage to the components and affect the Mac mini's performance.

Step 6: Placing the Mac mini in Its Ideal Location

Once you've unboxed your Mac mini and identified all the components, it's time to find the right place to set it up. The Mac mini is a compact device, so finding a place for it shouldn't be too difficult, but keep these considerations in mind:

1. **Ventilation**: Ensure the Mac mini has good airflow around it. Placing it in an area with plenty of space around the vents will prevent it from overheating.

2. **Accessibility**: While the Mac mini is small, make sure you can easily access the ports on the back, such as the USB-C ports and HDMI ports, for when you need to connect external devices.

3. **Workspace Organization**: Keep your workspace neat and organized. The Mac mini is designed to fit seamlessly into modern, minimalist desks. Pair it with a wireless keyboard and mouse, and consider placing it next to a monitor that's easily accessible.

Step 7: Moving Forward

With everything unboxed and set up, you're now ready to begin the initial setup and configuration of your Mac mini. In the next sections, we'll guide you through connecting it to your display, setting up macOS Sequoia, and configuring your Mac mini M4 Pro for optimal performance.

But before you get started, take a moment to enjoy the smooth and professional design of your new Mac mini. You've just taken the first step toward unlocking a whole new world of productivity and creativity.

By following these steps, you've successfully completed the unboxing and component identification of your Apple Mac mini M4 Pro. With careful handling and a bit of patience, you've ensured that everything is ready for the next phase of setting up your powerful new desktop. Now it's time to explore into the exciting world of macOS Sequoia and make the most of your Mac mini M4 Pro!

Setting Up Your Mac mini M4 Pro

Setting up your Mac mini M4 Pro is an exciting and straightforward process, but it's essential to do it right to ensure everything runs smoothly. In this section, we'll walk you through the steps—from unboxing to the first boot-up—making sure you know exactly what to do. If you encounter any bumps along the way, we've included troubleshooting tips to get you back on track. Let's get started!

Step 1: Unbox Your Mac mini M4 Pro

When you first open the box, you'll be greeted with the sleek Mac mini M4 Pro, along with a few accessories. Take your time and carefully remove the contents from the box. Here's what you should expect to find:

- **Mac mini M4 Pro**: The star of the show, this is where all the magic happens.

- **Power Cord**: This is the cord that connects your Mac mini to the power outlet.

- **Quick Start Guide**: Apple's quick setup manual to help you get started (though we'll go into detail here).

- **Apple Stickers**: Because, well, it's Apple.

Take a moment to remove the packaging and make sure everything is in place. If something feels off or you're missing any parts, double-check the box or contact Apple support. Sometimes, items like the power cord can be hidden underneath other packing materials.

Step 2: Choose a Location for Your Mac mini

The Mac mini is compact and portable, but it's important to pick a good spot for it. Since it's a desktop device, you'll need to place it on a flat surface with good ventilation. Avoid stacking things on top of it or placing it in tight spaces where airflow is restricted, as that can cause it to overheat.

Consider these points when choosing the right place:

- **Ventilation**: Ensure that the area is well-ventilated. The Mac mini has passive cooling, so it's important that the air can circulate around it.

- **Cable Management**: Make sure the location allows you to easily connect and manage all of your cables—power, monitor, and peripherals.

- **Accessibility**: It's also useful to place it somewhere easy to access for occasional plugging/unplugging or cable adjustments.

Once you've chosen your spot, gently place the Mac mini on the desk. You're ready for the next step.

Step 3: Connect the Power Cord

The first physical connection is to plug the power cord into the back of the Mac mini. Locate the power port on the back (it's the one labeled with a power icon). Carefully plug the power cord in, ensuring it fits snugly.

Next, plug the other end of the cord into a wall outlet or a power strip. Make sure the outlet is working by testing it with another device (like a lamp or phone charger) if you're unsure.

Step 4: Connect Your Display

The Mac mini M4 Pro supports a wide range of displays, and you have a few options for connecting your monitor.

- **Thunderbolt 4/USB-C Display**: If you're using a modern display that supports Thunderbolt or USB-C, use a Thunderbolt 4 (USB-C) cable. Plug one end of the cable into one of the Thunderbolt 4 ports on the back of the Mac mini and the other end into your display.

- **HDMI Display**: If your display uses HDMI, the Mac mini M4 Pro has an HDMI 2.0 port. Simply connect an HDMI cable between your Mac mini and the monitor.

- **Multiple Displays**: You can connect up to three 6K displays using the Thunderbolt 4 ports, or a combination of Thunderbolt and HDMI displays. If you're planning on a multi-monitor setup, follow the same process for each monitor.

After the display is connected, power on the monitor using the button on the side or bottom (depending on the model). Ensure the monitor is set to the correct input source (HDMI or Thunderbolt). If the display doesn't show an image right away, check the cables and connections to make sure everything is securely plugged in.

Step 5: Connect Your Keyboard and Mouse

For this step, you have two options: wired or wireless peripherals. Either way, setting them up is quick and easy.

- **Wired Keyboard and Mouse**: If you're using wired devices, simply plug them into any of the USB-A ports on the back of the Mac mini. The Mac mini will automatically recognize them, and you'll be ready to go.

- **Wireless Keyboard and Mouse**: If you're using Bluetooth peripherals (like Apple's Magic Keyboard and Magic Mouse), turn them on. You'll need to pair them with your Mac mini during the setup process.

To connect via Bluetooth:

1. Turn on your keyboard and mouse.

2. On your Mac mini's screen, the macOS setup will prompt you to pair the devices. Follow the on-screen instructions to complete the pairing.

It's a good idea to test your keyboard and mouse before moving on to ensure everything is working correctly. If your wireless devices aren't responding, try moving closer to the Mac mini to ensure a strong Bluetooth connection.

Step 6: Power Up and Boot the Mac mini

Now comes the exciting part—powering up your Mac mini for the first time! Press the power button located on the back of the Mac mini, and within a few seconds, the device should start to boot.

The display should light up and show the macOS Sequoia setup screen. If you don't see anything on the screen, double-check your connections and ensure the display is set to the correct input source.

Step 7: Configure macOS Sequoia

Once the Mac mini boots up, you'll be guided through a series of setup steps.

1. **Language and Region**: The first thing you'll need to do is choose your preferred language and region. This will determine the default settings, including time zone and currency.

2. **Wi-Fi Connection**: Next, you'll connect to a Wi-Fi network. Select your network and enter the password. If you don't have Wi-Fi available, you can connect using an Ethernet cable.

3. **Sign in with Apple ID**: Apple will prompt you to sign in with your Apple ID, which allows you to access services like iCloud, the App Store, and Apple Music. If you don't have one, you can create a new account.

4. **Data Migration**: If you're transferring data from an old Mac or another device, this is where you can choose to migrate your files, apps, and settings. You can do this via Time Machine, network transfer, or a direct connection to the old device.

5. **Privacy Settings**: macOS will guide you through some privacy options. These are important to review, so take a moment to enable or disable features based on your preferences.

Troubleshooting Tips

While setting up, you may encounter a few hiccups. Here are some common issues and how to resolve them:

- **No Display Signal**: If your Mac mini is powered on, but the display stays black, check the connection between the Mac mini and the monitor. Make sure the monitor is set to the correct input. Try using a different cable or port if needed.

- **Keyboard or Mouse Not Responding**: If your wired keyboard or mouse isn't working, try plugging them into different USB ports. For Bluetooth devices, ensure they're powered on and within range. Restart the Mac mini if necessary to trigger the pairing process.

- **Wi-Fi Not Connecting**: If the Mac mini doesn't detect your Wi-Fi network, ensure the router is working correctly. Restart the router and try again. If the network is password-protected, double-check the password for any typos.

- **System Not Booting**: If your Mac mini doesn't boot, make sure the power cord is securely plugged in. If the system is still unresponsive, perform a hard reset by holding the power button for 10 seconds and then powering it back on.

Step 8: Complete Setup and Start Using Your Mac mini

After completing the setup process, your Mac mini will be ready for use. From here, you can begin customizing it to suit your needs—installing apps, managing system preferences, and personalizing your workspace.

Connecting to Power, Display, and Peripherals

Getting your Mac mini M4 Pro up and running for the first time is an exciting experience, and it's all about making sure everything is properly connected and ready to go. Whether you're a first-time Mac user or a seasoned pro, understanding the correct ports and connection methods is key to ensuring you get the most out of your Mac mini.

In this section, we'll walk through the steps of connecting your Mac mini M4 Pro to a power source, monitor, and peripherals. We'll also highlight some best practices to make sure everything runs smoothly.

USB-C ports   Status indicator light

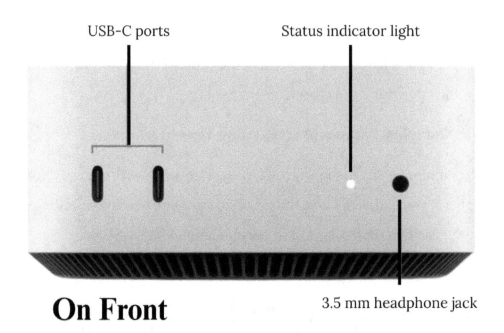

On Front

3.5 mm headphone jack

HDMI port

Gigabit Ethernet   Thunderbolt (USB-C)

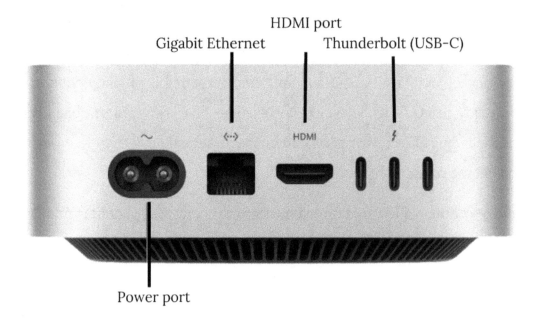

Power port

On Back

APPLE M4 PRO MAC MINI USER GUIDE

1. Connecting to Power

First things first—let's make sure your Mac mini M4 Pro is powered up and ready to go. The power connection is straightforward, but there are a couple of things to keep in mind.

Step-by-Step Guide to Connecting Power:

1. **Locate   the   Power   Cable:** When you unbox your Mac mini, you'll find a power cable included. It's a standard power cord designed to plug into the back of the Mac mini and into a power outlet.

2. **Find   the   Power   Port   on   the   Mac   mini:** On the back of your Mac mini, you'll notice a small power port located on the left side (when facing the back). This is where you'll connect the power cable.

3. **Plug   the   Cable   Into   the   Mac   mini:** Insert the power cable into the power port on the back of the Mac mini. You should feel a gentle click when it's securely in place.

4. **Connect   the   Power   Cable   to   the   Outlet:** Plug the other end of the power cable into a wall outlet or surge protector. If you're using a surge protector, make sure it's switched on and properly connected to the power source.

5. **Turn   On   the   Mac   mini:** After the power cable is securely plugged in, press the small power button located next to the power port on the back of the Mac mini.

The Mac mini will begin to boot up, and you'll see the familiar Apple logo on the screen once it powers up.

2. Connecting to Your Display

Now that the Mac mini M4 Pro is powered on, the next step is connecting it to your monitor or display. The Mac mini M4 Pro supports high-resolution displays, including up to three 6K displays, so you have plenty of options for creating the perfect workspace.

Step-by-Step Guide to Connecting Your Monitor:

1. **Choose the Right Cable:** The Mac mini M4 Pro offers two main options for connecting to a display: **HDMI** and **Thunderbolt 4** (USB-C). These ports offer different advantages depending on your display and cable setup.

   o **HDMI**: If you're using a standard TV or monitor, you'll likely be using an **HDMI to HDMI cable**. This is the easiest option if your display has an HDMI input.

   o **Thunderbolt 4 / USB-C**: For high-resolution monitors (such as 4K or 6K displays), Thunderbolt 4 or USB-C is the way to go. If your monitor supports these types of connections, you'll get faster data transfer speeds and higher quality images. Thunderbolt ports support **DisplayPort** connections, so you can use a **Thunderbolt to DisplayPort** cable for optimal performance.

APPLE M4 PRO MAC MINI USER GUIDE

2. **Plug the Cable into the Mac mini:** On the back of your Mac mini, you'll find **one HDMI port** and **two Thunderbolt 4 (USB-C) ports**. The HDMI port is great for simpler, more traditional setups, while the Thunderbolt ports offer the best performance for high-end displays.

   o For **HDMI**, simply plug one end of the HDMI cable into the HDMI port on the back of the Mac mini.

   o For **Thunderbolt 4 / USB-C**, connect one end of the Thunderbolt cable into one of the Thunderbolt 4 ports on the back of the Mac mini and the other end into the compatible port on your display.

3. **Connect Your Display to the Power Source:** Make sure your monitor is plugged into a power outlet and turned on. Depending on your display, it might automatically recognize the Mac mini's signal. If it doesn't, don't worry—continue with the next steps.

4. **Adjust Display Settings:** Once your display is connected and powered on, your Mac mini should recognize it automatically. If you have multiple displays, you may need to adjust the settings.

   o On macOS, go to **Apple Menu > System Preferences > Displays**. Here, you can configure the resolution, arrange your displays if you're using more than one, and even enable features like night shift for a more comfortable viewing experience at night.

- o **Tip**: If your Mac mini is connected to a 4K or 6K display, make sure you're using the correct resolution for the best picture quality. You can adjust this under **Display Preferences**.

3. Connecting Peripherals (USB Devices, Printers, etc.)

Finally, let's connect your other essential peripherals—things like your keyboard, mouse, printer, external storage, or any other USB devices. The Mac mini M4 Pro has multiple ports to handle these devices, but it's important to know which ones to use for optimal performance.

Step-by-Step Guide to Connecting Peripherals:

1. **Connecting a Keyboard and Mouse (USB or Bluetooth):**

   - o **Wired USB Keyboard/Mouse**: If you're using wired peripherals, simply plug the keyboard and mouse into one of the **USB-A** ports on the back of the Mac mini. The ports are conveniently located for easy access.

   - o **Bluetooth Keyboard/Mouse**: If you're using Bluetooth devices, press the power button on your keyboard or mouse to put it in pairing mode. On your Mac mini, go to **System Preferences > Bluetooth**, and the Mac mini will scan for nearby Bluetooth devices. When your keyboard or mouse appears, click **Connect**.

2. **Connecting Printers and Scanners (USB or Wi-Fi):**

   o **USB Printer/Scanner**: If you're using a USB printer or scanner, plug it into one of the **USB-A** or **USB-C** ports on the back of the Mac mini. You may need to install drivers, which can be done through **System Preferences > Printers & Scanners**.

   o **Wi-Fi Printer/Scanner**: If your printer or scanner supports Wi-Fi, make sure it's connected to the same Wi-Fi network as your Mac mini. You can add it by going to **System Preferences > Printers & Scanners** and clicking the + button to add a networked device.

3. **Connecting External Storage (Hard Drives, SSDs, etc.):**

   o The Mac mini M4 Pro comes equipped with **USB-A** and **USB-C** ports for connecting external hard drives or SSDs. For best performance, especially with high-capacity drives, use the **USB-C** or **Thunderbolt 4** ports for faster data transfer speeds.

   o After connecting your external drive, it should show up on your desktop or in **Finder**, ready to use. You can also manage your external drives in **Disk Utility**.

4. **Connecting Other Devices (Speakers, Cameras, etc.):**

   o For **USB speakers** or **webcams**, you can plug them directly into the **USB-A** or **USB-C** ports.

o   If you're using **audio output** devices like speakers or headphones, the Mac mini also has a **3.5mm headphone jack**. For high-end audio, use **USB or Bluetooth speakers** for the best sound quality.

5. **Best Practices for Port Management:**

o   While the Mac mini offers plenty of connectivity options, it's important to avoid overloading the ports. Try to use a **powered USB hub** if you have multiple USB devices. This will ensure that each device gets the power it needs without straining the Mac mini.

o   For **Thunderbolt 4** devices (such as external monitors or high-speed storage), it's best to plug them directly into the **Thunderbolt ports** to ensure maximum data transfer rates. If you're using a lot of peripherals, consider a **Thunderbolt docking station** to keep everything organized and connected.

Best Practices to Ensure Smooth Connections:

•   **Cable Management:** Keep your cables organized to avoid tangling and accidental disconnections. Cable ties or organizers can help you maintain a clean workspace.

•   **Port Accessibility:** The ports on the back of the Mac mini might be a bit harder to reach, so consider how often you'll need to plug and unplug devices. For frequently used peripherals, you may want to use a **USB hub** that sits on your desk.

- **Surge Protection:** Always plug your Mac mini and peripherals into a surge protector to safeguard them from electrical surges and outages.

- **Regular Maintenance:** Clean the ports and cables regularly to avoid dust buildup, which can lead to poor connections or damage over time.

Initial Boot and macOS Sequoia Setup

Welcome to your new Apple M4 Pro Mac mini! The moment you power it on, you'll begin an exciting journey into the world of macOS Sequoia, Apple's latest operating system. Don't worry – this step-by-step guide will help you smoothly navigate through the initial boot-up and setup process. By the end of this section, you'll be ready to use your Mac mini with all your settings configured and your apps up and running.

Step 1: Turning On Your Mac mini

When you're ready to begin, press the power button on your Mac mini. The power button is located on the back of the device, just beside the ports. You should see the power indicator light up, and shortly after, the screen will display the macOS startup sequence.

- **What to Expect**: Your Mac mini will show the Apple logo followed by the loading screen. It may take a minute or two to get things rolling.

This is completely normal – your Mac mini is preparing everything in the background so that your experience is as smooth as possible.

Step 2: Language and Region Selection

Once your Mac mini has booted up, the first screen you'll see is where you'll choose your **language** and **region**. This sets the tone for the rest of your setup.

1. **Select Language**: On the welcome screen, you'll be prompted to select your preferred language. For most users, English will be the default, but you can choose from a wide range of languages, so select whichever you're most comfortable with.

2. **Choose Your Region**: After selecting the language, you'll need to choose your **region**. Your region helps the Mac mini configure things like date, time, and currency settings. This is important for ensuring that your experience matches the location-specific features of macOS Sequoia.

- **Pro Tip**: If you're unsure which region to choose, pick the one that matches your country of residence. This will automatically adjust things like your keyboard layout and the formatting of numbers and dates.

Step 3: Connecting to Wi-Fi

Next, your Mac mini will prompt you to connect to a Wi-Fi network. This is essential, as your Mac mini needs to be connected to the internet to complete the setup process.

APPLE M4 PRO MAC MINI USER GUIDE

1. **Choose Your Network**: A list of available Wi-Fi networks should appear. Select your Wi-Fi network from the list.

2. **Enter Wi-Fi Password**: If your network is password-protected, you'll need to enter your Wi-Fi password. Make sure you enter it correctly, paying attention to capitalization and special characters.

3. **Confirm Connection**: Once you've entered the password, click **Join** to connect. If your connection is successful, the screen will show a confirmation message. Your Mac mini will now have access to the internet, allowing it to download any necessary software updates.

- **Pro Tip**: If you have trouble connecting to Wi-Fi, try moving your Mac mini closer to your router. Sometimes, Wi-Fi signals can be weak depending on the distance.

Step 4: Signing In with Your Apple ID

Now that your Mac mini is connected to the internet, you'll be asked to sign in with your **Apple ID**. Your Apple ID is the key to unlocking all the great features Apple offers, from iCloud storage to the App Store and beyond.

1. **Enter Apple ID Email and Password**: Type in the email address associated with your Apple ID and your password. If you don't have an Apple ID yet, you'll have the option to create one. You can easily do this by clicking on **Create New Apple ID**.

2. **Enable Two-Factor Authentication**: If you've enabled two-factor authentication on your Apple ID (which we highly recommend for

extra security), you'll need to verify your identity using another Apple device or phone number.

3. **Agree to Terms and Conditions**: Once logged in, you'll be asked to agree to Apple's terms and conditions. Read through them (or just skim, we know), and click **Agree** to continue.

4. **iCloud Integration**: After logging in, your Mac mini will ask if you want to enable iCloud for syncing data across all your Apple devices. iCloud is a great way to back up your documents, photos, and app data. We recommend enabling it, but if you're not ready yet, you can skip this step.

• **Pro Tip**: Signing in with your Apple ID will automatically link your Mac mini to services like Apple Music, iMessage, FaceTime, and the App Store. It's a great way to keep everything synchronized across all your Apple devices.

Step 5: Setting Up System Preferences

Next, you'll move on to configuring your **system preferences**, which include some essential customizations for your Mac mini. These settings help personalize the Mac mini to your liking.

1. **Enable Location Services**: macOS Sequoia allows apps to use your location for things like weather, maps, and time zone updates. You'll be asked whether you want to enable **Location Services**. It's entirely up to you, but enabling this feature can make your experience a lot smoother, especially for apps like Maps.

2. **Choose Your Time Zone**: macOS will try to set your time zone automatically based on your region. If it doesn't get it right, you can easily change it to match your location.

3. **Create a User Account**: You'll be asked to create a **user account** on your Mac mini. This account will have administrative privileges by default, allowing you to install apps, manage settings, and perform other tasks. You'll create a username and password here. Make sure your password is strong for security reasons.

- **Pro Tip**: Use a memorable username (like your name) and a strong password to keep your Mac mini secure. Consider using the **password manager** feature in macOS to help you manage and generate secure passwords.

4. **Set Up Touch ID (If Applicable)**: If your Mac mini came with a keyboard that has **Touch ID** capabilities, you'll be prompted to set it up. This is a convenient way to unlock your Mac mini and authorize purchases with just a fingerprint.

- **Pro Tip**: If you don't have a Touch ID-enabled keyboard, you can skip this step and configure it later.

Step 6: Completing Setup

Once you've configured the basic system preferences, macOS Sequoia will finalize the setup process. Your Mac mini may download updates during this step, and it may take a few minutes depending on your internet speed.

- **What to Expect**: During this process, macOS Sequoia will update the system with the latest security patches and software. If you're using a fresh installation of macOS, expect this process to take a few minutes. Once complete, your Mac mini will be ready for use.

Step 7: Enjoy Your New Mac mini M4 Pro!

After completing these steps, you'll be greeted by the **macOS Sequoia desktop**, ready for you to dive into your new Mac mini experience. You can now explore the **Dock**, launch apps, or head to **System Preferences** to further fine-tune your setup.

- **Pro Tip**: If you want to make your Mac mini feel like home, consider personalizing it with your favorite wallpapers, app icons, and widgets. macOS Sequoia offers a wide range of customization options that can make your workspace feel unique.

Wrapping It Up

The initial boot and macOS Sequoia setup is a seamless process designed to get you up and running quickly. By following these steps, you'll have a personalized Mac mini ready to handle everything from everyday tasks to professional-level projects. Whether you're new to macOS or a seasoned Apple user, this guide has helped you set up your Mac mini M4 Pro, ensuring you can dive into your new setup with confidence.

Enjoy exploring your new device, and remember that this guide is here to help you every step of the way! If you have any questions or run into issues during setup, don't hesitate to consult the troubleshooting section or get in touch with Apple Support.

Connecting to Wi-Fi and Apple ID Setup

Getting connected to the internet is one of the first essential steps when setting up your Mac mini M4 Pro. A reliable Wi-Fi connection is necessary not only for browsing the web but also for downloading important system updates, accessing your iCloud account, and setting up your Apple ID. In this section, we'll walk you through the entire process of connecting to Wi-Fi and setting up your Apple ID, with easy-to-follow instructions. We'll also go over some troubleshooting tips in case you run into any issues along the way.

Step 1: Connecting Your Mac mini to Wi-Fi

When you power up your Mac mini for the first time, macOS will guide you through the setup process. One of the first things you'll need to do is connect to a Wi-Fi network. Here's how you can do it:

1. **Power on Your Mac mini**

   o Press the power button on the back of your Mac mini to turn it on. Wait for a moment as the system boots up, and soon you'll see the macOS welcome screen.

2. **Select Your Language and Region**

   o After the initial welcome screen, the setup assistant will ask you to choose your preferred language and region. Make your selection and click "Continue."

3. **Choose Your Wi-Fi Network**

   o Next, you'll be asked to connect to a Wi-Fi network. A list of available Wi-Fi networks should appear on the screen. These are the networks within range of your Mac mini.

   o If you don't see your network, make sure that your router is turned on and broadcasting its signal. You might need to move your Mac mini closer to the router if you are too far away.

4. **Enter Your Wi-Fi Password**

   o Click on the network name you want to connect to. You'll be prompted to enter the Wi-Fi password for that network. Type in the password carefully (Wi-Fi passwords are case-sensitive), then click "Join."

   o If your Wi-Fi password is incorrect or your network is hidden, macOS will prompt you to retry or recheck your credentials.

5. **Check the Wi-Fi Status**

   o Once connected, your Wi-Fi status will be displayed at the top right of your screen. You should see the Wi-Fi icon, which will turn solid once the connection is successful.

APPLE M4 PRO MAC MINI USER GUIDE

- If the Wi-Fi icon doesn't turn solid or you see an error message, double-check your password and router settings.

Step 2: Setting Up Your Apple ID

An Apple ID is essential for accessing Apple's services, including iCloud, App Store, Apple Music, and more. It's tied to all the services and content you'll need. If you already have an Apple ID, this process is quick. If not, you'll be able to create one during setup.

Here's how to set up your Apple ID:

1. **Sign in with an Existing Apple ID**

   - After your Wi-Fi connection is established, the setup assistant will prompt you to sign in with your Apple ID.

   - If you already have an Apple ID, enter your **Apple ID** (typically an email address) and **password** in the respective fields and click "Next."

   - If you've forgotten your password, you can reset it by clicking "Forgot Apple ID or Password?" and following the instructions.

2. **Create a New Apple ID (If You Don't Have One)**

   - If you don't already have an Apple ID, you can create one during setup.

   - Click on **Create a Free Apple ID**.

- You'll be asked for some basic information, such as your **name**, **birthdate**, and **email address**. This email address will become your Apple ID, so make sure it's one you regularly check.

- Set a **password** for your Apple ID. This password must contain at least eight characters, a number, and a symbol. Make sure it's something secure but memorable.

3. **Set Up iCloud**

- iCloud is Apple's cloud service that stores your photos, documents, contacts, and more, keeping them synced across all your devices.

- During the Apple ID setup, you'll be prompted to turn on iCloud. Make sure to select "Turn On iCloud" to back up your data securely. You can choose to sync only certain apps (such as Mail, Contacts, Calendar, etc.), or you can sync everything for a complete cloud backup.

- If you have two-factor authentication set up for your Apple ID, you'll be prompted to verify your identity through your trusted device or phone number.

4. **Agree to Terms and Conditions**

- Once you've signed in or created your Apple ID, you'll be asked to agree to Apple's Terms and Conditions. Make sure to read through the agreement, then click **Agree** to proceed.

APPLE M4 PRO MAC MINI USER GUIDE

5. **Set Up Payment and Billing (Optional)**

    o   You'll also be asked to add a payment method (credit card, debit card, or PayPal) for purchases in the App Store or other Apple services. This is optional, and you can skip it if you don't want to add a payment method right away.

6. **Finish Setup**

    o   After your Apple ID is set up, macOS will prompt you to set up a few other options like Siri, location services, and Apple Pay. You can choose to set these up now or later. Once done, click **Continue**.

Troubleshooting Tips: What to Do If You Have Trouble Connecting to Wi-Fi or Setting Up Your Apple ID

Even though connecting to Wi-Fi and setting up your Apple ID is usually a straightforward process, some users may encounter issues along the way. Below are some troubleshooting steps to help you resolve common problems:

Issue 1: Can't Connect to Wi-Fi

*   **Check Your Router**: Ensure that your router is turned on and working. Try connecting another device to the same Wi-Fi network to see if the issue is with the Mac mini or your Wi-Fi.

- **Re-enter the Password**: Double-check that you've entered the correct password for your network. If the password is incorrect, you will not be able to connect. Try typing it again carefully.

- **Forget Network and Reconnect**: If you're still having trouble, go to **System Preferences > Network > Wi-Fi**. Find the network you're trying to connect to, click the **"-"** button to remove it, and then try connecting again.

- **Restart Your Mac mini**: A simple restart can often fix connection issues. Try restarting your Mac mini and reconnecting to Wi-Fi.

- **Reset Network Settings**: If nothing works, try resetting the network settings on your router. This will refresh your connection and may resolve any connection problems.

Issue 2: Can't Set Up Apple ID

- **Check Your Internet Connection**: An unstable or slow internet connection can cause issues when setting up an Apple ID. Ensure that your Wi-Fi connection is stable and try again.

- **Check for Existing Apple ID**: If you're having trouble creating a new Apple ID, make sure you don't already have one. You can check this by visiting the Apple ID account page (https://appleid.apple.com/) and trying to recover your account.

- **Password Reset**: If you've forgotten your Apple ID password, go to the **Apple ID account page** and follow the steps to reset your password.

APPLE M4 PRO MAC MINI USER GUIDE

- **Two-Factor Authentication Issues**: If you're having trouble with two-factor authentication (e.g., not receiving verification codes), make sure your phone number or trusted device is up-to-date in the Apple ID settings.

Final Thoughts

Connecting to Wi-Fi and setting up your Apple ID on your Mac mini M4 Pro is an important first step in fully configuring your new device. By following these instructions, you should be able to get connected and start exploring the incredible capabilities of your Mac mini.

If you run into any issues during the process, don't hesitate to consult Apple Support or check their online forums for help. With your Mac mini now connected and your Apple ID set up, you're ready to enjoy the full experience of macOS and the Apple ecosystem.

CONFIGURING MACOS AND SYSTEM PREFERENCES

Navigating macOS Sequoia Features

macOS Sequoia, the operating system designed specifically for the Apple M4 Pro Mac mini, is more than just an update. It's a transformation of how you interact with your computer, blending power, intelligence, and seamless integration. If you're familiar with macOS from earlier versions, you'll notice significant changes in how things look, feel, and work. But even if you're new to Mac, the new features are intuitive enough to make the transition smooth and enjoyable.

Here's a detailed look at the unique features of macOS Sequoia on the M4 Pro Mac mini and how they elevate your user experience.

1. AI-Driven User Experience: Meet the New Apple Intelligence

Apple has incorporated a more advanced version of its AI into macOS Sequoia, which significantly enhances the user experience. This feature is designed to adapt to your daily workflow and optimize your system based on your usage patterns. For example:

- **Smart Suggestions**: macOS Sequoia can suggest actions, apps, or documents you're likely to need based on your habits. If you've been working on a particular project or document, the system will remind you to continue your work or offer quick access to files you're most likely to open next.

- **Adaptive Performance**: The AI automatically adjusts the Mac mini's performance depending on the task. For instance, if you're working on a video edit, the system will prioritize the GPU for high-intensity tasks. If you're reading emails or browsing the web, it'll switch to a more power-efficient mode to preserve battery life (though, in the case of the Mac mini, that means efficiency without compromising performance).

- **Proactive Notifications**: Instead of bombarding you with every notification, macOS Sequoia smartly prioritizes what's important. It will send you relevant reminders and alerts based on your preferences, ensuring you're not distracted by unnecessary notifications.

2. The New Control Center

The Control Center in macOS Sequoia is more refined than ever before. Inspired by the simplicity and usability of iOS, it brings essential settings into one easy-to-access place, making your workflow smoother and faster. Here's what you'll find:

- **Quick Access**: Instead of opening multiple menus to adjust brightness, sound, Wi-Fi, or Bluetooth, everything is now accessible from the menu bar via the Control Center. You can even customize it to include your favorite settings.

- **Dynamic Display Controls**: For the M4 Pro Mac mini, managing multiple high-resolution displays is easier. You can adjust display settings like brightness, contrast, and even the color profile directly from the Control Center. No more fiddling with display preferences in the System Preferences panel — everything you need is right at your fingertips.

- **Do Not Disturb & Focus Modes**: The Control Center also integrates "Do Not Disturb" and "Focus" modes. These features allow you to silence notifications based on the time of day or the tasks you're working on, which is perfect for those who prefer uninterrupted productivity or need some quiet time to focus.

3. Enhanced Multitasking with Stage Manager

Stage Manager is a game-changing feature in macOS Sequoia. If you've struggled with organizing windows across multiple screens or have found yourself constantly switching between apps, this feature is here to help.

- **Organized Workspace**: Stage Manager automatically groups windows by app and task. So, if you're working on a research paper and a spreadsheet, Stage Manager will group all the related windows together for easy access. You no longer have to manually resize or move windows around to keep things organized.

- **Simplified Switching Between Apps**: Whether you're using one or multiple displays, Stage Manager makes it effortless to switch between tasks. You can quickly access all open apps through the window previews on the side, minimizing the time you spend navigating between apps. It's perfect for power users who juggle between several programs.

- **Customizable Layouts**: Stage Manager allows you to customize how apps are arranged. For example, you can have your email app open alongside a web browser, and the system will remember this layout when you return. It feels less like managing multiple tasks and more like managing a personalized workspace.

4. macOS Sequoia's New Widgets & Personalization

Widgets have always been a part of macOS, but in Sequoia, they take center stage with even more customization options.

- **Interactive Widgets**: The widgets now offer much more than just static information. You can interact with them directly from the Notification Center. For example, you can adjust the volume, control music, or even update your calendar events without opening the apps themselves.

- **Smart Stacks**: Smart Stacks automatically organize your widgets based on your activity. If you tend to check the weather first thing in the morning, your weather widget will appear at the top of the stack during that time of day. As your day progresses, the system will rearrange the widgets to reflect the tasks you're likely to engage with next.

- **Customizable Widget Sizes**: You can now resize widgets to suit your preferences, whether you want to show more detailed information or just a simple glance of a specific task. The customizability here makes macOS Sequoia feel truly personalized to how you work and live.

5. Live Text and Visual Look-Up

If you've ever wanted to interact with text within an image, macOS Sequoia makes that possible with **Live Text**. This feature brings real-time text recognition to your photos, screenshots, or even images in Safari. Here's how it can make a difference:

- **Text Recognition in Images**: Using the power of Apple's AI, Live Text can recognize and allow you to interact with text in images. For example, you could highlight phone numbers, addresses, or URLs in a picture and tap to call, visit a website, or open the address in Maps.

- **Instant Translations**: Live Text also offers instant translation of text within images, allowing you to quickly translate foreign language signs, menus, or documents. It's like having a translator in your pocket.

- **Visual Look-Up**: In addition to text, Sequoia's Visual Look-Up feature allows you to get details about objects in your photos or images. Point at a picture of a landmark, animal, or flower, and

Sequoia will offer relevant information or even suggest similar images from the web.

6. Spotlight Enhancements: More Powerful Search

Spotlight has always been one of the standout features of macOS, but with Sequoia, it's even better. The enhanced Spotlight search in Sequoia gives you a more powerful and intuitive way to find exactly what you're looking for, no matter where it is.

- **Rich Previews**: You can now preview documents, images, videos, and even web pages directly in the Spotlight search results. This saves you time by allowing you to access content without having to open an app or window.

- **Advanced Filters**: Spotlight search now supports filters for more refined results. For instance, you can filter your search by file type, date, or location, making it easier to find exactly what you need, whether it's a photo, a presentation, or a document.

- **Web and Siri Integration**: Spotlight now integrates more seamlessly with Siri, pulling up relevant web results, news, and even recommendations. The best part? The results are contextual, meaning Spotlight can learn what you're likely searching for based on your activity.

7. Privacy and Security: A New Level of Control

Apple continues its commitment to privacy with new features in macOS Sequoia that give you more control over your personal data. Here's what you need to know:

- **App Privacy Reports**: Sequoia includes a new feature where users can see detailed reports about how their apps access data such as location, contacts, and photos. You can even review when and how often apps are requesting access to your data, giving you more control over what information is shared.

- **Mail Privacy Protection**: In Sequoia, Mail offers more robust privacy features, such as blocking senders from tracking when your emails are opened. This ensures that you're not unknowingly giving away personal information just by opening an email.

- **Enhanced Security Features**: With the addition of more granular security options, users have better control over app permissions and security settings. From the initial system setup to real-time monitoring, Sequoia makes sure your Mac mini stays protected from external threats.

Conclusion: The Evolution of macOS

macOS Sequoia on the Apple M4 Pro Mac mini is more than just a software update. It's a fundamental shift in how we interact with technology. With its seamless integration of powerful AI, intuitive multitasking features, enhanced privacy controls, and unmatched personalization, Sequoia makes

APPLE M4 PRO MAC MINI USER GUIDE

the M4 Pro Mac mini a true powerhouse for creative professionals, power users, and everyday consumers alike.

What truly sets Sequoia apart from its predecessors is how it's designed to adapt to you. It learns from your habits, automates routine tasks, and ensures your data is protected while maximizing performance. Whether you're editing a video, drafting a report, or simply browsing the web, Sequoia is here to make everything feel more effortless and intuitive.

Personalizing System Preferences

When you first set up your Mac mini M4 Pro, you'll notice that macOS Sequoia provides a highly polished and clean interface. But why settle for the default when you can make your Mac truly feel like *yours*? Personalizing your system settings not only makes your device more visually appealing but also enhances your productivity and makes your daily experience smoother. Whether it's tweaking the sound settings, adjusting the layout of your desktop, or simply giving your Mac mini a more personal touch with a custom wallpaper, macOS Sequoia offers a wealth of options to make everything just right.

Let's walk through how to make these adjustments and tailor your Mac mini M4 Pro to fit your preferences.

1. Customizing the Sound Settings

One of the first things you'll probably want to adjust is your sound settings. Your Mac mini is packed with powerful speakers, but depending on your environment and needs, you may want to make some tweaks to suit your preferences.

a. Changing the Output Device

If you have external speakers or headphones, you'll want to ensure that the sound is directed to the right device. Here's how you can do that:

1. **Click the Apple menu** in the top left corner of your screen and select **System Preferences**.

2. Open the **Sound** preference panel.

3. Under the **Output** tab, you'll see a list of available sound output devices.

4. Select the one you want, such as **Built-in Output** for your Mac mini's internal speakers, or any external devices like headphones or Bluetooth speakers that are connected.

b. Adjusting Volume and Alerts

You can tweak how loud or soft the sound is, as well as how your Mac responds to various alerts:

1. In the **Sound** panel, adjust the **Output volume** slider to increase or decrease the volume.

2. If you want to adjust the alert sounds, check the **Play sound effects through** option and select your preferred output device.

3. For a more refined experience, you can also tweak the **Balance** slider if you have external speakers and want to adjust the left-right balance for a better listening experience.

c. Setting Up Sound Effects and Alerts

To give your Mac a more personalized feel, you can change the system sounds and notifications:

1. In the **Sound** preferences, go to the **Sound Effects** tab.

2. From here, you can adjust the alert sounds for system events (like when you receive a notification or error).

3. You can even choose a custom sound from the dropdown list to replace the default "pop" sound that plays when you interact with system alerts.

2. Customizing the Dock

The Dock is one of the most iconic features of macOS, and it's where you can access all of your favorite apps and documents. Let's make sure that it's as functional and stylish as you need.

a. Adjusting the Size and Position of the Dock

By default, the Dock is placed at the bottom of your screen, but macOS gives you the flexibility to move it around to suit your workflow. Additionally, you can resize it to make it more accessible.

1. Open **System Preferences** from the Apple menu.

2. Click on **Dock & Menu Bar**.

3. In this panel, you can adjust the **Size** slider to make the Dock smaller or larger based on your preference.

4. You can also change the **Position on screen** to place the Dock on the left, bottom, or right of your screen, depending on how you like to organize your desktop.

b. Adding and Removing Items from the Dock

The Dock can hold an array of icons, from apps to folders to files you use frequently. To make your Mac mini more personalized, you can add or remove items to keep it as streamlined as possible.

- **To add an app**: Open **Finder**, find the app you want to add, and simply drag the app icon to the Dock.

- **To remove an app**: Right-click (or Control-click) on the app icon in the Dock and select **Options > Remove from Dock**.

c. Customizing the Appearance of the Dock

macOS Sequoia lets you further customize the appearance of your Dock with a few options:

APPLE M4 PRO MAC MINI USER GUIDE

- **Magnification**: Enable magnification to make icons larger when you hover over them. This can be useful if you have a lot of apps in your Dock and want a quick way to see their icons more clearly.

- **Minimize windows using**: You can choose to minimize windows using either the **Genie effect** (the traditional 'sucking' effect) or the **Scale effect**, which is more subtle. Experiment with both to see which one you prefer.

- **Hide the Dock automatically**: If you want to maximize your screen space, enable the option to **Automatically hide and show the Dock**. This way, the Dock will only appear when you move your cursor to the bottom (or side) of the screen.

3. Personalizing the Wallpaper and Lock Screen

Now that the system sounds and Dock are set, let's focus on giving your Mac mini a more personal touch by changing its wallpaper and lock screen. This is a simple way to make your Mac feel uniquely yours.

a. Changing the Desktop Wallpaper

You can customize the look of your Mac's desktop with a wallpaper that suits your style. Whether you prefer a solid color, a scenic view, or an artistic design, macOS makes it easy to switch it up.

1. Right-click on your desktop and select **Change Desktop Background**.

2. The **Desktop & Screen Saver** preferences will open.

3. In the **Apple default wallpapers** tab, you'll find a range of beautiful images to choose from. Or, if you have your own image, click the + sign to browse and add it from your files.

4. You can even set your wallpaper to change automatically by selecting a folder of images, and macOS will cycle through them at your preferred interval.

b. Customizing the Lock Screen

Your lock screen can also reflect your personal style, offering a snapshot of your aesthetic before you even sign in.

1. Open **System Preferences** and go to **Lock Screen** under the **Desktop & Screen Saver** section.

2. You can select from Apple's default wallpapers or upload your own photo.

3. Adjust the settings for things like showing the time, date, and other information, so it's personalized just the way you like.

4. Additional Customizations for Visuals and Performance

macOS Sequoia offers more granular settings to customize your Mac mini's interface, including visual and accessibility settings that cater to your unique preferences.

a. Dark Mode and Light Mode

One of the most popular features in macOS Sequoia is the **Dark Mode** option, which provides a sleek and modern interface that's easier on the eyes, especially in low-light environments.

1. Open **System Preferences** and go to **General**.

2. In the **Appearance** section, choose **Light**, **Dark**, or **Auto** (which switches between Light and Dark mode depending on the time of day).

b. Enabling Accessibility Features

macOS also offers a wide array of accessibility options to make your Mac mini even easier to use, whether you need visual aids, hearing aids, or motor controls. Here's how you can fine-tune your system:

1. Open **System Preferences** and select **Accessibility**.

2. In the **Display** tab, you can adjust contrast, enable "Reduce Transparency," and even add filters for color blindness.

3. Explore other settings such as **VoiceOver** (screen reader), **Zoom** (screen magnification), and **Keyboard** options for a tailored experience that meets your needs.

Adjusting Display Settings for Single and Multi-Display Setups

When setting up your **Apple M4 Pro Mac mini**, one of the most important things to configure is your display settings. Whether you're using a single monitor or a multi-monitor setup, getting the right display settings will ensure you have an optimized and efficient workspace. In this section, we'll walk you through how to adjust your display settings for both single and multi-display configurations, focusing on how to set the correct resolution, orientation, and use macOS's 'Displays' preferences to achieve the best viewing experience.

Single Display Setup: Configuring Resolution and Orientation

For most users, a single monitor setup is the standard. This setup is straightforward, but it's essential to ensure that your display settings are tailored to your needs, whether you're working on documents, browsing, or enjoying media.

1. Connecting Your Monitor

- **Step 1**: Start by connecting your Mac mini to your monitor using an HDMI or Thunderbolt cable. If your monitor supports Thunderbolt, this connection will also allow faster data transfer and can provide more reliable performance, especially if you're working with high-resolution content.

- **Step 2**: Power on your Mac mini and the monitor. Your Mac should automatically detect the display, but if it doesn't, proceed to the next steps.

2. Configuring Resolution

macOS should detect your monitor's optimal resolution automatically, but sometimes you might want to adjust it to fit your preferences or improve performance.

- **Step 1**: Click on the **Apple menu** in the top-left corner of your screen and choose **System Preferences**.

- **Step 2**: In **System Preferences**, select **Displays**. This will open the display configuration window where you can adjust the display settings.

- **Step 3**: Under the **Display** tab, you'll see the "**Default for display**" setting selected by default. This is the recommended resolution for your monitor. However, if you need more screen real estate or sharper text, you can select the "**Scaled**" option.

- **Step 4**: After selecting "Scaled," you will see several resolution options. Choose the one that best fits your needs:

APPLE M4 PRO MAC MINI USER GUIDE

- o **Larger Text**: This resolution option makes everything appear larger on screen, which is helpful for those with visual impairments or if you prefer larger UI elements.

- o **More Space**: This option increases the resolution and makes everything smaller, allowing more windows and applications to fit on the screen at once.

- **Step 5**: Once you've chosen the desired resolution, macOS will automatically apply the changes. If the changes don't look right, you can quickly switch back to the default or another resolution.

3. Adjusting Display Orientation

Sometimes, you might want to rotate your screen's orientation. This is especially useful for graphic designers, coders, or people who use their computer for reading documents or web browsing.

- **Step 1**: In the **Displays** preferences window, under the **Display** tab, find the **Rotation** drop-down menu. This menu allows you to choose the screen orientation.

- **Step 2**: Select one of the available options:

  - o **Standard**: The default landscape orientation.

  - o **90°**: Rotate the display to portrait mode (good for reading long documents or coding).

  - o **180°**: Inverts the display upside down.

APPLE M4 PRO MAC MINI USER GUIDE

o **270°**: Rotate the display to portrait mode, but the other side.

- **Step 3**: Once you've chosen the appropriate orientation, your screen will rotate accordingly. If it looks off, simply return to the display settings and select a different orientation.

Multi-Display Setup: Configuring Multiple Monitors

Many users prefer multi-monitor setups, especially for tasks that require multitasking, like editing, coding, or professional content creation. Here's how to properly configure display settings for multi-monitor setups, so you can make the most of your workspace.

1. Connecting Multiple Monitors

- **Step 1**: Connect your second (or third) monitor to your Mac mini using available ports (Thunderbolt, HDMI, etc.). macOS will automatically detect each connected monitor.

- **Step 2**: Once connected, the display should automatically extend, but it might be mirrored or display a default configuration. We'll adjust that in the following steps.

2. Adjusting Display Arrangement

In macOS, you can arrange your displays in the **Displays** preferences to reflect your physical setup. This allows you to seamlessly move the mouse and windows between screens, just as you would in a physical multi-monitor arrangement.

- **Step 1**: Click the **Apple menu** and select **System Preferences** > **Displays**.

- **Step 2**: In the **Displays** window, go to the **Arrangement** tab. This shows a graphical representation of how your monitors are arranged.

- **Step 3**: To move the displays around, simply drag the display icons to match their physical arrangement on your desk. For example, if you have a second monitor positioned to the right of your Mac mini's display, drag the second display icon to the right of the primary display on the screen.

- **Step 4**: Once your displays are arranged to your liking, you can move your mouse across screens smoothly. You can also drag windows from one monitor to another by clicking and holding the window's title bar.

3. Configuring Resolution for Each Display

Each display connected to your Mac mini might have different resolutions or sizes. macOS allows you to customize the resolution for each screen independently, ensuring they look their best.

- **Step 1**: Under the **Displays** preferences window, click on each monitor icon in the **Display** tab to configure the settings for each individual screen.

- **Step 2**: Select the **Scaled** option to adjust the resolution, as we did for the single display setup. You'll find different options for each monitor, so be sure to set the resolution based on the size and capabilities of each screen.

APPLE M4 PRO MAC MINI USER GUIDE

4. Using the Menu Bar on Multiple Displays

If you're using multiple monitors, the **menu bar** will be shown on the primary display by default. However, you can choose which display gets the menu bar, which is helpful for productivity.

- **Step 1**: Go back to the **Arrangement** tab in **Displays** preferences.

- **Step 2**: Simply drag the white bar at the top of the primary display's icon to the monitor you want to set as the new primary display. This will make that display your new primary monitor, and the menu bar will appear on it.

5. Mirroring Displays

In some cases, you may want to mirror the displays, meaning both monitors show the same content. This is useful for presentations or when you want to display your screen to a larger audience.

- **Step 1**: In the **Displays** preferences window, under the **Display** tab, check the **Mirror Displays** checkbox. This will make both monitors show the same content.

- **Step 2**: Uncheck the box if you want to return to the extended display setup.

Optimizing Display Performance for Productivity

To further improve your multi-display setup, you can adjust settings like **Night Shift** for reducing blue light exposure, or enable **True Tone** (if supported by your monitors) for a more natural color balance.

- **Night Shift**: Night Shift adjusts the color temperature of your display, reducing blue light to make it easier on your eyes during evening hours. To enable Night Shift:

  o Go to **System Preferences** > **Displays**.

  o Select the **Night Shift** tab and choose your preferred settings for color temperature and scheduling.

- **True Tone**: True Tone automatically adjusts the white balance on your display based on the ambient light in your room. To enable True Tone:

  o In **System Preferences** > **Displays**, go to the **Display** tab and check **True Tone** (if supported by your monitor).

Managing Storage and Files on Your Mac mini M4 Pro

One of the most essential aspects of getting the most out of your Apple Mac mini M4 Pro is managing its storage and organizing your files efficiently. As you begin to explore your Mac mini, you'll quickly notice how seamless and intuitive macOS makes file management. In this section, we'll take a closer look at how to monitor disk space, use Finder to stay organized, and ensure your files are properly synced with iCloud, making sure you never lose a file again.

Monitoring Your Disk Space

Whether you're working on large creative projects or simply keeping a lot of files on your Mac mini, it's crucial to regularly monitor your disk space. macOS makes this easy, giving you access to a visual overview of your storage.

Here's how to check your storage:

1. **Click the Apple Icon in the Top Left Corner:** Start by clicking the Apple logo in the top left corner of your screen and select **"About This Mac."**

2. **Go to the "Storage" Tab:** Once you're in the "About This Mac" window, click on the **"Storage"** tab. Here, you'll get a clear overview of your Mac mini's available storage and how much space is being used by different categories such as **System**, **Apps**, **Documents**, **Photos**, and more.

3. **Understanding the Storage Breakdown:** The storage panel will show you a color-coded bar, which provides a visual representation of your disk's contents. You'll be able to see exactly how much space is being used for:

   o **System** (macOS files)

   o **Apps** (Applications you've installed)

   o **Documents** (Word files, PDFs, presentations, etc.)

- o **Photos** and **Media** (Photos, videos, music, and other media files)

- o **Other** (Files that don't fit into these categories)

4. **Free Up Space:**

   If you're running low on storage, you can use this panel to help make decisions on what to remove. You may want to delete old applications you no longer need, clear out old documents, or remove large video files that are taking up too much space.

   - o **Empty the Trash**: Files that you've deleted are still taking up space in the Trash. To free up that space, go to the **Trash** icon in the Dock and choose **Empty Trash**.

   - o **Manage Storage**: If you click the **"Manage..."** button next to the storage graph, macOS will open a new window with additional recommendations on how to free up space. It might suggest optimizing storage by moving files to iCloud or deleting old iTunes movies and TV shows that you've already watched.

By regularly checking your disk space, you ensure that your Mac mini continues to run smoothly, without unnecessary clutter.

Using Finder to Organize Files

Finder is your go-to file management tool on the Mac mini, and it's where you'll spend most of your time organizing, viewing, and searching for files.

It's easy to get overwhelmed with all your files piling up, but Finder offers several powerful tools to help you stay organized.

Here's how to make the most out of Finder:

1. **Launch Finder**

   You can open Finder by clicking on the **Finder** icon (a smiling face) in the Dock or by pressing **Command + Space** to open **Spotlight**, then typing "Finder" and hitting **Enter**.

2. **Creating Folders**

   Just like on any other computer, organizing your files into folders is key. You can easily create a new folder by:

   o **Right-clicking** in any directory and selecting **New Folder**, or

   o Pressing **Command + Shift + N** to create a new folder instantly.

Organizing your files into folders will help you find documents more efficiently and keep your Mac mini's storage tidy.

3. **Using   Tags   to   Organize   Files**

   One of Finder's coolest features is its **Tags**. Tags let you color-code and label files based on their relevance to specific projects or categories. To add a tag:

   o **Right-click** on a file and select a color or tag name (e.g., "Work," "Personal," "Important").

o You can search for tagged files later by simply typing the tag name in Finder's sidebar.

4. **Quick   Look   for   Previewing   Files**
Sometimes you need to quickly check the contents of a file without opening the entire app. **Quick Look** allows you to do just that:

   o **Select** the file in Finder.

   o Press the **Spacebar** to see a preview of the file. You can even scroll through documents and images without fully opening them.

This is an excellent time-saver when you're working with many files and don't want to waste time opening each one individually.

5. **Search and Sort Files**
Finder's search bar is an incredibly powerful tool that helps you find files in an instant. As you start typing, Finder will begin showing results, filtering them by file name, type, or even content inside the file.

   o You can also **sort files** by different criteria like **Name**, **Date Modified**, **Size**, and **Kind**. Sorting your files regularly will help you maintain a clean and easily navigable file system.

6. **Storing Files in iCloud Drive**
iCloud Drive allows you to store files in Apple's cloud, ensuring that they're available on all of your Apple devices. This feature is ideal

for those who want to keep their files safe, but also need access to them on the go.

- o To store files in iCloud Drive, simply **drag and drop** them into the **iCloud Drive** folder in Finder, or save directly from applications like Pages or Keynote to iCloud.

- o **Accessing Files Across Devices**: Once your files are in iCloud Drive, they can be accessed not only on your Mac mini but also on your iPhone, iPad, and even on a Windows PC (via iCloud for Windows).

The beauty of iCloud Drive is that it keeps your files synced across all your devices. For example, if you edit a document on your Mac mini, it will automatically sync and be available for viewing or editing on your iPhone or iPad.

7. **Optimizing   Storage   with   iCloud**
   If you're low on storage, macOS will suggest moving files to iCloud. This allows you to **offload** files from your Mac mini to the cloud without losing access to them.

- o **Store Files in iCloud**: You can enable this feature by going to **System Preferences** > **Apple ID** > **iCloud** and then checking the **Optimize Mac Storage** box. This will ensure that files you haven't used in a while are stored in iCloud, while only recently accessed files remain on your Mac mini.

File Management Best Practices

Now that you know how to monitor your storage and organize your files with Finder and iCloud, here are some best practices to keep your file management system running smoothly:

1. **Use Descriptive File Names**

   A good habit is to name your files descriptively so that you can easily find them later. Instead of naming a file "Document1," name it something like "Project_Proposal_2025" or "Vacation_Photos_June." This will make it easier for you to locate files using Finder search.

2. **Regularly Clean Up Your Files**

   Make it a habit to go through your files at least once every couple of months and remove what you no longer need. Old apps, duplicate files, and forgotten documents can pile up quickly and eat into your storage space.

3. **Backup Important Files**

   Use Time Machine or another backup solution to keep your files secure. Backing up your important documents, photos, and videos will protect them in case something goes wrong with your Mac mini.

APPLE M4 PRO MAC MINI USER GUIDE

Setting Up iCloud and Syncing Devices

When you set up your Mac mini M4 Pro, you're not just getting a new device—you're stepping into the heart of Apple's ecosystem. One of the most powerful features that make the Apple experience seamless across devices is **iCloud**. iCloud allows you to sync data, apps, and files across all your Apple devices, from your Mac mini to your iPhone, iPad, and even Apple Watch. It creates a unified experience, so you never feel disconnected, even when you're moving from one device to another.

In this section, we'll walk you through setting up iCloud on your Mac mini, syncing data with your other Apple devices, and configuring iCloud Drive for file storage and management. With iCloud, you can keep your emails, contacts, photos, notes, and apps updated automatically—no matter what Apple device you're using.

Step 1: Setting Up iCloud on Your Mac mini M4 Pro

The first step to integrating iCloud into your Mac mini M4 Pro is to make sure you're signed in with your Apple ID. iCloud is tied to your Apple ID, so without signing in, you won't be able to take full advantage of its features.

1. **Sign In to iCloud**

    o Open **System Preferences** by clicking the Apple logo at the top left of your screen and selecting **System Preferences** from the drop-down menu.

- Click on **Apple ID** at the top right of the window. If you're not signed in, you'll see an option to **Sign In**. Enter your Apple ID and password (this is the same ID you use on your iPhone or other Apple devices).

- Once signed in, you'll be taken to a page that shows your Apple ID details. If you're signed in correctly, you'll be able to see all the iCloud services you can enable.

2. **Enable iCloud Services**

- In the **iCloud** tab under **Apple ID**, you'll see a list of options you can choose to sync with iCloud. Here are the most popular services:

  - **iCloud Drive**: This is the central place where all your files from apps like Pages, Numbers, Keynote, and others will be stored. It allows you to access files from any Apple device.

  - **Photos**: Keep all your photos and videos synced across devices. If you take a photo on your iPhone, it will automatically appear on your Mac mini, and vice versa.

  - **Contacts, Calendars, and Reminders**: Sync your contacts, events, and to-dos so they are accessible on all devices.

  - **Mail**: Enable iCloud Mail to keep your emails in sync.

- **Safari**: If you're a fan of Apple's browser, Safari can sync your bookmarks and open tabs across all devices.

- **Notes and Messages**: Sync your notes and iMessages, so no matter where you're working from, you can pick up exactly where you left off.

   o   To enable any service, simply check the box next to it.

3. **Verify iCloud Settings**

   o   After selecting the services you'd like to sync, click **Done** to finalize your settings.

   o   It's important to periodically verify that iCloud is working properly. If you notice any syncing issues, you can always come back here to check or troubleshoot.

Step 2: Syncing Data Across Your Apple Devices

iCloud's true power lies in its ability to sync data across all your Apple devices seamlessly. Whether it's your iPhone, iPad, or Mac mini, once iCloud is set up, you can work across devices without missing a beat.

1. **Syncing iPhone, iPad, or Other Apple Devices**

   o   **iPhone/iPad Setup**: On your iPhone or iPad, go to **Settings**, then tap on your name at the top of the screen. Next, select **iCloud**, and from there, enable the same iCloud features that you did on your Mac mini, such as iCloud Drive, Photos,

Contacts, and more. As long as you're signed in with the same Apple ID, these features will sync across all your devices.

- o **Apple Watch**: If you have an Apple Watch, it will sync with your iPhone, and in turn, with iCloud. Ensure your iPhone is syncing with iCloud, and the watch will automatically follow suit.

- o Once set up on all devices, your data, apps, and settings will sync automatically. For example, if you add a new contact on your Mac mini, it will instantly appear on your iPhone.

2. **Keeping Apps in Sync**

- o **App Sync**: Many Apple apps are built to work seamlessly across devices. For instance, when you create a note on your Mac mini using the **Notes** app, it will instantly appear on your iPhone. The same goes for **Contacts**, **Calendar events**, and even **Reminders**. Any updates made on one device will show up on all others within seconds.

- o **Messages and FaceTime**: iCloud also syncs your **Messages** and **FaceTime** across all devices. If you receive a text on your iPhone, you can continue the conversation on your Mac mini without skipping a beat. This makes staying connected a lot easier when using multiple devices.

APPLE M4 PRO MAC MINI USER GUIDE

Step 3: Setting Up iCloud Drive for File Storage

iCloud Drive is Apple's cloud storage service, offering a place where you can store documents, photos, videos, and other files, and access them from any device.

1. **Enable iCloud Drive**

   o On your Mac mini, go back to the **Apple ID** settings under **System Preferences**, and check the box for **iCloud Drive**. This will enable cloud storage and allow you to start syncing files across all devices.

2. **Using iCloud Drive on Your Mac mini**

   o You'll see **iCloud Drive** appear in the **Finder** sidebar. Simply drag and drop your files or folders into this location, and they will automatically sync with your other Apple devices.

   o iCloud Drive works just like a regular folder. You can access, edit, or move files, and any changes will be reflected across your devices in real-time.

3. **Accessing iCloud Drive on Your iPhone or iPad**

   o On your iPhone or iPad, open the **Files** app. Here, you'll see a folder labeled **iCloud Drive**. Tap into it to view all the files stored in your cloud. Any document saved here will sync between your Mac mini, iPhone, and iPad, so you can start working on one device and finish on another.

4. **Managing iCloud Storage**

    o iCloud offers 5GB of free storage, but depending on how much data you store, you may need to upgrade. You can manage your iCloud storage by going to **System Preferences > Apple ID > iCloud > Manage Storage**. Here, you can see how much space is being used and what is consuming the most space. If you need more storage, you can upgrade your plan directly from this page.

Step 4: Syncing Apps via iCloud

In addition to files, iCloud also syncs apps across all your devices. Here's how to ensure that your apps remain consistent across devices:

1. **App Store Purchases**

    o All apps you purchase from the **App Store** are linked to your Apple ID. If you've purchased an app on your iPhone, you can download the same app on your Mac mini without having to pay again. The best part is that your app data—like game progress or notes in a productivity app—syncs automatically, so you're always up to date.

2. **App Data Syncing**

    o Many apps now use iCloud to sync data. For example, if you use a third-party note-taking app like Evernote or Microsoft OneNote, these apps can sync with iCloud, allowing you to access your notes from any device. Be sure to enable iCloud

APPLE M4 PRO MAC MINI USER GUIDE

syncing within the app's settings to ensure data flows across devices.

Step 5: Troubleshooting iCloud Syncing Issues

Even though iCloud works seamlessly for most users, there are occasional hiccups. If you notice that your files or apps aren't syncing properly, here are some troubleshooting tips:

1. **Check iCloud Storage**

   o Sometimes syncing stops if your iCloud storage is full. Visit **System Preferences > Apple ID > iCloud > Manage Storage** to see if you need to free up space.

2. **Ensure Devices Are Signed Into iCloud**

   o Double-check that all your devices are signed into iCloud with the same Apple ID. If they aren't, syncing won't happen. You can verify this in the **Settings** app on your iPhone or iPad, or in **System Preferences > Apple ID** on your Mac mini.

3. **Ensure Wi-Fi Connection**

   o Syncing data between devices relies on a stable Wi-Fi connection. Make sure that both your Mac mini and your other Apple devices are connected to the same Wi-Fi network.

4. **Check iCloud Status**

   o   Sometimes Apple's iCloud servers may experience downtime.
       You can visit the Apple System Status page to see if there are
       any issues with iCloud services.

MAXIMIZING PERFORMANCE

Understanding the Apple M4 Pro Chip

When you first open up your Apple M4 Pro Mac mini, you're not just unboxing a computer—you're unveiling a powerhouse designed to deliver top-tier performance for a wide range of tasks. The beating heart of this incredible machine is the Apple M4 Pro chip, a marvel of modern engineering that brings the power of both the CPU and GPU together in perfect harmony.

In this section, we're going to dive deep into what makes the M4 Pro chip tick, specifically looking at the architecture, the role of the 14-core CPU, and the 20-core GPU. But don't worry, we'll break everything down so it's easy to understand. Whether you're a casual user or someone who relies on heavy-duty tasks like video editing, gaming, or software development, understanding the M4 Pro chip will help you get the most out of your Mac mini.

The Evolution of Apple's Silicon

Apple's transition from Intel processors to its own Apple Silicon, starting with the M1 chip and followed by the M1 Pro and M1 Max, was a game-changer. But the M4 Pro takes things even further. With each new generation,

Apple has fine-tuned its processors to be faster, more energy-efficient, and, most importantly, more capable of handling the tasks that matter most to users. The M4 Pro is a major leap in performance and efficiency, setting the stage for an entirely new level of computing power.

At its core, the Apple M4 Pro chip is an integrated system-on-a-chip (SoC), meaning it combines the CPU, GPU, memory, and other essential components into one single piece of hardware. This architecture eliminates the need for separate parts, creating a smoother, more efficient experience for the user.

The 14-Core CPU: Power Meets Efficiency

When you hear "14-core CPU," it might sound like something only found in high-end gaming PCs or workstations, but the M4 Pro is engineered to use these cores more efficiently than ever before.

What is a Core?

A core is the part of the CPU that does the heavy lifting when it comes to processing tasks. Having more cores means that your computer can handle more tasks simultaneously, especially those that require a lot of processing power—think complex calculations, rendering, or compiling code.

The Apple M4 Pro chip's 14-core CPU is divided into two different types of cores: **performance cores** and **efficiency cores**.

- **Performance Cores**: These are the heavy hitters of the CPU. They're designed to handle demanding tasks like running intensive software or multitasking with large files. The M4 Pro chip features **10**

APPLE M4 PRO MAC MINI USER GUIDE

performance cores, meaning these cores are optimized for speed and power. Whether you're editing high-resolution video, running virtual machines, or doing 3D modeling, these cores are up for the job.

- **Efficiency Cores**: These are more power-conscious. The M4 Pro has **4 efficiency cores** designed to handle lighter tasks like browsing the web, checking email, or running background processes. The beauty of having efficiency cores is that they can operate without draining the battery or wasting energy, allowing the Mac mini to run smoothly and coolly during less demanding tasks.

How They Work Together

The magic of the M4 Pro chip is how these two types of cores work together. The chip uses a process called **dynamic task switching**, meaning it knows when to shift demanding tasks to the performance cores and when to delegate lighter tasks to the efficiency cores. This ensures that your Mac mini always delivers the right amount of power while staying energy-efficient. The result? A machine that doesn't just handle tasks; it adapts to your needs in real-time, offering seamless performance across the board.

The 20-Core GPU: Graphics Performance Like Never Before

Now let's turn our attention to the graphics power of the M4 Pro chip. The **20-core GPU** is another reason why this Mac mini is a powerhouse. If you're into graphics-intensive tasks like video editing, 3D rendering, or gaming, the GPU is a crucial component.

What Makes the GPU So Powerful?

Graphics processing units, or GPUs, are specialized hardware designed to handle the calculations required for rendering images and video. While CPUs are designed to handle a wide variety of tasks, GPUs are focused specifically on rendering visuals. Having more cores in the GPU means that more calculations can happen at once, which directly impacts the speed and quality of the graphics.

The M4 Pro's **20-core GPU** delivers exceptional graphics performance, capable of handling 3D rendering, high-end gaming, and complex visual effects with ease. This is particularly beneficial for creative professionals who rely on intensive software like **Final Cut Pro**, **Adobe Premiere Pro**, or **Blender**. For instance, when editing video, the GPU can accelerate real-time previews and render video faster, allowing users to work more efficiently without frustrating delays.

The Power of Unified Memory

What truly sets Apple's M4 Pro GPU apart is its integration with the CPU and RAM via **unified memory architecture**. Instead of having separate memory pools for the CPU and GPU, both components share the same memory. This results in faster data transfer, which is especially noticeable when you're working with large files like 4K video footage or high-resolution 3D models.

This unified memory architecture means that your Mac mini can access the data it needs without waiting for it to be copied back and forth between different memory pools. It also reduces the overall power consumption because everything is working from the same memory space, cutting down on the amount of energy required for these intensive tasks.

How the CPU and GPU Work Together

What really elevates the performance of the Apple M4 Pro chip is the seamless collaboration between the CPU and GPU. While each component is powerful on its own, their ability to work in tandem creates an exceptional user experience. For instance:

- **Video Editing**: When you're editing a video, the CPU handles the core computations (such as cutting, trimming, and adjusting video clips), while the GPU takes over the visual tasks (like applying effects or rendering previews). With 10 performance cores and 20 GPU cores working together, you get a smooth and responsive editing experience, even with high-resolution footage.

- **3D Rendering and Gaming**: When rendering complex 3D models or playing graphically intense games, both the CPU and GPU contribute to the task. The CPU handles the logic and physics calculations, while the GPU does the heavy lifting of rendering the visuals. Together, they can process millions of calculations at once, making your Mac mini capable of handling professional-level 3D rendering or gaming at high settings.

- **Machine Learning and AI**: Another area where the CPU and GPU work together is in **machine learning** tasks. The M4 Pro chip leverages the combined power of both the CPU and GPU to accelerate AI and machine learning processes. The GPU's parallel processing capabilities allow it to handle the vast amounts of data required for AI tasks, while the CPU manages the logic and decision-making process.

Performance Benchmarks: Real-World Impact

So, how does all of this translate into real-world performance? Let's take a look at a few examples:

- **Video Editing**: If you're working with 4K or even 8K video, the M4 Pro chip will allow you to scrub through footage and edit in real time without lag. You'll notice significantly faster export times as well.

- **Gaming**: While the Mac mini M4 Pro isn't marketed as a gaming machine, its 20-core GPU delivers an exceptional experience for graphically demanding games. You'll be able to play the latest titles with smooth frame rates and high-quality visuals, all while maintaining a low temperature and quiet operation.

- **Software Development**: If you're a developer, compiling large codebases or running virtual machines becomes much faster with the 14-core CPU, allowing you to test and deploy applications in record time.

Optimizing the GPU and CPU for Intensive Tasks

The Apple Mac mini M4 Pro is an absolute powerhouse, particularly when it comes to handling demanding tasks like video editing, gaming, and 3D rendering. With its M4 Pro chip that combines a 14-core CPU and a 20-core GPU, this little box of performance is built to handle intensive workloads with ease. However, to make sure you're extracting every ounce of power from your Mac mini, it's essential to understand how to optimize the CPU and GPU for the best performance.

Whether you're a video editor working with 4K footage, a gamer diving into graphically intense games, or a 3D artist rendering complex models, optimizing your Mac mini M4 Pro for these tasks can make a noticeable difference. Let's break it down and help you get the most out of your machine.

1. Understanding the CPU and GPU

Before we dive into optimization tips, it's important to understand what exactly you're working with. The **CPU (Central Processing Unit)** and **GPU (Graphics Processing Unit)** are the two main components that handle most of your computer's work.

- The **CPU** is responsible for handling general tasks such as running programs, calculations, and most of the system operations. It's your

Mac mini's brain, taking care of everything from organizing files to handling input/output requests.

- The **GPU**, on the other hand, is responsible for handling graphics-heavy tasks such as rendering images, processing visual effects, and powering smooth video playback. It's particularly important in tasks like video editing, gaming, and 3D rendering, where graphical processing is intensive.

2. Configuring Your Mac mini for Optimal CPU Performance

While macOS automatically allocates system resources between the CPU and GPU, there are a few things you can do to ensure that the CPU is performing at its peak when you need it most.

2.1. Managing Processor Usage Through Activity Monitor

The Activity Monitor in macOS gives you an overview of how your system is using CPU resources. This tool is essential for keeping track of which processes are consuming the most processing power.

- **How to Use It**:

  o Go to Applications > Utilities > Activity Monitor.

  o Select the "CPU" tab to see a breakdown of the processes using the CPU.

  o Pay attention to any processes that are consuming an unusually high amount of CPU. If you're running video editing software, for example, you'll likely see that the software is using a significant portion of the CPU.

2.2. Close Unnecessary Applications and Processes

One of the easiest ways to ensure the CPU isn't being overloaded is by quitting unnecessary applications running in the background.

- **How to do it**: If you're working on a heavy task like video editing or rendering, ensure that only essential applications are open. The fewer the apps, the more CPU resources will be available for your demanding task.

- **System Preferences**: Navigate to **System Preferences > Users & Groups > Login Items** and disable any apps that automatically start up when you log in that you don't need.

2.3. Enable 'Automatic Graphics Switching' (for Laptop-Style Mac mini)

If you're using a Mac mini that supports dynamic switching between integrated and discrete GPUs (like MacBook Pros), enabling this feature ensures your system balances power consumption and performance.

- **Where to find it**: Go to **System Preferences > Energy Saver**, then check the box labeled **Automatic Graphics Switching**. This will allow the system to dynamically switch between power-saving modes and high-performance modes, depending on the task.

2.4. CPU Performance in Activity Settings

For advanced users, the **Energy Saver** settings can influence CPU performance. If you're running intensive tasks that require all of your CPU's power, go ahead and disable some of the battery-saving settings.

- **How to do it**: Go to **System Preferences** > **Energy Saver**, and select **High Performance** (if applicable). This ensures that the CPU runs at full power, without any throttling.

3. Configuring Your Mac mini for Optimal GPU Performance

The GPU is where the real magic happens for video editing, gaming, and 3D rendering. Here's how to ensure that it's working at full throttle for your demanding tasks.

3.1. Prioritize GPU-Heavy Apps with Activity Monitor

Just like you did with the CPU, Activity Monitor is also helpful for keeping tabs on GPU usage. If you're doing something that requires a lot of graphics processing (e.g., editing high-res videos), it's essential to ensure that your GPU is taking the lead.

- **How to monitor it**: Open **Activity Monitor** and switch to the **GPU** tab to view GPU usage. Some apps might require more GPU resources than others, so be sure to check that your demanding app is using the GPU effectively.

3.2. Using Metal for Enhanced GPU Performance

macOS uses a graphics API called **Metal**, which is specifically designed for high-performance graphics tasks. Metal allows apps like Final Cut Pro, Logic Pro, and other professional software to take full advantage of the M4 Pro chip's 20-core GPU.

- **For video editors**: If you're using video editing software like Final Cut Pro, make sure that you've enabled **Metal** rendering. This ensures that your Mac mini M4 Pro uses the GPU for rendering, speeding up the process significantly.

- **How to enable it**: Most professional apps, such as Final Cut Pro, automatically use Metal when available. However, always check the settings of the application you're using to confirm that Metal is enabled for optimal GPU usage.

3.3. Using External GPUs (eGPU)

If you're working on a project that demands even more graphics power, you might consider using an **eGPU (external graphics processing unit)**. While the Mac mini M4 Pro already comes with a powerful 20-core GPU, an eGPU can be a game-changer for extremely demanding tasks like complex 3D rendering.

- **How to use an eGPU**: Connect your eGPU to one of the Thunderbolt 4 ports, and your system should automatically recognize it. Some apps allow you to select which GPU to use for rendering, so be sure to configure your settings accordingly.

3.4. Update Graphics Drivers and Software

For both CPU and GPU optimization, ensuring your system is up-to-date is essential. Apple regularly releases updates for macOS and driver support, which can improve performance and fix bugs related to graphics processing.

- **How to update**: Go to **System Preferences** > **Software Update** to ensure you're running the latest version of macOS and that all hardware drivers are up-to-date.

4. Managing Workload Distribution Between CPU and GPU

Now that you have both your CPU and GPU optimized, the next step is to manage how your Mac mini allocates resources between the two for the best performance in specific applications.

4.1. Use Software That Automatically Balances CPU and GPU Workloads

Most professional software, such as **Adobe Premiere Pro**, **Blender**, and **Final Cut Pro**, is optimized to intelligently distribute workloads between the CPU and GPU. However, understanding how these applications interact with the hardware can help you optimize your workflow.

- **Example for video editors**: In **Final Cut Pro**, you can configure the rendering settings to prioritize **GPU rendering** over CPU, which can speed up the process. For software that handles both CPU and GPU processing, make sure the task is split effectively to minimize bottlenecks.

4.2. Prioritize Multithreading for CPU-Intensive Tasks

For tasks that are CPU-bound, such as complex calculations, rendering, or compiling code, macOS does a good job of distributing workloads across the cores. However, you can enhance this by ensuring that the application you're using is set to **multithread** properly.

- **How to check**: In your application's settings, look for options to enable multithreading or high-performance mode. Many programs allow you to assign how many CPU cores to dedicate to specific tasks. This ensures that the CPU's 14 cores are working to their full potential without overloading one single core.

4.3. Optimize Software-Specific Settings

Certain software applications allow you to customize CPU and GPU performance based on your current needs. Here's what to look out for:

- **Video Editing**: Software like **Adobe Premiere Pro** and **Final Cut Pro** allows you to choose between **CPU rendering** and **GPU acceleration**. When working on large video files, GPU acceleration should be prioritized as it greatly reduces rendering time.

- **Gaming**: For gaming, make sure your game is set to run at **High Performance** mode, ensuring that the GPU is fully utilized. Games like **Shadow of the Tomb Raider** or **Cyberpunk 2077** will automatically adjust settings for you, but always double-check the in-game settings to ensure you're getting the most out of your Mac mini.

- **3D Rendering**: If you're using software like **Blender** or **Cinema 4D**, ensure that the renderer is set to use your **GPU** instead of your CPU for faster rendering times. Check the settings within your software to ensure GPU acceleration is enabled.

5. Conclusion: Get the Most Out of Your Mac mini M4 Pro

Optimizing your Mac mini M4 Pro for demanding tasks is all about understanding the strengths of both the CPU and GPU and configuring them in a way that maximizes performance without causing overheating or bottlenecks. With the right adjustments, your Mac mini can handle the most resource-heavy tasks with ease, whether you're editing 4K videos, playing the latest games, or rendering 3D models.

By following the tips outlined here, you can ensure that your Mac mini M4 Pro is always ready to tackle even the most intensive workflows. With powerful CPU and GPU optimizations, this machine is capable of doing it all – now it's up to you to harness that power and take your creative or professional work to the next level.

Configuring Memory for Speed and Efficiency

When it comes to performance, **memory** is at the heart of it all. Whether you're working on a creative project, developing software, or simply managing a few tabs in your browser, how your Mac mini uses memory can make all the difference in speed and efficiency. With the Mac mini M4 Pro, you've got a powerful machine under the hood, but maximizing that power means understanding how memory works in **macOS Sequoia** and knowing how to optimize it for the best possible performance.

Let's dive into how macOS uses memory, and more importantly, how you can make sure it's being used efficiently to give you a smooth, responsive experience.

How Memory is Utilized in macOS Sequoia

At its core, **macOS Sequoia** is designed to manage memory intelligently. Unlike older operating systems that might leave you manually managing memory usage, macOS is built to automatically allocate RAM in the most efficient way possible. It does this by using a system called **unified memory**.

In traditional computer systems, CPU and GPU each have their own separate memory (RAM). This can lead to inefficiencies, as data needs to be transferred between the two whenever a program calls on resources from both the CPU and GPU. With **unified memory**, however, macOS can let both the CPU and GPU share the same pool of memory, which makes accessing and processing data faster and more efficient.

For your Mac mini M4 Pro, this means that no matter what task you're working on—whether it's video editing, coding, or gaming—the system allocates memory where it's needed, when it's needed, reducing delays and optimizing overall performance.

But this doesn't mean you can just let your Mac mini handle everything. Even though macOS does a lot of the heavy lifting for you, there are still things you can do to ensure that memory is being used in the best possible way.

Tips for Optimizing Memory Usage on Your Mac mini

1. Keep an Eye on Activity Monitor

First things first, get familiar with **Activity Monitor**. Think of it as the "control center" for managing memory and resources on your Mac mini. This tool shows you what apps and processes are running, how much memory they're using, and whether any programs are hogging too many resources.

To open Activity Monitor:

1. Go to your **Applications** folder.

2. Click on **Utilities**.

3. Open **Activity Monitor**.

You'll see the **Memory** tab at the top of the window. This section tells you exactly how much memory is being used and which apps are consuming the most. If you spot any apps taking up an unusually high amount of memory, you can close them from within Activity Monitor to free up space.

Memory Pressure: This graph is particularly helpful. It shows you the pressure on your memory, which helps you assess whether your Mac mini is using memory efficiently. A green bar means things are running smoothly, while yellow or red indicate high memory usage, which could slow things down.

APPLE M4 PRO MAC MINI USER GUIDE

2. Manage Open Apps and Windows

We've all been there—too many apps, too many tabs, and everything starts to slow down. While macOS tries to handle memory efficiently, the more apps you have running, the more memory your Mac mini has to divide between them. If you're working on something that requires a lot of resources (like video editing or 3D rendering), you'll want to ensure that you only have essential apps open.

Here are a few tips:

- **Close unused apps**: If you're not using an app, close it. Even though macOS suspends inactive apps, they can still use up valuable memory.

- **Use tabs instead of windows**: If you're working with a lot of documents or web pages, use tabs instead of opening multiple windows. Tabs are typically lighter on memory usage.

3. Use the "Memory Usage" View to Prioritize Important Apps

macOS lets you prioritize apps based on how much memory they're using. If you're working on a task that requires a lot of resources, such as running a design program or compiling code, make sure that these apps have enough memory to work without being interrupted by others.

To manage this:

- **Limit unnecessary processes**: If a background process or app is using memory but you don't need it running, disable or quit it.

- **App usage**: Some apps, like browsers, can consume a lot of memory when you have multiple tabs open. Consider using a browser like **Safari** for fewer memory issues, as it's optimized for macOS and typically uses less memory than others.

4. Manage Memory-Hungry Software

Certain software programs are particularly resource-intensive, such as video editing programs (e.g., **Final Cut Pro**), graphic design tools (e.g., **Photoshop**), and 3D modeling applications (e.g., **Blender**). These programs require a lot of memory to operate smoothly, but there are ways to optimize how they use memory.

Here are some tips:

- **Close all other apps**: When working with memory-hungry programs, close any unnecessary apps running in the background to ensure these programs get as much memory as possible.

- **Increase RAM (if possible)**: Although the Mac mini M4 Pro has unified memory, some users might need to upgrade their system if they plan to use demanding applications regularly. If your model supports upgrades, consider boosting your RAM to handle more tasks simultaneously.

- **Use disk storage for overflow**: Some apps allow you to store temporary data (like cache files) on disk instead of in RAM. Check the settings of your applications to see if you can adjust how they use memory.

5. Enable Virtual Memory Management

macOS uses **virtual memory** to simulate more memory than what's physically installed in your system. When your Mac runs out of physical memory, it uses disk space to act as additional memory. This is a great backup, but it's much slower than real RAM. To ensure macOS is using virtual memory effectively, here are a few tips:

- **Keep enough free storage space**: Virtual memory requires free disk space to swap data in and out of RAM. If your Mac mini's storage is almost full, it might cause slowdowns.

- **Don't overfill your hard drive**: Aim to keep at least 10–20% of your disk space free for macOS to use as virtual memory.

Understanding Memory Management in macOS

macOS handles memory management in a way that's largely invisible to the user, but understanding a few key concepts can help you make smarter decisions about how to optimize performance. For example, macOS uses something called **memory compression**, which automatically reduces the size of inactive apps and data to make room for more active ones.

If you've ever wondered why your Mac mini doesn't seem to slow down even with a lot of apps open, that's because macOS is working behind the scenes to compress memory and use it more efficiently. This is where your Mac mini's **unified memory architecture** really shines—it allows the system to prioritize resources dynamically, based on what's active and most needed.

Using Apple Intelligence for Enhanced Productivity

Apple's dedication to integrating artificial intelligence (AI) into its devices has taken a major leap forward with **macOS Sequoia**. This new version of macOS is not just about improved hardware performance but also about a more intuitive, personalized, and productive user experience. **Apple Intelligence**—which includes features like **enhanced Siri**, **smart notifications**, and **AI-powered task management tools**—is designed to help users get more done with less effort. These tools not only make your Mac mini M4 Pro smarter, but they also streamline your workflow, making daily tasks easier and faster.

In this section, we'll break down the key Apple Intelligence features in macOS Sequoia and explain how they can boost your productivity in tangible ways. Whether you're a creative professional, a busy student, or a business user, understanding how to use these features will save you time and help you work more efficiently.

1. Enhanced Siri: Your Voice-Powered Personal Assistant

Siri, Apple's intelligent voice assistant, has come a long way since its early days. With macOS Sequoia, Siri is not only faster and more accurate, but it has also become a central part of Apple Intelligence. Siri's capabilities are now deeply integrated into macOS, offering powerful tools to help manage your tasks, automate routines, and search your system more efficiently.

How Siri Can Boost Productivity:

- **Smart Commands for Daily Tasks:** Siri now understands a wider range of commands, making it easier to control your Mac mini hands-free. For example, you can ask Siri to open specific apps, send emails, set reminders, or even adjust system settings—all without lifting a finger. This is especially useful for multitasking or when you're deep into work and can't stop what you're doing to type.

- **Contextual Understanding:** Siri can now follow the context of your conversations better than ever. You can ask for information in a more conversational manner, and Siri will understand what you mean. For example, if you ask, "What's my next meeting today?" Siri will pull up your calendar events for that day. If you follow it with "What time is it?" Siri will respond with the current time, seamlessly understanding you're asking for the time in relation to your schedule.

- **Multi-Step Automation:** One of the most exciting ways Siri can enhance productivity is through multi-step automation. With Siri Shortcuts, you can create custom workflows to handle multiple tasks at once. For example, if you're a content creator, you can set a shortcut that automatically opens your video editing software, adjusts your Mac's display settings for editing, and even pulls up your project files. This eliminates the need to manually navigate multiple steps, saving you time and keeping you in your creative flow.

Pro Tip: Use Siri to set Focus Modes. When you're in deep work mode, tell Siri to "Activate Focus Mode" or "Set Do Not Disturb." Siri will silence notifications, ensuring you're not distracted by pings or alerts during important work sessions.

2. Smart Notifications: Less Interruptions, More Focus

With smart notifications, macOS Sequoia has taken the user experience up a notch by offering more personalized, context-aware notifications. Rather than being bombarded with endless alerts, you'll only be notified about the things that truly matter to you at any given moment.

How Smart Notifications Improve Productivity:

- **Context-Aware Alerts:** Thanks to machine learning, macOS can now prioritize notifications based on your habits. If you're in the middle of a meeting, Siri won't distract you with irrelevant notifications. Instead, it will focus on showing you high-priority messages or reminders that align with your current task. This reduces the mental load of constantly checking notifications, allowing you to focus more on the work at hand.

- **Notification Grouping:** Smart notifications also come with grouping features that ensure your screen isn't cluttered. Similar notifications—such as app updates, social media alerts, or messages—will be grouped together in one notification, instead of interrupting your workflow with multiple individual pings. You can then review them at your convenience without being disturbed.

- **Snooze and Time-Based Reminders:** You can now manage your notifications more effectively by setting them to snooze for a period of time or until a certain event. For example, if you need to concentrate for the next hour, simply snooze notifications from certain apps until after your focused work session. This helps maintain productivity by preventing distractions at the wrong moments.

Pro Tip: Make use of the Focus Mode and combine it with Do Not Disturb. Customize your Focus Mode so that you only receive notifications from work-related apps or essential contacts during work hours, while silencing everything else.

3. AI-Powered Task Management Tools: Getting Things Done, Smarter

macOS Sequoia brings powerful AI-driven task management tools to your Mac mini. These tools, backed by Apple Intelligence, help you organize, prioritize, and complete your tasks in an efficient, almost effortless way.

How AI Task Management Features Enhance Productivity:

- **Task Suggestions and Reminders:** macOS Sequoia can suggest tasks based on your past behavior. For instance, if you frequently draft reports every Monday morning, your Mac may prompt you with a reminder or even automatically create a task for you to start preparing for it. Siri can also suggest tasks from your calendar, emails, or reminders, helping you stay on top of your schedule without having to manually check.

- **Smart Calendar Integration:** macOS Sequoia has an enhanced **Calendar** that uses AI to automatically detect scheduling conflicts or upcoming deadlines. The AI can suggest optimal times for meetings based on your existing schedule, and if you need to adjust something, it will help you find the best alternative slot. It's a seamless way to keep everything on track without the hassle of double-checking your calendar.

- **Focus Scheduling:** AI doesn't just manage tasks, it helps manage your mental focus too. Through **Focus Scheduling**, macOS will help you identify when you're most productive during the day (based on your usage patterns) and suggest times for tackling more challenging tasks. This can help you schedule deep work sessions when you're least likely to be distracted.

- **Smart Reminders:** When you set reminders, macOS can now recommend the optimal time for you to tackle them, depending on your work habits. For example, if you have a reminder to draft an email but macOS detects you're in a meeting, it may suggest to reschedule the reminder for later or adjust the timing based on your free slots.

Pro Tip: Use Focus Time to block off specific hours dedicated only to work-related tasks, and then schedule automatic reminders to check in on your progress. This ensures that your day stays organized, with a perfect balance between focused work and necessary breaks.

4. Automating Routine Tasks: Doing More with Less Effort

Apple Intelligence isn't just about managing tasks—it's about **automation**. With **macOS Sequoia**, you can automate many of your daily routines, freeing up valuable time for more important work.

How Automation Improves Productivity:

- **Automator and Shortcuts:** macOS Sequoia comes with **Automator**, an app that allows you to create custom workflows to streamline repetitive tasks. For instance, you can create a workflow that automatically opens the apps you need for work, arranges them in specific positions on your screen, and loads your most recent project files—all with a single command.

- **AI-Powered Siri Shortcuts:** With Siri Shortcuts, you can automate even more specific actions. If you're constantly adjusting settings or repeating a series of actions every day, Siri Shortcuts allows you to program these sequences with simple voice commands. For example, if you frequently update your project management tool and then check your email, you can create a shortcut that performs both actions at once, minimizing manual input.

- **Custom Workflows for Creative Tasks:** If you're a creative professional, you can set up workflows that automatically organize files, run batch editing tasks, or even apply specific filters to images in Adobe Photoshop. These workflows, powered by Apple's AI, can save you hours every week.

Pro Tip: Create time-saving shortcuts for commonly used apps and tasks. Whether you need to open a set of apps in the morning or perform a series of editing steps, Siri Shortcuts can be your secret weapon to boost efficiency.

Managing System Resources for Peak Performance

When it comes to maximizing the performance of your **Apple M4 Pro Mac mini**, understanding how to manage system resources is key to ensuring that your device runs smoothly, even during heavy tasks. The Mac mini M4 Pro, with its cutting-edge **M4 Pro chip**, **20-core GPU**, and up to **64GB of RAM**, is a powerhouse that can handle anything from professional video editing to complex development tasks. However, like any high-performance machine, it needs a bit of management to run at its best.

The good news is that with a little know-how, you can monitor and manage CPU, GPU, and RAM usage effectively to make sure your Mac mini handles even the most demanding workloads with ease. Below, we'll break down the most effective methods to monitor system performance and optimize resource usage.

1. Monitoring System Performance

Before you can optimize your system's performance, it's important to understand how your Mac mini is using its resources. Fortunately, macOS provides several built-in tools that help you track and manage **CPU**, **GPU**, and **RAM** usage.

Using Activity Monitor

Activity Monitor is the macOS tool that shows how your Mac mini is utilizing system resources. It's your first stop when you want to see how much processing power, memory, or storage your Mac is using at any given moment.

1. **Open Activity Monitor**

   o You can find Activity Monitor by searching for it in Spotlight or navigating to **Applications > Utilities > Activity Monitor**.

2. **CPU Usage**

   o The **CPU tab** in Activity Monitor shows how much of your Mac mini's processing power is being used by different apps and processes. If you're working on a resource-heavy task like video editing, you may notice that the CPU usage spikes, and that's perfectly normal. However, you want to avoid the CPU being maxed out for prolonged periods, as it could lead to overheating or lag.

What you can do:

- o If a particular app or process is using too much CPU, check the app's preferences and consider lowering its workload (e.g., reducing resolution in a video editing app). You can also quit unnecessary background processes to free up CPU power.

3. **GPU Usage**

- o For tasks like 3D rendering or gaming, the **GPU tab** shows how much of your graphics card is being used. The Mac mini's **20-core GPU** should handle heavy graphics tasks smoothly, but some apps may demand more GPU power.

What you can do:

- o Like with the CPU, if an app is using an excessive amount of GPU, check for settings that can be adjusted, such as lowering graphics quality or turning off unnecessary visual effects. For video editing or 3D applications, ensure that hardware acceleration is enabled, as it helps offload processing to the GPU.

4. **Memory (RAM) Usage**

- o The **Memory tab** in Activity Monitor shows how much RAM is being used and by which processes. If you're running multiple apps at once, you may notice RAM consumption increase. Running out of memory can slow down your Mac mini and cause apps to crash.

What you can do:

- o If you find your Mac mini running low on RAM, consider closing apps or processes you're not actively using. For heavy workflows, increase your system's RAM capacity if possible (though, keep in mind that the **M4 Pro Mac mini** has fixed RAM, so upgrading would require purchasing a different model).

- o You can also use the **Memory Pressure** graph at the bottom of the Memory tab in Activity Monitor to see how well your system is managing RAM. If it's in the green zone, everything's fine. If it's in the red, your system might be struggling to keep up.

2. Managing CPU, GPU, and RAM Usage

Now that you know how to monitor your system, the next step is optimizing it to ensure peak performance during heavy tasks. Here are some best practices to help you manage CPU, GPU, and RAM usage effectively.

Managing CPU Usage for Optimal Performance

The CPU is the brain of your Mac mini, and keeping it working efficiently is crucial. Here are some tips to avoid overloading the CPU:

1. **Close Unnecessary Apps and Processes**
   When you're working on something that requires a lot of power, like rendering a video or compiling code, close any apps or background

processes you aren't actively using. These apps can silently take up CPU power, even when you're not aware of it.

2. **Use Activity Monitor to Identify Problematic Apps**
If your CPU usage is constantly high, check the **CPU tab** in Activity Monitor to identify which apps are using the most processing power. Look for apps that you don't need to run at that moment and consider closing them.

3. **Update Software**
Software updates often include performance improvements, bug fixes, and optimizations. Keeping your apps and macOS up to date can ensure that your Mac mini is using CPU resources more efficiently.

4. **Limit Background Processes**
Background tasks such as syncing with iCloud, checking for updates, or running scheduled backups can eat up CPU power. Turn off any unnecessary background tasks that may not be crucial to your immediate work.

Optimizing GPU Performance

The 20-core GPU on the Mac mini is designed to handle demanding visual tasks, but even it needs to be managed for peak performance.

1. **Enable Hardware Acceleration**
Many creative and professional applications like Adobe Premiere Pro or DaVinci Resolve offer a setting to enable **hardware**

APPLE M4 PRO MAC MINI USER GUIDE

acceleration, which allows the GPU to handle rendering tasks instead of the CPU. This significantly speeds up processes like video rendering or real-time preview.

2. **Adjust Graphics Settings in Apps**

   Many apps, especially games or video editors, let you adjust the quality of graphics. Lowering the resolution or turning off certain visual effects (such as shadows or reflections) can reduce GPU load without significantly impacting your work.

3. **Use External Monitors Wisely**

   If you're working with multiple displays, consider how your Mac mini handles them. The **M4 Pro chip** can support up to three 6K displays, but adding more monitors or higher resolutions may place additional stress on the GPU. If performance starts to degrade, try reducing the number of active displays or lowering the resolution.

Optimizing RAM for Heavy Tasks

Your Mac mini's **RAM** is essential for multitasking and keeping apps responsive. When you're working on resource-heavy tasks, like editing large video files or running virtual machines, here's how to manage memory effectively:

1. **Keep Track of Memory Usage**

   Use the **Memory tab** in Activity Monitor to monitor how much memory is being used. If your memory pressure is consistently high, your system may need more RAM to perform efficiently.

2. **Close   Unused   Apps   and   Tabs**
Each app and browser tab you open uses a portion of your RAM. Close any apps, documents, or browser tabs that you're not using to free up memory for the tasks that matter.

3. **Use   Virtual   Memory   Efficiently**
macOS uses **virtual memory** to compensate when RAM is full, but this comes at the cost of performance. Avoid running too many apps that drain your RAM, as macOS will start swapping data to disk (which is much slower than RAM).

4. **Consider   Upgrading   RAM   (If   Possible)**
While the **Mac mini M4 Pro** has fixed RAM, the next model in line might provide the memory upgrade you need. If your system regularly runs out of RAM during heavy workflows, consider upgrading to a version with more RAM when possible.

3. Performance Boosting Tools and Tips

Beyond monitoring and managing resources manually, there are several tools and tips that can give your Mac mini an extra boost when needed.

Use Disk Cleanup Tools

Having enough free storage is crucial for smooth system performance, especially when working with large files or running resource-heavy applications. Use **Disk Utility** or third-party apps to clear up cache, old files, and unnecessary data.

Consider Using an SSD for Storage

If you're working with large files, using an external SSD to store them can free up space on your internal drive, ensuring macOS can use that space for caching and virtual memory.

Reset SMC and PRAM/NVRAM

If your Mac mini is feeling sluggish despite following these optimization techniques, try resetting the **System Management Controller (SMC)** and **PRAM/NVRAM**. These resets can help clear out any lingering settings or issues affecting performance.

4. Keeping Your Mac Mini Cool

High performance naturally leads to higher temperatures, especially during intense workloads. To maintain optimal performance, it's important to ensure your Mac mini stays cool.

1. **Ensure   Proper   Ventilation**
   Place your Mac mini in a well-ventilated area to allow for proper airflow. Avoid stacking objects on top of it that could obstruct airflow.

2. **Use   Cooling   Stands   or   Pads**
   If your Mac mini tends to get hot during extended use, consider using a cooling pad or stand to help dissipate heat.

3. **Monitor Temperature**
   Use third-party tools like **iStat Menus** to monitor the temperature of

your Mac mini's components. If you notice excessive heat, stop resource-heavy tasks until the temperature drops.

ADVANCED FEATURES AND CUSTOMIZATION

Unlocking the Power of the 20-Core GPU

The **Apple M4 Pro Mac mini** comes packed with impressive processing power, and at the heart of that power is its **20-core GPU**. Whether you're a professional working with high-resolution video, a gamer craving fluid gameplay, or a creator pushing your graphics software to its limits, the 20-core GPU provides the raw muscle to handle resource-intensive tasks with ease. In this section, we'll dive deep into how to unlock the full potential of the 20-core GPU, optimizing your Mac mini for the most demanding applications and workflows.

What Makes the 20-Core GPU Special?

Before we dive into the settings and tips, it's helpful to understand what makes the 20-core GPU stand out in the Apple M4 Pro chip. This GPU features 20 cores that work together to deliver ultra-fast rendering speeds, enabling smooth performance in applications that require heavy graphics processing.

- **Parallel Processing Power**: The 20-core GPU can perform multiple tasks simultaneously, making it perfect for video editing, 3D rendering, and other professional-grade creative tasks. This architecture enables the GPU to handle complex computations faster, allowing your system to work more efficiently.

- **Real-Time Rendering**: For creatives working in fields like 3D modeling or video production, the GPU's real-time rendering capabilities allow for smoother previews while editing. Whether it's applying special effects or rendering frames in real time, the GPU minimizes lag, giving you a seamless experience.

- **Gaming**: The 20-core GPU isn't just for professional work—it's also a powerhouse for gaming. With support for higher frame rates and detailed graphics, gaming on the Mac mini M4 Pro is smooth and immersive, even in graphically demanding titles.

Maximizing the 20-Core GPU for Video Rendering

When working with video editing software, such as **Final Cut Pro** or **Adobe Premiere Pro**, the GPU's power can make a significant difference in rendering times, video effects, and playback quality. Here's how to make the most of the 20-core GPU for these high-performance tasks:

1. Enable Hardware Acceleration

Both Final Cut Pro and Adobe Premiere Pro leverage hardware acceleration, which offloads certain tasks from the CPU to the GPU. This not only speeds up the rendering process but also ensures a smoother playback experience.

- **Final Cut Pro**: Go to **Final Cut Pro > Preferences > Playback**, and make sure **Better Performance** is selected under **Video Processing**.

This allows the GPU to handle video effects and rendering, giving you faster previews and quicker exports.

- **Adobe Premiere Pro**: Navigate to **Premiere Pro > Preferences > Media**, then check the option **Enable GPU Acceleration**. Make sure your system recognizes the 20-core GPU for accelerated video playback and rendering.

2. Optimize Video Export Settings

When exporting your videos, use settings that are designed to fully utilize the 20-core GPU. Exporting with higher resolution and bitrate settings demands more from your system, but the GPU's processing power allows you to handle it effectively.

- **Final Cut Pro**: In the export settings, choose **H.264 or ProRes 422** as your codec to make full use of the GPU's power. ProRes 422 in particular is optimized for high-quality video rendering, ensuring you get a professional-grade output without lag.

- **Adobe Premiere Pro**: For exporting in **4K** or **HDR** formats, ensure that **Hardware Encoding** is selected under the **Export Settings > Video** tab. This uses the GPU to speed up the export process without compromising quality.

3. Utilize GPU for Effects and Color Grading

Both **Final Cut Pro** and **Adobe Premiere Pro** use GPU acceleration to apply video effects, including color grading, transitions, and special effects. By tapping into the GPU's cores, these effects are rendered faster and more efficiently.

- **Final Cut Pro**: Use the **Color Board** or **Color Wheels** for color grading. With the 20-core GPU, you'll notice smoother adjustments, especially when applying LUTs (Look-Up Tables) or correcting footage.

- **Adobe Premiere Pro**: When adding color effects or using advanced grading techniques with **Lumetri Color**, the GPU ensures that each adjustment is rendered without significant delay, even for 4K or HDR footage.

Taking Advantage of the 20-Core GPU for Gaming

The **20-core GPU** is not just for professionals—it's an absolute beast when it comes to gaming, too. Whether you're a casual gamer or a dedicated streamer, here's how to set up your Mac mini for the best gaming performance:

1. Set the Graphics Settings in Games

Most modern games give you the ability to tweak graphics settings for optimal performance. When gaming on your Mac mini M4 Pro, you'll want to adjust the settings to ensure that the 20-core GPU delivers smooth gameplay.

- **Resolution**: Choose a resolution that balances graphical detail and performance. For smoother performance, you may want to stick to

1080p or **1440p** for more demanding games, while the 20-core GPU can handle **4K** gaming without much strain for less intensive games.

- **Graphics Quality**: Opt for **High** or **Ultra** settings for most games, but if you notice any lag, you can dial back settings like shadows, reflections, or anti-aliasing. The 20-core GPU is designed to handle most games at **high settings**, so you should be able to enjoy immersive visuals without sacrificing frame rates.

2. Enable Metal API for Graphics Optimization

Apple's **Metal API** is optimized for the Mac mini's hardware, allowing the 20-core GPU to work efficiently with games and applications. Ensure that Metal is being utilized in your games to get the best possible performance.

- **Metal API**: Most modern games and game engines, such as **Unity** or **Unreal Engine**, support Metal by default on macOS. If you're developing your own game or using a game engine, make sure Metal is the selected graphics API to maximize GPU performance.

3. Adjust Game-Specific Settings

Some games, like **Shadow of the Tomb Raider** or **Diablo III**, offer specific settings that work best with high-end GPUs like the one in the Mac mini M4 Pro. Check the settings to enable **V-Sync** or **Adaptive Sync** to reduce screen tearing, ensuring a smoother gaming experience.

Fine-Tuning the GPU for High-Performance Workloads

1. Monitor GPU Usage with Activity Monitor

macOS has a built-in tool called **Activity Monitor** that lets you track GPU usage, among other system resources. Keeping an eye on GPU usage can help you determine if the 20-core GPU is being fully utilized during resource-heavy tasks.

- Open **Activity Monitor** from the **Utilities** folder. Click on the **Window** menu and select **GPU History**. This shows real-time graphs of GPU usage, which can help you identify if the system is underutilized or if you need to adjust your settings.

2. Use External Displays for Increased GPU Load

If you're working with multiple monitors or high-resolution displays, the 20-core GPU will be able to handle the increased graphical load, especially with macOS' seamless multi-display support.

- Use **multiple 4K or 6K monitors** to get the most out of the GPU. The Mac mini M4 Pro supports up to three 6K displays, allowing you to create a powerful, expansive workspace for tasks like video editing, design, or gaming.

3. Keep Software and macOS Updated

Apple frequently releases updates to macOS and its software, including optimizations for the GPU. Make sure your system is up to date to get the best performance from the 20-core GPU.

- Regularly check for updates under **System Preferences > Software Update**. These updates can include bug fixes, performance

APPLE M4 PRO MAC MINI USER GUIDE

improvements, and new GPU optimizations that will make the most of the 20-core GPU.

Managing External Devices and Thunderbolt Connections

When you buy an Apple M4 Pro Mac mini, you're not just getting a powerful desktop machine; you're also unlocking the ability to connect a whole range of external devices that can expand its functionality. Whether it's high-speed storage, external monitors, or peripherals like printers, audio interfaces, or external GPUs, the Mac mini's Thunderbolt and USB-C ports provide the fast and flexible connectivity you need.

In this section, we'll take you through how to connect, manage, and get the most out of your external devices. Whether you're working from home, creating content, or handling professional tasks, you'll find that the Mac mini's Thunderbolt ports can make life a lot easier by offering lightning-fast data transfers, reliable connections, and expanded capabilities.

Understanding Thunderbolt and USB-C Ports

Before diving into how to connect devices, let's first break down what Thunderbolt and USB-C really are. The M4 Pro Mac mini comes with **four Thunderbolt 5 (USB-C)** ports. These are incredibly versatile and allow for high-speed data transfer, video output, and power delivery—all through a single cable.

Here's a quick breakdown of their capabilities:

- **Thunderbolt 5 (USB-C)**: These ports can transfer data at speeds of up to **40 Gbps**, which means you can connect devices like external SSDs, high-definition monitors, and even eGPUs (external graphics processing units) without worrying about slowdowns. Thunderbolt ports can also **daisy-chain** up to six devices, making it easy to set up a multi-device workflow.

- **USB-C**: A bit like Thunderbolt, but with a few differences. While not as fast as Thunderbolt 5, USB-C still offers great transfer speeds, up to **10 Gbps** (depending on the device). It's perfect for peripherals like printers, mice, and cameras that don't require the highest speeds but need reliable and stable connections.

Connecting High-Speed Storage Devices

One of the first things you'll likely want to connect to your Mac mini is an external storage drive—especially if you're working with large files, such as video editing projects or high-resolution photography. Thunderbolt and USB-C are both great choices for storage, but let's start with **Thunderbolt storage**:

- **Thunderbolt SSDs**: These drives are ideal for high-speed data access. For example, if you're editing 4K video or managing large databases, a Thunderbolt 5 SSD will let you transfer files between your Mac mini and storage device almost instantly. Thunderbolt 5's blazing fast **40 Gbps** transfer speed ensures no lag between reading and writing data, which is crucial for workflow efficiency.

- **Connecting Your SSD**: Simply plug your external Thunderbolt SSD into one of the **Thunderbolt 5** ports. You'll likely need to install the drive's software if required by the manufacturer, but macOS will typically recognize the device right away.

Tip: Always eject external drives properly before unplugging them. Just drag the device icon to the trash or right-click it in Finder and select "Eject." This helps prevent data corruption.

- **USB-C Storage**: USB-C drives are also an excellent choice, especially for tasks that don't require ultra-fast transfer speeds. They're also cheaper compared to Thunderbolt drives but still offer great performance for most everyday tasks. If you're just backing up documents or handling medium-sized files, a **USB-C** external SSD or hard drive is more than adequate.

Tip: If your USB-C storage device isn't recognized immediately, check if it's formatted correctly. If not, you can use **Disk Utility** to reformat it to **APFS** or **ExFAT** depending on your needs.

Connecting External Monitors

Another great feature of the M4 Pro Mac mini is its ability to support up to **three 6K displays** simultaneously—thanks to the **20-core GPU** and Thunderbolt ports. This is perfect for professionals who need lots of screen real estate, whether you're into graphic design, video editing, or multitasking across different applications. Here's how you can set up and manage multiple monitors:

- **Plugging In**: To connect an external monitor to your Mac mini, use a Thunderbolt 5 port to link your display to the Mac mini via a **USB-C to DisplayPort** or **USB-C to HDMI** cable, depending on your monitor's port. Remember, Thunderbolt 5 also supports **DisplayPort 2.0** for high-resolution monitors, so you can enjoy ultra-sharp visuals without any compromise.

Tip: If you're connecting more than one display, make sure each one is plugged into a separate Thunderbolt port. The Mac mini can support three external displays in addition to its built-in display, if you're using an external monitor for a portable setup.

- **Adjusting Display Settings**: After connecting your monitor, go to **System Preferences > Displays**. Here, you can adjust the resolution, refresh rate, and display arrangement (for multi-monitor setups). For instance, if you're using two monitors side by side, you can adjust the arrangement to match their physical positions on your desk.

Tip: Use **macOS's Display Mirroring** feature if you want to display the same screen across multiple monitors. This can be useful for presentations or meetings.

Managing Multiple Devices Simultaneously

With Thunderbolt ports capable of daisy-chaining up to six devices, you can easily manage a multi-device setup. For example, you could connect a high-speed SSD, a monitor, and a peripheral like a printer or camera—all through just one port.

- **Daisy-Chaining Devices**: Start by connecting your primary Thunderbolt device (such as an SSD) to one of the Thunderbolt 5 ports. Then, connect your second device (such as a monitor) to the first device's **second Thunderbolt port**. This allows multiple devices to share the same Thunderbolt port without reducing their speed. Thunderbolt is smart enough to manage bandwidth between the connected devices.

Tip: If you're using a Thunderbolt hub or dock, these can provide multiple ports, making it easier to connect more devices. Just plug the hub or dock into a single Thunderbolt port and enjoy the extra connections.

- **Using USB-C Peripherals**: Thunderbolt and USB-C devices are fully compatible, meaning you can easily plug USB-C peripherals like keyboards, mice, printers, and cameras into any available USB-C port. While the USB-C ports don't offer the same transfer speed as Thunderbolt 5, they are still great for low- to moderate-speed devices that don't require extreme bandwidth, like a printer or external mouse.

- **Switching Between Devices**: The beauty of Thunderbolt connections is how easy it is to switch between devices. For instance, if you're working with a Thunderbolt SSD for fast storage but need to hook up an eGPU for graphics-intensive tasks, simply unplug one device and plug in the next. The Mac mini will automatically detect and switch between devices as needed.

Tip: When switching between devices that rely on Thunderbolt, you may need to adjust your system settings. For example, if you're using an eGPU, you may need to change the graphics settings in **System Preferences > Displays > Graphics**.

Troubleshooting Common Issues

Even with the robust Thunderbolt and USB-C connections, you may occasionally run into problems. Here are a few tips for troubleshooting common issues:

- **Device Not Recognized**: If your external device isn't showing up, check the physical connection first. Is the cable firmly plugged in? Try using a different cable to rule out a faulty one. If the device still isn't recognized, restart your Mac mini and try again.

- **Slow Transfer Speeds**: If you notice that your Thunderbolt or USB-C device is running slower than expected, ensure that it's plugged into a **Thunderbolt 5** port (for maximum speed). For USB-C devices, check that they support **USB 3.1** or higher for faster transfers.

- **Display Issues**: If your monitor is not displaying correctly, check that the cable is securely connected and that the display is set to the right input source (e.g., DisplayPort or HDMI). Sometimes, a quick reboot will fix any display issues caused by a software glitch.

Customizing Security Settings (FileVault, Privacy, Firewall)

As we look deeper into customizing your Mac mini M4 Pro, one of the most important areas to address is **security**. Apple places a strong emphasis on user privacy, and the Mac mini M4 Pro is equipped with a suite of security features to protect your data from unauthorized access. In this section, we'll walk through the process of setting up **FileVault** for disk encryption, configuring **privacy settings** to control what apps can access, and managing the **Firewall** to block unwanted network connections.

1. Enabling FileVault for Disk Encryption

FileVault is macOS's built-in encryption tool that ensures the data on your Mac mini's hard drive is secure. This feature encrypts everything on your disk, making it much harder for anyone to access your files without your password. Here's how to enable it:

Step-by-Step Instructions:

1. **Open System Preferences:**

   o Click on the **Apple logo** in the top left corner of your screen.

- o Select **System Preferences** from the dropdown menu.

2. **Go to Security & Privacy:**

   - o In the **System Preferences** window, click on **Security & Privacy**.

3. **Unlock to Make Changes:**

   - o At the bottom left of the window, you'll see a lock icon. **Click on it** and enter your **administrator password** to unlock the settings.

4. **Enable FileVault:**

   - o In the **FileVault** tab, you'll see the option to turn on disk encryption. Click **Turn On FileVault**.

   - o A window will appear asking you to select a recovery option. You can either:

     - ▪ **Use your Apple ID** to unlock your disk if you forget your password.

     - ▪ **Create a recovery key** (write it down and store it somewhere safe).

5. **Restart to Start Encryption:**

   - o Once you've selected a recovery option, your Mac will need to restart. The encryption process will begin automatically, but depending on how much data is on your Mac, it might take some time to complete. You can still use your Mac while it's encrypting, but make sure it's plugged into a power source.

6. **Complete the Process:**

   o After encryption is complete, your Mac mini M4 Pro will be fully encrypted. You'll need to enter your password to unlock the computer when it restarts.

2. Configuring Privacy Settings

macOS allows you to customize what apps and services can access your personal data. By configuring **privacy settings**, you can control what apps have access to things like your location, contacts, photos, microphone, camera, and more. Here's how to set up privacy controls:

Step-by-Step Instructions:

1. **Open System Preferences:**

   o Click on the **Apple logo** and select **System Preferences**.

2. **Go to Security & Privacy:**

   o In the **System Preferences** window, click on **Security & Privacy** again.

3. **Select the Privacy Tab:**

   o In the **Security & Privacy** window, click on the **Privacy** tab at the top.

4. **Review App Permissions:**

   o On the left sidebar, you'll see a list of categories, such as **Location Services**, **Contacts**, **Photos**, **Camera**, **Microphone**, etc.

   o Select each category to see which apps have access to that data.

5. **Adjust Permissions:**

   o For each category, you can check or uncheck the boxes next to the apps that should or should not have access.

   o For example, if you don't want a certain app to use your camera or microphone, simply uncheck the box next to that app in the **Camera** or **Microphone** section.

6. **Enable Location Services (if needed):**

   o If you need apps like Maps or Find My Mac to use your location, make sure **Location Services** is enabled. You can select which apps are allowed to access your location by checking or unchecking the boxes next to each app.

7. **Control Advertising and Analytics:**

   o Scroll to the bottom of the **Privacy** tab to find **Advertising** and **Analytics** settings. You can opt out of personalized ads and limit tracking by unchecking the options for **Limit Ad Tracking** and **Share with App Developers**.

8. **Manage Health Data (if applicable):**

   o If you use health-related apps (e.g., Apple Health), you can grant or restrict access to your health data from this Privacy tab.

9. **Lock Changes:**

   o After making your adjustments, click the **lock icon** again to prevent unauthorized changes to your privacy settings.

3. Managing the Firewall to Block Unwanted Network Connections

The **Firewall** is an essential security feature that helps block unauthorized connections to your Mac mini over the internet or local network. By managing the Firewall, you can control which apps or services are allowed to receive incoming connections.

Step-by-Step Instructions:

1. **Open System Preferences:**

   o Click on the **Apple logo** and go to **System Preferences**.

2. **Go to Security & Privacy:**

   o Click on **Security & Privacy** once more.

3. **Select the Firewall Tab:**

   o In the **Security & Privacy** window, click the **Firewall** tab.

4. **Unlock to Make Changes:**

   o As with the previous steps, click the **lock icon** at the bottom left and enter your administrator password to unlock the settings.

5. **Turn On the Firewall:**

   o If the Firewall is not already enabled, click **Turn On Firewall**. This will start protecting your Mac mini from unauthorized incoming network connections.

6. **Customize Firewall Options:**

   o Click on **Firewall Options** to customize your Firewall settings. Here, you can:

     - **Allow or block specific apps**: For example, if you're using an app that you trust but you don't want other apps to communicate with it over the network, you can manually add or block apps here.

     - **Enable stealth mode**: This option will make your Mac less visible on the network, reducing the chance of it being discovered by malicious users or bots.

7. **Enable Automatic Firewall Configuration:**

   o If you're unsure which apps should be allowed or blocked, you can let macOS automatically configure the Firewall for you. It

APPLE M4 PRO MAC MINI USER GUIDE

will allow necessary apps while blocking any unauthorized ones.

8. **Lock Changes:**

   o Once you've configured the Firewall to your liking, don't forget to click the **lock icon** again to prevent further changes.

Extra Tips for Enhanced Security:

- **Use Strong Passwords**: Ensure that you use strong, unique passwords for your Mac mini and Apple ID. A good password includes a mix of uppercase and lowercase letters, numbers, and special characters.

- **Enable Two-Factor Authentication (2FA)**: For your Apple ID, enable two-factor authentication for an added layer of security. This will require a second device or authentication method to access your Apple account.

- **Regular Backups**: Use **Time Machine** to regularly back up your files. This way, even if you ever face a security issue or data loss, you'll have a backup of your important documents.

- **Security Updates**: Always keep your macOS up-to-date by enabling automatic updates. These updates frequently contain important security patches to protect your Mac mini.

Exploring Hidden macOS Features for Power Users

When you first unbox your Apple Mac mini M4 Pro, you're greeted with a sleek, user-friendly interface, and a range of powerful features ready to be put to work. But for those who want to unlock the full potential of their Mac, there are several hidden gems tucked away in macOS that can supercharge your productivity and streamline your workflow. These are tools that may not be immediately visible, but for advanced users, they are indispensable for getting things done faster and more efficiently.

In this section, we'll dive into some of these hidden macOS features that can significantly boost your efficiency. These features include Terminal, Automator, macOS shortcuts, and other lesser-known utilities that power users often rely on to work smarter, not harder.

1. Terminal: The Command Line Powerhouse

One of the most powerful tools on macOS is the Terminal. It's a gateway to the Unix underpinnings of macOS, offering deep control over your system. For those who love precision and speed, Terminal allows you to execute commands that can do everything from managing files and directories to automating processes and debugging your system.

What is Terminal?

Terminal is the command-line interface of macOS, where you type commands instead of clicking through graphical user interfaces (GUIs). It's a direct way to communicate with your Mac, bypassing the usual menus and buttons.

Why should you use Terminal?

Terminal can be intimidating at first, but once you learn how to use it, it becomes an incredibly powerful tool that gives you full control over your system. It allows you to perform tasks much faster than navigating through the GUI. For example, creating, renaming, moving, or deleting files can be done in a matter of seconds using commands.

Examples of Useful Terminal Commands:

- **Navigating the File System:**

  o cd – Change directory. For example, cd Desktop takes you to the Desktop folder.

  o ls – Lists the contents of a directory.

- **Managing Files:**

  o touch – Creates a new, empty file. For example, touch newfile.txt creates a new text file.

  o rm – Deletes files. Use with caution: rm file.txt will remove the file permanently (without moving it to Trash).

- **Getting System Information:**

  - top – Displays real-time system resource usage (CPU, memory).

  - df – Shows disk usage for mounted file systems.

By using Terminal, you can execute commands much faster and, in some cases, automate tasks that would be tedious to do manually through the GUI.

2. Automator: Streamlining Repetitive Tasks

Automator is an underappreciated macOS tool that allows you to automate repetitive tasks without needing to write a single line of code. Whether it's renaming multiple files at once, resizing images, or moving files between folders, Automator can save you time and effort.

What is Automator?

Automator is a built-in macOS application that lets you create workflows for automating tasks. These workflows can be simple or complex, depending on your needs, and they can be triggered by you manually or set to run automatically under certain conditions.

Why should you use Automator?

Automator allows you to automate tasks that you perform regularly, reducing the amount of time you spend on mundane work. For example, if you frequently resize images before uploading them, you can create a workflow that automatically resizes and exports images in the correct format with just a few clicks.

Examples of Useful Automator Workflows:

- **Batch Rename Files:** If you have a large collection of files (e.g., photos, documents) that need to be renamed in a specific format, Automator can handle this in bulk. You can create a workflow that renames files by adding a prefix, suffix, or even changing the case of all file names.

- **Convert Files to PDF:** You can create an Automator workflow that takes any selected images or documents and converts them into a PDF file with just one click.

- **Resize Multiple Images:** Another great use case for Automator is image resizing. If you have a bunch of images you need to resize before emailing them, you can automate the process. Create a workflow that resizes all selected images to a predefined size and saves them in a specific folder.

To start using Automator, open the app and choose from a variety of pre-built actions, or build your own custom workflows by dragging and dropping actions into the workspace. Once your workflow is ready, you can save it as an app or run it from within Automator.

3. macOS Shortcuts: Speeding Up Everyday Tasks

Introduced in macOS Monterey, Shortcuts bring the power of automation right to your desktop and integrate seamlessly with your other Apple devices. With Shortcuts, you can create complex automations to handle tasks that you do often, such as opening multiple apps at once, controlling your smart home devices, or sending predefined messages to friends and family.

What are macOS Shortcuts?

macOS Shortcuts are a feature that lets you combine multiple actions into a single task, reducing the need for manual intervention. These shortcuts can perform actions like launching apps, sending messages, adjusting system settings, or even controlling other apps on your Mac.

Why should you use Shortcuts?

Shortcuts are great for those who want to save time on tasks that can easily be automated. Whether it's sending a text to your friend at a specific time or creating a daily report with a few clicks, Shortcuts makes it easy to set up and trigger workflows with minimal effort.

Examples of Useful macOS Shortcuts:

- **Open Multiple Apps at Once:** If you regularly use a set of apps (such as your email, calendar, and web browser), you can create a shortcut to open all of them at once. This saves you from having to open each app manually every time you start your day.

- **Send Scheduled Text Messages:** Set up a shortcut that sends a text message to a contact at a specific time. For instance, you can create a shortcut that automatically texts your spouse every evening to check if they need anything from the store.

APPLE M4 PRO MAC MINI USER GUIDE

- **Control Your Smart Home:** If you have smart home devices, you can create shortcuts that let you control them directly from your Mac. For example, a shortcut could adjust the lighting in your home or turn off your thermostat when you leave the house.

To get started with Shortcuts, open the Shortcuts app, explore the pre-built actions, or create your own by dragging and dropping actions. Once a shortcut is set up, you can trigger it using Siri, from the menu bar, or through a keyboard shortcut.

4. Hidden macOS Features You Should Know About

In addition to Terminal, Automator, and Shortcuts, macOS has a few hidden gems that can further enhance your efficiency. Let's take a look at some of the lesser-known features that power users should be aware of.

Quick Actions:

Quick Actions allow you to perform simple tasks directly from Finder, such as rotating images, converting files to PDFs, or adding items to your Notes app. You can access Quick Actions by right-clicking on a file in Finder and selecting one of the available options. You can customize these Quick Actions to suit your needs.

Hiding the Menu Bar:

If you're someone who values minimalism, you might appreciate the ability to hide the menu bar while working. By holding down the Command key, you can hide the menu bar temporarily when using full-screen apps, giving you a cleaner and more focused workspace.

Mission Control and Spaces:

Mission Control provides an overview of all your open windows, making it easy to switch between them. You can create multiple desktops (called Spaces) to organize your work and switch between different tasks seamlessly. Use the F3 key or swipe up with three fingers to open Mission Control and start using Spaces to manage your workflow better.

Optimizing macOS for Specific Tasks (Video Editing, Development, etc.)

When you own an Apple Mac mini M4 Pro, you're holding a machine that's more than just a piece of hardware—it's a powerful tool that can be customized and optimized for specific professional tasks. Whether you're a video editor, a software developer, a graphic designer, or anyone working with demanding applications, macOS Sequoia offers various features and settings that can maximize your Mac mini's potential.

In this section, we'll explore how to fine-tune your Mac mini M4 Pro running macOS Sequoia for specific professional tasks, with particular attention to video editing and software development. These optimizations will help you unlock the full potential of your machine and ensure your workflow is as smooth and efficient as possible.

1. Optimizing macOS for Video Editing

Video editing is one of the most demanding tasks for any computer. But with the right optimizations, your Mac mini M4 Pro can deliver a seamless, high-performance editing experience. macOS Sequoia, paired with the power of the M4 Pro chip, is a fantastic platform for editing everything from home videos to professional-grade content. Here's how you can optimize your Mac mini for this task:

1.1. Use Optimized Video Editing Software

Start by choosing video editing software that works harmoniously with the M4 Pro chip and macOS. The most popular video editing software for macOS includes **Final Cut Pro**, **Adobe Premiere Pro**, and **DaVinci Resolve**.

- **Final Cut Pro**: Apple's own video editing software is deeply optimized for macOS, taking full advantage of the M4 Pro's hardware acceleration and powerful GPU. It's particularly efficient for handling high-resolution 4K and 8K footage, delivering smooth playback and fast rendering times.

- **Adobe Premiere Pro**: While Premiere Pro isn't as tightly integrated with macOS as Final Cut, it's a powerful choice for cross-platform editors. To ensure maximum performance, be sure to use the latest version that supports hardware acceleration for rendering and playback.

- **DaVinci Resolve**: Known for its professional color grading tools, DaVinci Resolve also benefits from the GPU-accelerated performance of the M4 Pro chip.

1.2. Adjust System Preferences for Video Editing

To get the most out of your Mac mini, you need to adjust macOS settings to optimize for high-performance video tasks. Here's how you can do it:

- **Energy Saver Preferences**: Set your Mac mini to never sleep during video editing. You don't want your system to go to sleep in the middle of rendering a project. Go to **System Preferences > Energy Saver** and set **Computer Sleep** to **Never**.

- **Graphics Performance**: macOS should automatically use the 20-core GPU when required, but in some cases, you can manually optimize your settings by going to **System Preferences > Displays**. Here, make sure your display settings are set to match your editing setup (e.g., 4K or 6K displays for ultra-high-definition content).

- **Disable Unnecessary Background Processes**: Before starting an intensive video editing session, close any unnecessary applications running in the background. You can use **Activity Monitor** (found in **Applications > Utilities**) to check which processes are consuming CPU, GPU, and memory resources.

1.3. Optimize External Storage

Video editing requires a lot of disk space, and using your Mac mini's internal storage can quickly become inefficient. Using an external SSD or RAID

APPLE M4 PRO MAC MINI USER GUIDE

setup will not only provide ample storage but also improve your editing speed.

- **External SSD/RAID**: For faster read/write speeds, opt for a Thunderbolt 3 or 4 external SSD or RAID array. Thunderbolt connections offer the speed you need for handling large video files in real-time.

- **Set Your Scratch Disk**: In most video editing software, you can designate an external drive as the "scratch disk" for temporary file storage. By doing this, you ensure that your Mac mini's internal storage isn't bogged down with large media files.

1.4. Enable Hardware Acceleration

Many video editing applications can utilize your Mac mini's hardware acceleration capabilities to process video faster. Hardware acceleration offloads demanding tasks from the CPU to the GPU, providing smoother performance and faster render times.

- **Final Cut Pro**: This application has built-in optimization for macOS hardware, and it will automatically use the M4 Pro's GPU for video rendering and playback. You can check hardware acceleration settings by going to **Final Cut Pro > Preferences > Playback** and ensuring **High Quality Playback** is selected.

- **Adobe Premiere Pro**: In Premiere Pro, go to **Preferences > Playback**, and make sure to enable **GPU Acceleration** under the **Video Rendering and Playback** section.

1.5. Use Proxy Media for High-Resolution Footage

Editing 4K or 8K footage can be challenging, even for a powerful system like the Mac mini M4 Pro. A great solution is using proxy media—lower-resolution versions of your footage—while editing. This drastically reduces the strain on your system during the editing process. Once your edits are complete, you can relink the project to the original high-res footage for rendering.

2. Optimizing macOS for Software Development

The M4 Pro chip in the Mac mini makes it a powerhouse for software development. Whether you're working with Swift, Python, JavaScript, or any other language, macOS offers a smooth and efficient environment for coding. Here's how to optimize your Mac mini for a seamless development experience:

2.1. Install Xcode for Swift Development

Xcode is Apple's integrated development environment (IDE) and is essential for building macOS, iOS, and watchOS apps. To make your experience with Xcode as fast and efficient as possible:

- **Use the Latest Xcode Version**: Always ensure that you have the latest version of Xcode to take advantage of the M4 Pro's performance improvements. You can update Xcode through the **Mac App Store**.

- **Install Command-Line Tools**: If you're using the terminal for software development, make sure you install the necessary

Command Line Tools by running the following command in Terminal:

"xcode-select –install"

2.2. Optimize Your Development Environment

Having the right tools and settings configured on your Mac mini is key to optimizing development performance.

- **Enable Developer Mode**: Enable **Developer Mode** in **System Preferences > Security & Privacy > Developer Tools**. This will allow you to build and test applications without interruptions.

- **Use Virtual Environments for Python Projects**: For Python development, consider using **virtual environments** to isolate dependencies and avoid performance issues caused by installing packages globally. This can be done with the **venv** module in Python.

- **Install Package Managers**: For JavaScript developers, installing package managers like **Homebrew** (for macOS) and **npm** (for Node.js) will streamline the process of installing libraries and dependencies. In Terminal, install Homebrew with:

```
/bin/bash -c "$(curl -fsSL https://raw.githubusercontent.com/Homebrew/install/HEAD/install.sh)"
```

2.3. Utilize the M4 Pro's Multi-Core Performance

The M4 Pro chip features a 14-core CPU and 20-core GPU, which is ideal for software development tasks like compiling code, running simulations, or handling databases. Here's how to leverage the multi-core power of your Mac mini:

- **Parallel Compilation**: If you're compiling large codebases, use tools that can compile in parallel to utilize multiple cores. For example, you can configure **Makefiles** to run parallel jobs during compilation.

- **Swift Package Manager**: If you're building iOS or macOS apps using Swift, you can use the **Swift Package Manager** to speed up dependency resolution and package management. Swift's build system is optimized to take full advantage of multi-core CPUs.

2.4. Use Virtualization Tools for Testing

If you're working in a cross-platform environment, you may need to test your code on different operating systems. macOS offers several virtualization tools that can help you run multiple environments efficiently:

- **Docker**: For containerized applications, **Docker** is an excellent tool that works well with macOS. It uses minimal resources while providing isolated environments for each application, which is great for testing software in different configurations.

- **Parallels Desktop or VMware Fusion**: These tools allow you to run virtual machines (VMs) on macOS. With the M4 Pro's powerful hardware, running a VM with Linux or Windows will be fast and seamless.

2.5. Fine-Tune for Performance with System Preferences

Just like video editing, software development can demand a lot of system resources. By tweaking your system preferences, you can ensure your Mac mini runs at optimal speeds during development tasks:

- **Disable Automatic App Updates**: In **System Preferences > Software Update,** turn off automatic updates while you're working to avoid interruptions and slowdowns during critical coding sessions.

- **Configure Energy Preferences**: Set your Mac mini to not go to sleep while running long builds or tests. You can adjust this by going to **System Preferences > Energy Saver** and selecting **Never** for sleep settings.

2.6. Version Control and Collaboration

For developers working in teams, version control tools like **Git** are essential. Setting up a solid version control system will streamline collaboration and allow you to track code changes efficiently:

- **GitHub or GitLab Integration**: Install **Git** through Homebrew or **Xcode Command Line Tools** to easily manage repositories on GitHub or GitLab directly from your Terminal.

- **Git GUI Tools**: If you prefer graphical interfaces, tools like **GitHub Desktop** or **SourceTree** can simplify version control operations, providing an intuitive UI for managing branches and commits.

DISPLAY AND GRAPHICS SETUP

Connecting External Monitors and Configuring Resolutions on the Mac mini M4 Pro

The **Apple M4 Pro Mac mini** is a powerhouse designed to handle everything from creative tasks to complex software development. One of the most exciting features of the Mac mini M4 Pro is its ability to support high-resolution external displays — up to **three 6K displays simultaneously**. Whether you're connecting a single monitor or setting up a multi-display configuration, configuring your external monitors correctly is essential for getting the most out of your Mac mini.

In this section, we'll walk you through everything you need to know about connecting external monitors to your Mac mini M4 Pro and adjusting display settings to optimize your viewing experience. By the end, you'll be able to set up your displays to suit your needs — whether that's for work, gaming, or creative projects.

Step 1: Identify the Right Ports for Connecting Your Monitor

Before you connect anything, let's make sure you know which ports on your Mac mini M4 Pro you'll use for your external monitor(s).

The Mac mini M4 Pro comes with several ports that support external displays:

1. **Thunderbolt 5 (USB-C)**:
   These are your primary connection ports for high-resolution monitors. There are **two Thunderbolt 5 ports** on the back of the Mac mini. Thunderbolt 5 can handle 6K displays, so you'll likely use these ports if you're connecting high-end monitors.

2. **HDMI**   **2.1**:
   The Mac mini M4 Pro has **one HDMI 2.1 port** on the back as well. HDMI 2.1 supports up to **4K resolution at 120Hz** or **8K resolution at 60Hz**. This is a good option for standard monitors or TVs that support HDMI.

3. **USB-C/Thunderbolt to DisplayPort Adapters**:
   If your display uses **DisplayPort** and not HDMI or Thunderbolt, you can use **USB-C to DisplayPort adapters**. The adapters allow you to connect through the Thunderbolt ports.

Step 2: Connect Your Monitor to the Mac mini

Now that you know which ports to use, let's go ahead and connect the external monitor(s) to your Mac mini. This process is relatively simple, but it's important to connect everything properly to ensure optimal performance.

1. **Using Thunderbolt or USB-C**:

   o Plug one end of your **USB-C to USB-C cable** into one of the Thunderbolt 5 ports on your Mac mini.

              APPLE M4 PRO MAC MINI USER GUIDE

o Connect the other end to your monitor's USB-C port (or use an adapter if your monitor has DisplayPort or HDMI).

If your monitor supports 6K resolution, make sure to use the Thunderbolt 5 port for the best performance.

2. **Using HDMI**:

    o Plug one end of your **HDMI cable** into the HDMI port on the back of your Mac mini.

    o Connect the other end to your monitor or TV. Make sure that your HDMI cable is capable of supporting the resolution and refresh rate you intend to use (HDMI 2.1 is preferred for 4K and 6K displays).

Step 3: Power On the Monitor and Mac mini

Once everything is connected, it's time to turn on your devices:

1. Turn on your **external monitor**. You should see the display signal from the Mac mini appear after a few seconds.

2. Turn on your **Mac mini M4 Pro**. If the monitor is powered on and correctly connected, your Mac mini should detect it automatically.

If the monitor doesn't display anything right away, don't panic! It may take a moment for the Mac mini to recognize the external display. Try unplugging and plugging in the cable again to establish the connection.

Step 4: Adjusting Display Preferences and Resolutions

Once your monitor is connected, it's time to adjust the display settings. macOS is designed to automatically adjust the resolution to match your monitor's capabilities, but you may want to fine-tune things to ensure the best performance.

Configure Display Resolution:

1. **Go to the Apple Menu**: Click the **Apple logo** in the top-left corner of your screen and select **System Preferences**.

2. **Select Displays**: In the System Preferences window, click on the **Displays** icon. This opens the display settings for your Mac mini and connected monitors.

3. **Select the Display Tab**: If you're using multiple monitors, you should see the display settings for each screen. Choose the one you want to adjust.

4. **Adjust the Resolution**:

   o **Default for Display**: macOS typically defaults to the best resolution for your monitor. If you want to ensure the sharpest image, this is usually the best option.

   o **Scaled**: If you prefer more control, you can select "Scaled" to choose a custom resolution. macOS will display a set of recommended resolutions based on your monitor's capabilities. For high-res monitors, you may see options like

1920x1080, **2560x1440**, or **3840x2160 (4K)**, and if you're using a 6K monitor, you might also see a **6016x3384** resolution option.

Adjusting Display Refresh Rate:

For monitors that support higher refresh rates (e.g., gaming or professional displays), you can adjust the refresh rate for a smoother experience. To do this:

1. While in the **Display Preferences** window, click on the **Display** tab.

2. Hold down the **Option** key and click on the **Scaled** button.

3. You'll see an additional set of options for the refresh rate of your monitor.

4. Choose a refresh rate (e.g., 60Hz, 120Hz, or 144Hz) depending on your display and your needs.

A higher refresh rate is essential for smoother motion, especially if you're doing activities like gaming, video editing, or working with fast-moving content.

Step 5: Configuring Multi-Monitor Setups

If you're connecting more than one monitor to your Mac mini, macOS allows you to configure a multi-monitor setup with ease. You can arrange your displays in the **Displays Preferences** window to match your physical setup, making the transition between screens seamless.

1. **Arrange Displays**:

   o In the **Displays Preferences** window, click the **Arrangement** tab. This tab allows you to drag and drop the icons representing each connected display.

   o Arrange the display icons in the same way they are physically positioned on your desk. For example, if you have one monitor to the left and one to the right, make sure the display icons reflect that.

   o Drag the **Menu Bar** (the white bar at the top of one of the display icons) to the monitor where you want the **main display** to appear.

2. **Mirror Displays**:

   o If you want both monitors to display the same content (often used for presentations), click the **Mirror Displays** checkbox in the **Arrangement** tab. This will duplicate what's on your main display to the secondary monitor.

Step 6: Optimizing Display Preferences for Different Use Cases

Depending on what you're using your Mac mini M4 Pro for, you might want to tweak the display settings further to enhance your experience.

1. **For Creative Work (Photo/Video Editing)**:

   o Set the **color profile** for your monitor by going to the **Color** tab in **Displays Preferences**. Select the appropriate color profile for professional creative work (e.g., **Adobe RGB** or **P3**).

- o Adjust the **brightness** and **contrast** settings to match the lighting of your workspace for the best visual accuracy.

2. **For Gaming or High-Performance Work**:

- o If you're using a high-refresh-rate display for gaming, adjust the **refresh rate** to **120Hz** or **144Hz** (depending on your monitor's capabilities).

- o Turn on **True Tone** (if supported) for a more natural display of colors, or turn it off for the most accurate color representation.

3. **For Everyday Use**:

- o You can adjust the display to something more comfortable by choosing a resolution that provides larger text and icons for ease of reading (like 1440p or 1080p on a 4K monitor).

- o You may also want to enable **Night Shift** to reduce blue light and ease eye strain during evening hours.

Step 7: Troubleshooting Display Issues

If your monitor isn't displaying correctly, here are some common troubleshooting steps:

1. **No Signal**:

- o Check that the cable is properly connected.

o   Ensure that the monitor is powered on and set to the correct input source (e.g., HDMI, DisplayPort).

o   Try restarting your Mac mini and re-plugging the cable.

2. **Display Flickering**:

o   Check for any loose cables or connections.

o   Try lowering the display resolution or refresh rate to see if the flickering stops.

3. **Resolution Not Supported**:

o   If you're using a high-resolution monitor and macOS doesn't automatically select the best resolution, go into **System Preferences > Displays** and choose a different resolution or use "Scaled" to select an optimal setting.

Managing Multi-Monitor Setups (Up to 3 6K Displays)

Setting up a multi-monitor setup can dramatically enhance your workspace, whether you're working from home, editing videos, or developing software. If you've just upgraded to the Apple M4 Pro Mac mini, you're in for a treat. This powerhouse can easily handle up to three 6K displays simultaneously, providing you with an expansive, crystal-clear viewing experience. Whether you want to extend your desktop for more room to work, or mirror displays for presentation purposes, macOS Sequoia makes it relatively simple to configure your setup.

Why Use Multiple Monitors?

Before we dive into the technical setup, let's briefly discuss why you might want to use multiple monitors. Whether you're multitasking, doing creative work, or managing large sets of data, multiple monitors can:

- **Increase Productivity**: Having extra screen real estate means you don't have to constantly switch between tabs or applications. You can have all your essential tools open at once—an email inbox, your browser, and a word processor.

- **Enhance Creative Workflows**: Designers, video editors, and 3D artists can benefit from additional monitors to view large images or video files without sacrificing workspace.

- **Efficient Workspace Organization**: Organizing your windows into different screens helps keep your workspace uncluttered and minimizes distractions.

Now, let's get into how you can actually set up your Mac mini M4 Pro to take full advantage of these monitors.

Step 1: Preparing for the Multi-Monitor Setup

Before you plug anything in, make sure you've got the right equipment:

- **Cables**: You'll need the appropriate cables for each monitor, such as HDMI, Thunderbolt 5, or USB-C, depending on the ports your displays support.

- **Monitor Compatibility**: Verify that your monitors can support 6K resolution. You'll need displays that can handle 6016 x 3384 resolution for the best possible image quality.

- **Mac mini Ports**: The M4 Pro Mac mini has three Thunderbolt 5 ports and an HDMI 2.1 port, which means it can easily support up to three 6K displays with the right configuration.

Step 2: Connecting the Monitors

1. **Power Down and Plug In**:

   o First, power off your Mac mini and all your monitors.

   o Connect each monitor to the Mac mini using either a Thunderbolt 5 or HDMI cable, depending on your monitor's port. Thunderbolt 5 will provide the best performance for 6K displays, but HDMI can also work well if your monitor supports it.

   o Ensure that each monitor is powered on and set to the correct input mode (HDMI, Thunderbolt, etc.).

APPLE M4 PRO MAC MINI USER GUIDE

2. **Turn On the Mac mini**:

   o Power on your Mac mini. macOS Sequoia should automatically detect your monitors. If not, don't worry—there are easy steps to fix this.

Step 3: Configuring Displays in macOS

Now that your Mac mini recognizes the monitors, it's time to configure how they'll behave. macOS offers two main options for multi-monitor setups: **Extended Desktop** and **Mirrored Displays**.

Option 1: Extended Desktop (The Default Option)

In extended desktop mode, each monitor acts as an independent workspace. You can move windows between the monitors freely, which allows you to use them for different tasks.

1. **Open Display Settings**:

   o Go to **System Preferences** (click the Apple logo in the top left corner of your screen).

   o Click on **Displays**.

   o Here, you'll see a window that allows you to configure how your monitors behave.

2. **Arrange Displays**:

   o Under the **Arrangement** tab, you'll see a visual representation of your monitors. This is where you can drag and arrange the

APPLE M4 PRO MAC MINI USER GUIDE

monitor icons to match how they are physically placed on your desk.

o For example, if you have a monitor on the left, drag the left monitor icon to the left of the central one in the Arrangement tab.

o If you want one of the monitors to be above or below another, just drag it vertically in the Arrangement window.

3. **Set Display Resolution**:

o In the **Display** tab, you can choose the display resolution for each monitor. The Mac mini should automatically detect and set the best resolution (6K for your compatible monitors). But if you want to manually adjust it, simply select **Scaled** and choose a different resolution. However, for 6K displays, it's best to leave the resolution as default.

4. **Position the Dock**:

o If you want the Dock to appear on a particular monitor, simply drag it to the monitor of your choice in the **Arrangement** tab.

Option 2: Mirrored Displays

In mirrored display mode, all monitors show the exact same content. This is particularly useful for presentations or when you want to display the same screen on multiple monitors.

1. **Select Mirror Displays**:

    o   In the **Display** settings window, there is an option to **Mirror Displays**. Simply check the box, and all your monitors will display the same content.

    o   This can be useful for presentations or when you need to share what's on your screen with others.

2. **Choose the Primary Display**:

    o   When mirroring, you can select which screen will act as the primary display (the one that shows the menu bar and Dock). This can be done by dragging the white menu bar to your preferred screen in the **Arrangement** tab.

Step 4: Advanced Multi-Monitor Configuration Tips

Managing Different Resolutions and Refresh Rates

*   **Multiple 6K Monitors**: If you're connecting multiple 6K monitors, macOS should automatically scale the resolution properly. However, if you want to adjust the refresh rate for specific tasks like gaming or video editing, you can do this through the **Display** tab. Higher refresh rates are especially important for dynamic video content.

*   **Monitor Matching**: If you have mixed monitor types (e.g., a 4K and 6K monitor), macOS allows you to adjust each monitor's resolution independently. Just go to the **Scaled** option in the **Display** tab for each monitor.

APPLE M4 PRO MAC MINI USER GUIDE

Using DisplayCal for Color Calibration

- If you're doing color-sensitive work like photo editing or video production, you may want to calibrate your monitors to ensure accurate colors across all displays.

- You can use third-party tools like **DisplayCal** to calibrate each of your 6K displays individually for consistent color profiles.

Step 5: Troubleshooting Multi-Monitor Issues

Even though macOS is excellent at detecting multiple displays, issues can sometimes arise. Here are some common problems and how to fix them:

Monitors Not Being Detected

- **Check Cable Connections**: Ensure that the cables are securely connected to both your Mac mini and monitors.

- **Power Cycle Your Devices**: Sometimes, simply restarting the Mac mini and powering off/on the monitors can help them sync correctly.

- **Update macOS**: If the issue persists, check for macOS updates. Sometimes, updates contain fixes for display issues.

- **Use Different Ports**: If you're using a Thunderbolt port for one monitor and an HDMI port for another, try swapping them. The Mac mini may handle one port type better than another in certain setups.

Poor Resolution or Display Flickering

- **Adjust Resolution Settings**: Go into the **Display** tab in **System Preferences** and make sure the correct resolution is selected.

- **Update Graphics Drivers**: Ensure your graphics drivers are up to date. The Mac mini M4 Pro uses integrated Apple Silicon graphics, which should automatically update with macOS updates.

Step 6: Making the Most of Your Multi-Monitor Setup

- **Use Mission Control for Better Window Management**: macOS Sequoia includes a feature called **Mission Control** that allows you to easily switch between desktops and monitor different tasks across screens. Use it to organize apps and windows on your multi-monitor setup.

- **Third-Party Apps**: Consider using apps like **BetterSnapTool** or **Magnet** to further enhance your window management across multiple screens.

Using External Graphics Cards (eGPUs) with Your Mac mini M4 Pro

If you're someone who works with demanding graphical applications like 3D modeling, video editing, or high-end gaming, you might find that the built-in GPU of your Mac mini M4 Pro is enough for everyday tasks. However, when it comes to resource-intensive workflows, adding an **external graphics card** (eGPU) to your Mac mini can significantly boost its graphical performance. An eGPU allows you to offload GPU-heavy tasks from the built-in graphics processor, giving you more power for everything from rendering to gaming.

In this section, we'll walk through everything you need to know about setting up and using an eGPU with your Mac mini M4 Pro. Whether you're an enthusiast looking to take your creative work to the next level or a gamer wanting smoother graphics, this guide will ensure that your external GPU setup is seamless and optimized for peak performance.

What is an eGPU?

Before diving into the setup, let's quickly explain what an eGPU is. An eGPU, or **external graphics processing unit**, is a dedicated graphics card housed outside of your Mac mini. It's connected to the computer via a Thunderbolt 3 or 4 port (depending on your Mac mini model), which provides fast data transfer speeds. The eGPU is used to accelerate graphics-heavy tasks, taking the load off your built-in GPU.

In simple terms, think of it as adding a "booster" to your Mac mini's ability to handle demanding graphics. It can make a noticeable difference in applications like **Final Cut Pro**, **Adobe Premiere Pro**, **Blender**, and even **high-performance gaming**.

Why Use an eGPU with Your Mac mini M4 Pro?

The Mac mini M4 Pro comes with a powerful **20-core GPU**, but certain tasks, especially those involving **real-time rendering**, **3D simulations**, or **high-frame-rate gaming**, might push the system's capabilities. Here's why you might consider using an eGPU:

- **Enhanced Graphics Performance**: By connecting an eGPU, you can dramatically increase the graphical power available to your Mac mini, which is crucial for design work, animation, or gaming.

- **Better Support for Multiple Displays**: With an eGPU, you can connect additional monitors or high-resolution displays without compromising performance.

- **Future-Proofing**: External GPUs often come with upgrade options, allowing you to swap out the card as newer, more powerful options become available.

- **Specialized Workflows**: If your work involves **GPU-accelerated tasks** like AI modeling, scientific simulations, or other high-end computing, an eGPU can speed up your workflow dramatically.

Now that you understand why an eGPU could benefit your Mac mini M4 Pro, let's explore how to set one up.

Choosing the Right eGPU for Your Mac mini M4 Pro

Before you plug anything into your Mac mini, it's important to choose the right eGPU. There are two main components you'll need to select:

1. **The eGPU Enclosure**: This is a box that houses the external graphics card. The enclosure connects to your Mac mini via Thunderbolt, which is what allows for fast data transfer between the eGPU and the computer. Some popular eGPU enclosures include:

   o **Razer Core X**

   o **Sonnet eGFX Breakaway Box**

   o **Akitio Node**

These enclosures are designed to be compatible with macOS, and they offer enough power to support high-end graphics cards.

2. **The Graphics Card**: Once you've chosen an enclosure, the next step is selecting a compatible graphics card. Depending on your workflow, you'll want to pick one that balances performance with cost:

   o For **general video editing** or **light 3D rendering**, a **mid-range card** like the **AMD Radeon RX 6700 XT** should suffice.

   o For **high-end gaming** or **professional 3D rendering**, you'll want a **higher-end card** like the **AMD Radeon RX 6900 XT** or **Radeon Pro WX series**.

When selecting an eGPU, make sure that the graphics card is **compatible with macOS**. As of macOS Mojave (10.14.6) and later, Apple has improved support for AMD graphics cards, and they are the recommended choice for eGPU setups on Macs.

Setting Up Your eGPU with the Mac mini M4 Pro

Once you've selected your eGPU enclosure and graphics card, it's time to set up the eGPU. Let's break this down into simple steps:

Step 1: Install the Graphics Card into the Enclosure

Most eGPU enclosures come pre-assembled but will require you to **install the graphics card** into the enclosure. Follow these general steps:

- **Power off the eGPU**: Make sure the eGPU enclosure is not plugged in while you install the graphics card.

- **Open the enclosure**: Check the user manual for your specific enclosure to learn how to open it.

- **Insert the GPU**: Carefully insert the graphics card into the PCIe slot inside the enclosure, making sure it's seated properly.

- **Secure the card**: Some enclosures require you to screw the card into place for added stability.

- **Close the enclosure**: Once the card is secured, close the enclosure and connect the power cable to the eGPU.

Step 2: Connect the eGPU to the Mac mini

- **Plug the eGPU into the Thunderbolt Port**: Using the Thunderbolt 3 or 4 cable provided with your enclosure, connect the eGPU to one of the Thunderbolt ports on the back of your Mac mini.

- **Power on the eGPU**: Turn on the eGPU using the power button on the enclosure. You may see lights or hear fans start running, indicating that the device is powered on.

- **Wait for macOS to Detect the eGPU**: Once the eGPU is powered on and connected, macOS should automatically recognize it. This may take a minute or two.

Step 3: Configure the eGPU Settings

macOS should automatically detect the eGPU, but to ensure the best performance, you can configure a few settings:

- **Check for Driver Updates**: In most cases, macOS will download the necessary drivers for the eGPU automatically, but it's a good idea to check for updates by going to the **Apple Menu** > **System Preferences** > **Software Update**.

- **Set eGPU as Primary GPU for Specific Apps**: Some applications allow you to choose which GPU to use. For example, you might want Final Cut Pro or Adobe Premiere Pro to use the eGPU for rendering. To do this:

  1. Open the **Get Info** window for the app (right-click the app icon).

  2. Select the option "**Prefer External GPU**" if it's available.

- **Use eGPU for Metal and GPU-Accelerated Tasks**: macOS uses a framework called **Metal** for GPU-accelerated tasks. Make sure that

APPLE M4 PRO MAC MINI USER GUIDE

your creative software (like video editors or design tools) is set to utilize the eGPU for tasks that require heavy graphical power.

Step 4: Testing Your eGPU Setup

Once everything is connected and configured, it's time to test your eGPU setup:

- **Launch a GPU-Intensive Application**: Open a program that benefits from additional GPU power, like **Adobe After Effects**, **Blender**, or a game that pushes the graphical limits.

- **Check Activity Monitor**: Open **Activity Monitor** (found in **Applications > Utilities**) to see the GPU performance. If the eGPU is being utilized correctly, it should show higher levels of GPU usage compared to when using the internal GPU.

- **Performance Testing**: For the most accurate performance test, use benchmarking tools like **Unigine Heaven** or **Geekbench** to compare performance before and after connecting the eGPU.

Troubleshooting eGPU Issues

Sometimes, things don't go as smoothly as we'd like. Here are a few common issues and their fixes:

1. **eGPU Not Detected by macOS**:

   o Make sure the Thunderbolt cable is securely connected.

   o Try using a different Thunderbolt port on your Mac mini.

o   Restart your Mac mini and power cycle the eGPU (turn it off and then on again).

2. **Low Performance After Connecting eGPU**:

   o   Check if any macOS updates are available, as Apple frequently improves eGPU support in newer releases.

   o   Ensure that your app is using the external GPU (refer to Step 3).

   o   Make sure the eGPU's power supply is properly connected and functioning.

3. **App Crashes or Freezes When Using eGPU**:

   o   Some apps may not fully support eGPU acceleration. Check the app's settings or documentation for compatibility.

   o   Try disconnecting the eGPU and restarting the app to ensure there's no conflict.

Troubleshooting Display Issues

When setting up your Apple M4 Pro Mac mini, the display is one of the most important aspects to get right. Whether you're using a single monitor or a multi-display setup, a smooth and clear visual experience is essential.

APPLE M4 PRO MAC MINI USER GUIDE

However, sometimes things don't go as planned, and you might run into display issues such as a "no signal" error, blurry screens, or incorrect resolution settings. These issues can be frustrating, but don't worry – they're usually easy to solve.

In this section, we'll walk through some common display issues and provide detailed, step-by-step troubleshooting solutions. By following these tips, you'll be back to enjoying your Mac mini's stunning display in no time.

1. No Signal on Your Display

This is one of the most common display issues users face when setting up a new Mac mini. If your screen is black or shows a "no signal" message, here are the troubleshooting steps to follow:

Step 1: Check the Cable Connections

- **Loose or damaged cables** are often the culprit. Double-check that the HDMI, DisplayPort, or USB-C cables connecting your Mac mini to the monitor are securely plugged in. If the cable feels loose, try unplugging it and plugging it back in.

- If you're using a **Thunderbolt or USB-C** cable, make sure you're using a high-quality, compatible cable that supports video output. Some lower-quality cables may not work correctly.

- If possible, **try using a different cable** to see if the issue lies with the cable itself.

Step 2: Verify the Monitor's Input Source

- Some monitors have multiple input ports (HDMI, DisplayPort, VGA, etc.). Make sure your monitor is set to the correct input source. Check the monitor's on-screen menu and ensure it's set to the input that corresponds to the cable you're using.

- If your monitor has **multiple inputs,** you may need to press the **Input** or **Source** button on the monitor to switch to the right one.

Step 3: Restart Your Mac mini and Monitor

- Sometimes a simple restart can resolve the issue. Power off your Mac mini and monitor, then power them back on. This can help reset the connection and may fix the no signal error.

- If you're using a **multi-monitor setup**, try disconnecting one monitor to see if the issue persists on just the primary screen.

Step 4: Test the Monitor with Another Device

- To rule out the possibility that the problem lies with your Mac mini, try connecting the monitor to another device, such as a laptop, another desktop, or a gaming console. If the monitor works with other devices, the issue might be with your Mac mini or its connection settings.

2. Blurry or Distorted Display

A blurry or fuzzy display can make it difficult to use your Mac mini effectively. If your screen looks out of focus or distorted, follow these troubleshooting steps:

Step 1: Adjust Screen Resolution

- macOS automatically detects your display's optimal resolution, but sometimes this may not work correctly. To fix this:

  1. Open **System Preferences** from the Apple menu.

  2. Click on **Displays**.

  3. Under the **Display** tab, check if the resolution is set to **Default for display**. If it's not, select this option. This will set your Mac mini to the best possible resolution for your monitor.

  4. If you still notice blur, try manually adjusting the resolution from the list of available options and see if a lower resolution clears up the display.

Step 2: Check for Screen Scaling Issues

- If you're using a **retina display** or an external display with high resolution, macOS may scale the screen to make text and icons more readable, which can sometimes cause a blurry effect. To adjust:

  1. In the **Displays** preferences, click on **Scaled**.

  2. Try selecting a different scaling option to see if it improves the clarity of the display.

Step 3: Inspect the Display for Physical Damage

- If your monitor is showing consistent blurriness across the screen, it could be due to physical issues like **dead pixels**, **burn-in**, or **screen**

damage. Inspect your monitor closely for any visible signs of damage. If the monitor is damaged, you may need to replace it.

Step 4: Update macOS and Drivers

- Make sure that both macOS and any display-related drivers are up to date:

  1. Go to the **Apple menu** and select **System Preferences**.

  2. Click on **Software Update** to check for any available updates.

  3. If an update is available, install it and restart your Mac mini. This could fix bugs related to display settings.

3. Incorrect Resolution or Screen Cut-Off

If your screen resolution seems off, such as text being too large or small, or parts of the screen are cut off, follow these troubleshooting steps:

Step 1: Adjust Display Resolution and Aspect Ratio

- Incorrect screen resolution can often result in parts of the screen being cut off or icons appearing too large. To adjust this:

  1. Go to **System Preferences** > **Displays**.

  2. In the **Display** tab, make sure the resolution is set to **Default for display**.

  3. Alternatively, you can try **Scaled** to adjust the resolution. Be sure to pick a resolution that matches your monitor's

APPLE M4 PRO MAC MINI USER GUIDE

recommended settings (you can find this in the monitor's user manual or the manufacturer's website).

Step 2: Set the Correct Aspect Ratio

- If your monitor is **widescreen**, make sure the aspect ratio is set correctly. Some older monitors or projectors might not support newer aspect ratios automatically. You may need to adjust the settings to get a full-screen display.

Step 3: Check Your Monitor's Settings

- Some monitors have an **auto-adjust** or **auto-scaling** feature that can help automatically adjust the display to fit the screen. Look for an "Auto" or "Auto Adjust" button in your monitor's menu settings and try using it.

Step 4: Test with Another Monitor

- If the issue persists, try connecting your Mac mini to a different monitor. If the issue disappears with a new monitor, the problem is likely with your original display or its settings. If the problem occurs with both monitors, it may be a settings issue within macOS.

4. Screen Flickering or Flashing

Screen flickering or flashing is another common issue that can disrupt your Mac mini experience. If your screen is flickering or showing random flashes, follow these steps:

Step 1: Check the Refresh Rate

- Your monitor may not be syncing properly with your Mac mini's refresh rate. To fix this:

    1. Open **System Preferences** > **Displays**.

    2. Click on the **Display** tab and check the **Refresh Rate** option. Try switching to a different refresh rate (e.g., 60Hz or 120Hz) to see if it resolves the flickering.

Step 2: Test the Cables and Ports

- A **damaged cable** or faulty **port** can cause flickering. Try using a different cable or port (for example, switch between HDMI and Thunderbolt) to see if this stops the flickering.

Step 3: Check for External Interference

- Sometimes, external devices or **electrical interference** can cause screen flickering. If you have other devices like speakers, printers, or fluorescent lights near the Mac mini or display, try moving them away to see if the flickering stops.

Step 4: Reset the System Management Controller (SMC)

- A system reset can help fix certain display issues like flickering:

    1. Shut down your Mac mini.

    2. Unplug the power cord and wait 15 seconds.

    3. Plug the power cord back in and wait an additional 5 seconds.

APPLE M4 PRO MAC MINI USER GUIDE

4. Turn your Mac mini back on.

5. Color Distortion or Incorrect Colors

If your display is showing colors that don't look right—such as a greenish, reddish, or blue tint—here's how to fix it:

Step 1: Calibrate Your Display

- macOS has a built-in tool for display calibration. To use it:

    1. Go to **System Preferences** > **Displays**.

    2. Click on the **Color** tab.

    3. Select **Calibrate** and follow the on-screen instructions to adjust your display's color settings.

Step 2: Check Cable Connections

- Poor **cable connections** can cause color distortion. Make sure the cables are securely connected and free of damage. Try using a different cable to see if the color issue persists.

Step 3: Reset Display Settings

- If you've made custom adjustments to your display's color profile, try resetting it to default settings. Go to **System Preferences** > **Displays** > **Color**, and choose **Default**.

Step 4: Check for External Monitor Issues

- If you're using an external monitor, check if there's a **color setting** within the monitor's menu that's causing the distortion. Some monitors have a "Vivid" or "Cinema" mode that can skew colors, so set it to the default setting.

PERIPHERAL DEVICES AND CONNECTIVITY

Connecting and Configuring Bluetooth Devices

One of the major advantages of the Apple M4 Pro Mac mini is its seamless integration with Bluetooth devices, allowing you to connect peripherals like headphones, keyboards, and mice without the need for additional cables. Whether you're setting up a clean desk with wireless accessories or trying to reduce the clutter of wires, Bluetooth offers a convenient solution. Here's how you can easily connect and configure Bluetooth devices with your Mac mini M4 Pro, along with some troubleshooting tips to ensure a smooth experience.

Step 1: Turn On Your Bluetooth Device

Before anything else, make sure that the Bluetooth device you want to pair with your Mac mini is turned on and in pairing mode. Depending on the device, this might involve:

- **Headphones**: For many Bluetooth headphones, you'll need to press and hold the power button until the light flashes (usually in blue or red). This signals that the headphones are ready to pair.

- **Keyboard**: For Bluetooth keyboards, simply power it on. If the device has a dedicated "pairing" button, press and hold it. For Apple's Magic Keyboard, it should automatically enter pairing mode once powered on.

- **Mouse**: Similar to keyboards, most Bluetooth mice will go into pairing mode as soon as they are turned on. If your mouse has a pairing button, hold it down until the light flashes, indicating it's ready for connection.

Step 2: Enable Bluetooth on Your Mac mini M4 Pro

Next, you need to make sure Bluetooth is enabled on your Mac mini. Here's how:

1. **Open the Apple Menu**: Click on the **Apple logo** in the top-left corner of the screen.

2. **Select System Preferences**: From the dropdown, select **System Preferences**.

3. **Go to Bluetooth Settings**: In the System Preferences window, find and click on **Bluetooth**. If Bluetooth is off, click the **Turn Bluetooth On** button.

Alternatively, you can check if Bluetooth is turned on directly from the **menu bar**:

- Look for the **Bluetooth icon** in the top-right corner of your screen.

- If the icon appears gray, it means Bluetooth is off. Click it and select **Turn Bluetooth On**.

Step 3: Pair Your Bluetooth Device

Once Bluetooth is enabled, your Mac mini will automatically start searching for available devices. Now follow these steps to complete the pairing:

1. **Open Bluetooth Preferences**: After enabling Bluetooth, your Mac mini will display a list of nearby available devices under **Devices**. This includes everything from headphones and mice to keyboards and speakers.

2. **Select Your Device**: Find the device you want to pair in the list and click on it. A message will appear asking if you want to connect. Click **Connect** to begin the pairing process.

3. **Follow On-Screen Prompts**: For some devices, like keyboards and mice, macOS might ask you to enter a pairing code or confirm the pairing on both devices. If you're pairing a keyboard, you may be asked to type a code to confirm the connection. Follow any on-screen instructions to complete the process.

4. **Confirmation**: Once paired, your device will appear as connected in the Bluetooth preferences window, and the Bluetooth icon in the menu bar will change to indicate a successful connection.

Step 4: Test the Connection

Now that your device is paired, it's a good idea to test it to make sure everything is working properly:

- **Headphones**: Play some music or a video on your Mac mini to check if audio is being routed to your Bluetooth headphones. Adjust the volume using your Mac mini or your headphones.

- **Keyboard**: Try typing a few characters in a text field to ensure your Bluetooth keyboard is responding.

- **Mouse**: Move the cursor around the screen and click to ensure that your Bluetooth mouse is working properly.

Troubleshooting Bluetooth Pairing Issues

Even though pairing Bluetooth devices with your Mac mini is typically a smooth process, occasionally, you might run into issues. Don't worry—here are some common problems and troubleshooting steps to help you get your Bluetooth devices working.

1. Device Not Showing Up in Bluetooth Preferences

If your Bluetooth device isn't showing up in the list of available devices, it could be due to several factors:

APPLE M4 PRO MAC MINI USER GUIDE

- **Check the Device's Bluetooth Mode**: Make sure your Bluetooth device is in pairing mode. Refer to the user manual for your device to ensure it's ready to pair.

- **Make Sure Bluetooth is On**: Double-check that Bluetooth is enabled on your Mac mini. If it's turned off, your Mac won't be able to find your Bluetooth device.

- **Restart Your Mac mini**: Sometimes a simple restart can resolve connectivity issues. Reboot your Mac mini and try pairing the device again.

- **Move Closer to the Mac mini**: If your device is too far away, Bluetooth signals might be weak. Try moving the device closer to your Mac mini and see if it shows up.

2. Pairing Fails or Disconnects

If the pairing process fails or your device disconnects unexpectedly, try these steps:

- **Turn Bluetooth Off and On Again**: Go to your Mac mini's Bluetooth settings and turn Bluetooth off, wait for a few seconds, and turn it back on. Then try pairing again.

- **Reset the Bluetooth Device**: For headphones or other devices that don't seem to pair, try turning them off and then back on, or reset the device to factory settings (if applicable). Consult the user manual for specific reset instructions.

- **Delete Previous Pairings**: If the device has been paired with other devices in the past, this could cause interference. In the Bluetooth settings, click the **X** next to old devices you no longer need and try pairing again.

3. Audio Not Playing Through Bluetooth Headphones

If your Bluetooth headphones are paired but the sound isn't coming through, follow these steps:

- **Check Audio Output Settings**: Go to **System Preferences** > **Sound** and make sure your Bluetooth headphones are selected as the output device.

- **Reconnect the Headphones**: Disconnect and reconnect the Bluetooth headphones in your **Bluetooth preferences**. Sometimes this can refresh the connection and solve the issue.

- **Restart Your Mac mini**: If all else fails, restart your Mac mini, which can sometimes help resolve audio routing issues.

4. Slow or Unresponsive Bluetooth Device

If your Bluetooth device feels slow or unresponsive, it may be due to a poor connection:

- **Reduce Interference**: Bluetooth operates on the 2.4 GHz frequency, which can be crowded with other devices like Wi-Fi routers and microwaves. Try moving your Mac mini and Bluetooth device away from other electronics to reduce interference.

APPLE M4 PRO MAC MINI USER GUIDE

- **Update Your macOS**: Make sure you're running the latest version of macOS. Sometimes, software updates fix bugs related to Bluetooth connectivity.

- **Re-pair the Device**: Remove the Bluetooth device from your Mac mini's list of paired devices and re-pair it to refresh the connection.

5. Bluetooth Device is Out of Range or Keeps Disconnecting

If your Bluetooth device keeps disconnecting or you're getting a weak signal, it may be too far from your Mac mini:

- **Bring Devices Closer Together**: Ensure that your Bluetooth device is within range of your Mac mini. The typical Bluetooth range is about 30 feet (9 meters), but walls and obstacles can reduce this.

- **Check for Interference**: Devices like routers, microwaves, and even other Bluetooth devices can cause interference. Try turning off other wireless devices or moving them further away from your Mac mini.

Setting Up USB-C, Thunderbolt, and HDMI Connections on Your Apple M4 Pro Mac mini

The Apple M4 Pro Mac mini is designed to offer powerful and seamless connectivity with the latest technology. Among the various options for connecting external devices, USB-C, Thunderbolt, and HDMI are the most commonly used ports. Understanding how to use these ports effectively can greatly enhance your experience, whether you're setting up external displays, adding storage devices, or connecting peripherals like printers, cameras, or audio equipment.

Let's break down how to properly connect your Mac mini using these ports, while ensuring you get the best performance out of each.

USB-C Connections

USB-C is a versatile, fast, and compact port that has become the standard for modern devices, including the Mac mini M4 Pro. This port offers a lot of flexibility, and its speed is impressive for tasks ranging from transferring data to connecting external displays or peripherals.

What's   Special   About   USB-C?
USB-C is reversible, meaning you can plug the cable in either way, making it much easier to use compared to older USB ports. It supports both data transfer and power delivery, and on your Mac mini, it can deliver up to 40Gbps of data transfer speeds when connected to the right device. This is ideal for transferring large files, connecting fast external storage devices, or linking to a high-speed dock for multiple peripherals.

How to Connect USB-C Peripherals:

1. **Choose the Right Cable and Device**: Ensure that both your Mac mini and the peripheral (e.g., external hard drive, printer, or camera) support USB-C. Not all devices use USB-C for power and data, so it's essential to verify compatibility.

2. **Connect the Cable**: Plug one end of the USB-C cable into one of the USB-C ports on the back of the Mac mini and the other end into your device. These ports are typically located on the back of the Mac mini, but check your device's documentation for where to connect the USB-C cable.

3. **Ensure Maximum Speed**: For the fastest data transfer speeds, make sure your device supports USB 3.1 Gen 2 or USB 3.2 (the latter being faster). Also, when using an external SSD, this will ensure you're getting the full potential of the connection.

4. **Mounting the Device**: If you're connecting storage devices (external hard drives or SSDs), macOS should recognize the device almost immediately. Your external drive will show up in the Finder sidebar, ready for use.

Thunderbolt Connections

Thunderbolt is one of the most powerful connectivity options available today, and on the Mac mini M4 Pro, it is available via the USB-C port. Thunderbolt 4, which is the latest version supported by the Mac mini, brings significant speed improvements (up to 40Gbps), as well as more flexibility with connected devices. Thunderbolt can handle everything from high-definition video output to external GPU setups, while also supporting fast data transfer.

Why   Thunderbolt   Is   Different
Thunderbolt is not just a faster USB-C port; it offers added benefits like the ability to connect multiple devices in a daisy-chain configuration.

Thunderbolt also provides power delivery to compatible devices, reducing the number of cables you need to manage.

How to Connect Thunderbolt Devices:

1. **Connecting to High-Speed Storage**: One of the most common uses for Thunderbolt is to connect external drives. If you have a Thunderbolt-enabled external SSD, you can connect it to your Mac mini using a Thunderbolt cable. These drives will offer lightning-fast speeds, perfect for video editing, large file transfers, or working with data-heavy applications.

2. **Using Multiple Devices**: You can daisy-chain Thunderbolt devices, meaning you can connect one device to the next in a series without needing additional ports on your Mac mini. This is extremely useful for setups that require multiple peripherals like external displays, storage devices, and even an external GPU (eGPU) for more powerful graphics performance.

3. **Thunderbolt for Displays**: Thunderbolt also supports high-definition displays. If you have a Thunderbolt-compatible monitor (or one with a USB-C port that supports Thunderbolt), you can connect it to the Mac mini to display stunning visuals. It supports up to two 6K displays at 60Hz, giving you crisp, clear images on your workspace.

4. **Check for Thunderbolt 4 Support**: When purchasing Thunderbolt devices, make sure they're Thunderbolt 4 compliant, as this will

APPLE M4 PRO MAC MINI USER GUIDE

ensure the highest possible transfer speeds and compatibility with your Mac mini.

HDMI Connections

While USB-C and Thunderbolt ports are great for high-speed data transfers and additional display options, HDMI still plays a significant role in the world of peripheral connectivity. HDMI is especially common for connecting external displays and TVs, but it can also be used for soundbars and other multimedia devices.

HDMI on Your Mac mini

The Apple M4 Pro Mac mini comes equipped with a single HDMI 2.0 port, which allows you to connect an external monitor, TV, or projector with ease. While HDMI is typically slower than Thunderbolt or USB-C for data transfer, it remains the best option for video and audio output to external displays.

How to Connect via HDMI:

1. **Connecting External Displays**: Simply plug one end of an HDMI cable into the HDMI port on the back of your Mac mini and the other end into the HDMI port on your monitor, TV, or projector. Your Mac mini should automatically detect the display, and you can adjust the resolution and display settings by navigating to **System Preferences > Displays**.

2. **Setting Up Audio**: Many HDMI displays also support audio output. If you want the sound to come through your TV or speakers connected

via HDMI, go to **System Preferences > Sound**, and select the HDMI option as the output device.

3. **Configuring Multiple Displays**: Although Thunderbolt ports support multiple displays, if you have an HDMI display as well, you can use both ports (Thunderbolt for a monitor and HDMI for another) to set up a multi-monitor system. Just be sure to go into **System Preferences > Displays** and arrange the monitors to your liking.

4. **Resolution and Refresh Rate**: HDMI 2.0 supports resolutions up to 4K at 60Hz. If you want a better visual experience, ensure that your display supports the resolution you intend to use, and adjust accordingly in the **Display Settings**.

Maximizing Transfer Speeds and Connectivity

To make sure you're using these connections to their full potential, follow these tips:

- **Use High-Quality Cables**: While USB-C and Thunderbolt ports can deliver excellent performance, the cables you use play a significant role in transfer speeds. Always use certified, high-quality cables that support the maximum speeds for your devices.

- **Avoid Overloading Ports**: Each USB-C and Thunderbolt port on your Mac mini can handle multiple connections (especially when daisy-chaining Thunderbolt devices), but avoid overloading them. If you have several high-demand devices (e.g., external SSDs, eGPU, high-res monitors), try spreading them out across multiple ports to avoid bandwidth limitations.

- **Monitor System Resources**: If you notice slower speeds or lag when connecting external devices, check your Mac mini's **Activity Monitor** to see if any other processes are consuming excessive CPU or RAM resources. Freeing up resources may help improve the performance of connected devices.

- **Optimize Display Settings**: When connecting multiple monitors, make sure to select the correct resolution and refresh rate for each screen. Lowering the resolution on non-essential displays can help optimize performance.

- **Keep Your Mac mini Cool**: High-demand peripherals can generate a lot of heat, especially in a compact setup like the Mac mini. If you're running high-performance peripherals (such as an eGPU or 4K display), consider placing your Mac mini in a well-ventilated area to prevent overheating and ensure that performance remains optimal.

Managing Ethernet and Wi-Fi Connections

In today's digital world, a stable and fast internet connection is crucial for productivity, entertainment, and seamless work on your Mac mini M4 Pro. Whether you're using a wired Ethernet connection or relying on Wi-Fi, having the right setup and configuration is key to ensuring a reliable and smooth experience.

This section will guide you through setting up and managing your Ethernet and Wi-Fi connections on the Mac mini M4 Pro. We'll also discuss how to optimize your network settings for the best speed and reliability.

1. Setting Up Ethernet (Wired Connection)

A wired Ethernet connection provides the most stable and consistent internet experience. It's often the best choice when you need uninterrupted connectivity for tasks like video conferencing, large file transfers, or streaming high-definition content.

Step 1: Connect Your Ethernet Cable

First, ensure you have an Ethernet cable ready and plugged into your router or modem. The Mac mini M4 Pro comes with a Gigabit Ethernet port (or a 10Gb Ethernet option on certain models), which allows for fast wired connections.

- **Locate the Ethernet port on your Mac mini**: The Ethernet port is usually found on the back of the device, next to other ports like USB-C and HDMI. If you have the 10Gb Ethernet model, you'll get a faster connection speed.

- **Plug the cable in**: Insert one end of the Ethernet cable into the port on the Mac mini, and the other end into an available port on your router or switch.

Step 2: Enable Ethernet Connection on macOS

Once the cable is connected, your Mac mini should automatically detect the wired connection. However, you'll want to check that it's properly enabled in your system settings.

- **Open System Preferences**: Click on the Apple logo in the top-left corner of the screen, and select **System Preferences** from the drop-down menu.

- **Go to Network Settings**: In the System Preferences window, click on **Network**. This will take you to a list of available network interfaces.

- **Select Ethernet**: In the left-hand column, you should see **Ethernet** listed. If it's not already selected, click on it to make sure it's active.

- **Check Connection Status**: If your Mac mini is connected to Ethernet properly, you'll see a green indicator next to Ethernet, indicating that your connection is live. If it's not connected, macOS will let you know.

Step 3: Configure Your Ethernet Settings (Optional)

Most users won't need to change settings here, as macOS typically configures everything automatically using DHCP (Dynamic Host Configuration Protocol). However, if you want to manually set up your IP address or change DNS servers for faster browsing, you can do so here.

- **Click on the Advanced button**: This will open a new window where you can adjust settings like IP address, DNS, and more.

APPLE M4 PRO MAC MINI USER GUIDE

- **Manual Configuration**: If you prefer a static IP address, select **Manually** from the dropdown next to Configure IPv4. You can then enter your specific IP address, subnet mask, and router details.

Once you've made any necessary adjustments, click **OK**, and then **Apply** to save the changes.

2. Setting Up Wi-Fi (Wireless Connection)

If you prefer a wireless setup, the Mac mini M4 Pro has robust Wi-Fi capabilities. Whether you're in a large office or a home environment, connecting to Wi-Fi can provide flexibility and mobility without the need for physical cables.

Step 1: Connect to Your Wi-Fi Network

The first step is to make sure your Mac mini is within range of your Wi-Fi network. The M4 Pro supports Wi-Fi 6 (802.11ax), which means it can take advantage of faster speeds and better performance in crowded networks.

- **Open Wi-Fi Settings**: Click on the **Wi-Fi icon** located in the top-right corner of your screen, near the clock.

- **Choose a Network**: A list of available networks will appear. Click on your Wi-Fi network to select it.

- **Enter Password**: If your network is secured, you'll be prompted to enter the Wi-Fi password. Type it in and click **Join**.

Step 2: Check Wi-Fi Status

Once connected, the Wi-Fi icon in the top-right corner should show a solid connection, indicating that your Mac mini is online. If the icon has a warning sign, it means there is an issue with your connection.

Step 3: Optimize Wi-Fi Settings (For Better Speed and Reliability)

To get the most out of your Wi-Fi connection, especially with the Mac mini M4 Pro's Wi-Fi 6 capabilities, there are a few settings you can tweak to optimize the connection.

- **Use the 5 GHz Band**: If your router supports dual-band Wi-Fi (2.4 GHz and 5 GHz), make sure you're connected to the 5 GHz band. This band offers faster speeds and less interference, especially in crowded environments with lots of devices.

- **Keep Firmware Up-to-Date**: Make sure your Wi-Fi router firmware is up-to-date. This ensures that the latest performance improvements and security patches are applied.

- **Optimize Router Placement**: The physical placement of your router matters. Place it in a central location, away from walls and obstructions, for optimal coverage. Avoid placing your router near large metal objects or microwave ovens, which can interfere with the signal.

- **Check Your Wi-Fi Channel**: In areas with heavy Wi-Fi traffic, the channels may be crowded, leading to slower speeds. Some routers automatically switch channels, but if yours doesn't, you might want to manually adjust the channel for less interference. Apps like **Wi-Fi Analyzer** can help you identify the best channel to use.

Step 4: Configure Advanced Wi-Fi Settings

If you want more control over your Wi-Fi connection, you can access advanced settings within your network preferences.

- **Open Network Preferences**: Go to **System Preferences > Network**, and select **Wi-Fi** on the left panel.

- **Advanced Settings**: Click on **Advanced** to access additional options such as preferred networks, automatic joining, and DNS settings.

- **DNS Optimization**: You can configure DNS settings to use faster, more reliable servers. For instance, you can switch to Google's DNS (8.8.8.8 and 8.8.4.4) or Cloudflare's (1.1.1.1) for potentially quicker website load times.

3. Troubleshooting Ethernet and Wi-Fi Connections

Even with the best setup, you might encounter issues with either your Ethernet or Wi-Fi connection. Below are some troubleshooting steps to help you resolve common connection problems:

Ethernet Issues

- **Check the Cable**: If your Ethernet connection isn't working, make sure the cable is securely plugged in at both ends and isn't damaged.

- **Restart the Router**: If there's no internet connectivity, try restarting your router to refresh the network connection.

- **Check Your ISP**: Ensure your internet service provider (ISP) isn't experiencing an outage. You can check with them for status updates.

Wi-Fi Issues

- **Forget and Reconnect to Wi-Fi**: If you're having trouble connecting to Wi-Fi, go to **System Preferences** > **Network** > **Wi-Fi**, click on **Advanced**, select your network, and click the minus button to forget it. Then reconnect by selecting your Wi-Fi network and entering the password again.

- **Reset Network Settings**: If the issue persists, try resetting your network settings. Go to **System Preferences** > **Network**, select Wi-Fi, and click the minus button. Then add it back by clicking the plus button and selecting Wi-Fi again.

- **Interference**: If your connection is slow or unreliable, check if there are other devices or appliances causing interference. A busy Wi-Fi network with many devices can also cause slower speeds.

4. Optimizing Network Performance for Better Speed and Reliability

To get the best out of your Ethernet or Wi-Fi connection, consider the following tips:

- **Use a Wired Connection When Possible**: For the most stable and fastest internet experience, use a wired Ethernet connection, especially for tasks that require high bandwidth.

- **Limit Bandwidth-Hungry Apps**: Close unnecessary apps and tabs that consume excessive bandwidth. If you're working with video conferencing software or streaming services, ensure that no other device on the network is using excessive bandwidth.

- **Upgrade Your Router**: If you're still using an old router, upgrading to a Wi-Fi 6 router can significantly improve performance, especially if you have multiple devices connected to the network.

- **Monitor Your Network**: Use apps like **Activity Monitor** or third-party tools to monitor network activity and bandwidth usage. This will help you identify if certain apps or processes are slowing down your connection.

Using the Mac mini with External Storage and Media Devices

One of the strengths of the **Apple M4 Pro Mac mini** is its versatility, especially when it comes to expanding storage. Whether you're a creative professional who needs to store large video files, a software developer

APPLE M4 PRO MAC MINI USER GUIDE

looking to manage big project files, or just someone who prefers having their media stored externally, knowing how to connect and manage external storage devices can dramatically enhance your Mac mini experience.

External storage can take the form of traditional **hard drives** (HDDs) or the faster **solid-state drives** (SSDs). These devices are used for everything from backing up data to expanding your available storage when your internal drive starts filling up. Fortunately, the Mac mini's range of high-speed ports, including **USB-C**, **Thunderbolt**, and **USB-A**, makes it easy to connect external drives and media devices. Here's a detailed guide to help you get the most out of connecting and managing external storage on your Mac mini.

1. Understanding the Ports and Compatibility

Before diving into the step-by-step process of connecting external storage devices, it's important to understand the ports available on your Mac mini and the devices it supports:

- **USB-C/Thunderbolt Ports**: The Mac mini M4 Pro is equipped with multiple **Thunderbolt 5** and **USB-C** ports. These provide incredibly fast data transfer speeds, which is crucial for tasks like editing video or transferring large files quickly. They can support devices like external SSDs, high-performance hard drives, and other media devices.

- **USB-A Ports**: Older peripherals, like external hard drives, may require the traditional **USB-A** connection. The Mac mini M4 Pro includes at least one **USB-A** port, making it compatible with a wide range of external storage devices, including those from previous generations.

- **HDMI Port**: This port can also be used for connecting displays, but some storage devices, such as media players or cameras, may also use HDMI in specific setups for file transfers.

- **Ethernet**: While primarily used for internet connections, the Ethernet port can also be used for network-attached storage (NAS) devices.

2. Connecting an External Storage Device

Step 1: Prepare Your External Storage

First, make sure your external storage device is ready to use. Whether it's an **HDD** or an **SSD**, here are some things to consider:

- **Check the file system**: If you are using an external hard drive that was previously used on Windows, it might be formatted as **NTFS**. macOS can read NTFS drives but cannot write to them by default. In this case, you may need to reformat the drive to a macOS-compatible file system like **exFAT**, **HFS+**, or **APFS**.

To check and format a drive:

1. Open **Disk Utility** (you can search for it using Spotlight).

2. Select your external drive from the sidebar.

3. Click **Erase** and choose the appropriate file system (e.g., exFAT for cross-platform use or APFS for macOS-only use).

- **Power requirements**: Some external hard drives or SSDs require an external power source, while others, particularly SSDs, are powered directly through the USB connection. Make sure you connect the necessary power cable if your device requires one.

Step 2: Connect the Device to Your Mac mini

- For **USB-C/Thunderbolt drives**: Simply connect your external storage device to one of the **USB-C** or **Thunderbolt** ports on your Mac mini.

- For **USB-A drives**: If your drive has a USB-A connector and your Mac mini has a **USB-A port**, simply plug it in. If your device is USB-A but your Mac mini only has USB-C ports, you may need a **USB-C to USB-A adapter**.

Once connected, macOS will typically recognize the device automatically. A notification might pop up on your screen, asking what action you'd like to take (e.g., open the folder, ignore, or eject).

Step 3: Format (If Necessary)

If the external drive isn't formatted for macOS or you're connecting it for the first time, you may need to format it. Always remember that formatting will erase any existing data on the device, so make sure to back up important files before proceeding.

3. Accessing and Managing Files on External Storage

Step 1: Locating the External Drive

Once connected, you'll find your external storage in the **Finder**. This is the macOS file management system, and it allows you to see and organize all the files on your Mac mini, as well as any external devices connected.

- **Finder Sidebar**: Your external drive will appear under the **Devices** section in the Finder sidebar. Simply click on the drive's name to open it and view its contents.

- **Desktop**: In some cases, the external drive will also appear as an icon on your desktop for quick access.

Step 2: Copying and Moving Files

Now that you've located your external storage, you can start managing your files:

- **Copy Files to External Storage**: If you want to back up files or move them off your Mac mini, simply drag and drop the desired files or folders from your Mac's **Documents**, **Downloads**, or **Desktop** folders to the external storage device.

- **Copy Files from External Storage**: To retrieve files from the external drive, simply drag them from the drive back to your Mac mini, or open the file directly from the external storage (e.g., by double-clicking a document or opening a video in a media player).

You can also right-click files or folders and select **Copy** or **Move** to quickly copy files between your Mac mini and the external storage.

APPLE M4 PRO MAC MINI USER GUIDE

Step 3: Organizing Files on External Storage

It's important to keep your files organized, especially when you're working with large amounts of data. Here are some tips for organizing your external drive:

- **Create Folders**: Create new folders directly on the external drive to keep your files sorted by type or project. For example, create folders for **Documents**, **Videos**, **Photos**, etc.

- **Naming Files and Folders**: Name files and folders in a way that makes sense to you so that you can easily find what you need. For example, when working on a video project, you might create a folder named "Video_Editing_Projects" with subfolders for different parts of the project.

- **Use Tags**: In Finder, you can use color-coded tags to organize files. Right-click on a file, select **Tags**, and choose a color that corresponds to its status (e.g., red for urgent, green for complete).

4. Safely Ejecting External Storage Devices

Once you've finished using your external drive, it's important to eject it safely to prevent data corruption. Here's how:

- **Using Finder**: In the Finder sidebar, click the **Eject** icon next to your external storage device. Alternatively, you can drag the external drive's icon to the **Trash** (which will turn into an Eject icon).

- **Using the Desktop**: If the drive appears on your desktop, you can right-click on the drive's icon and select **Eject**, or drag the icon to the Trash.

Once the device disappears from Finder or the desktop, it's safe to physically disconnect it from your Mac mini.

5. Troubleshooting External Storage Devices

While connecting external storage devices to your Mac mini is usually straightforward, here are some common issues you might encounter and how to resolve them:

- **Drive Not Recognized**: If your external storage isn't showing up, ensure the device is properly connected. Try using a different USB port or cable. If you're using a USB-C to USB-A adapter, make sure it's functioning correctly. You can also restart your Mac mini and reconnect the device.

- **Slow Data Transfer**: If you're noticing slow data transfer speeds, check the type of connection (USB-A is slower than USB-C/Thunderbolt). If you're using a traditional hard drive (HDD), consider upgrading to an SSD for faster read/write speeds.

- **Permissions Issues**: If you're unable to write to the external drive, it could be due to file system compatibility or permission settings. Check the drive's format (NTFS is read-only on macOS), and in **Disk Utility**, you can change the permissions to allow writing (if supported).

APPLE M4 PRO MAC MINI USER GUIDE

- **Drive Not Mounting**: If the external drive doesn't mount, you can try accessing it via **Disk Utility**. Open Disk Utility from **Applications > Utilities**, select your external drive, and click **Mount**.

Troubleshooting Peripheral Connectivity

When setting up and using your **Apple M4 Pro Mac mini**, you might encounter issues with peripheral connectivity. These issues can be frustrating, but don't worry – most of the time, the problems are easy to fix with just a few troubleshooting steps. Whether it's a USB device that's not being detected or audio not playing through Bluetooth speakers, this section will guide you through common connectivity issues and how to resolve them.

Let's break it down into the most common problems and their simple solutions:

1. USB Device Not Detected

This is one of the most frequent issues users encounter. When you plug a USB device (like a keyboard, mouse, external hard drive, or USB flash drive) into your Mac mini and it doesn't show up, it can be frustrating.

Possible Causes:

- Loose or faulty USB connection.

- The device itself might be malfunctioning.

- Power issues (for devices that require external power).

- Software or OS issues.

- Incompatible or outdated drivers.

How to Fix It:

- **Check the USB Cable and Port**: Start by ensuring the USB cable is properly connected to both the device and the Mac mini. If the cable is damaged or worn out, replace it. Try plugging the device into a different USB port on the Mac mini to rule out a faulty port.

- **Test the Device on Another Computer**: If possible, try plugging the USB device into another computer or laptop. This will help you determine if the issue is with the Mac mini or the device itself.

- **Reboot Your Mac mini**: Sometimes a simple restart can resolve connectivity issues. Restart your Mac mini and check if the USB device is detected after the reboot.

- **Check for macOS Updates**: Make sure your macOS is up to date. Apple often releases updates that fix bugs, including connectivity issues with peripherals. Go to **System Preferences > Software Update** to check for any available updates.

- **Reset the SMC (System Management Controller)**: Resetting the SMC can resolve many hardware-related issues, including USB problems. To reset the SMC on your Mac mini:

    o Shut down your Mac mini.

APPLE M4 PRO MAC MINI USER GUIDE

- o   Unplug the power cord and wait for 15 seconds.

- o   Plug the power cord back in and wait for another 5 seconds.

- o   Turn your Mac mini back on.

- **Try a Different Device**: If none of the above steps work, the USB device might be the issue. Try using a different USB device (such as a different mouse or keyboard) to see if the issue persists.

2. Bluetooth Devices Not Connecting

Bluetooth devices, such as wireless keyboards, mice, headphones, and speakers, offer great flexibility, but sometimes they can have connectivity issues with the Mac mini.

Possible Causes:

- Bluetooth settings may not be configured correctly.

- Bluetooth devices may not be in pairing mode.

- Interference from other Bluetooth devices.

- Bluetooth software issues or outdated drivers.

How to Fix It:

- **Ensure Bluetooth is Enabled**: First, make sure Bluetooth is enabled on your Mac mini. Go to **System Preferences > Bluetooth** and ensure Bluetooth is turned on. If it's already on, try toggling it off and on again.

- **Put Your Bluetooth Device in Pairing Mode**: For Bluetooth headphones, speakers, or any other device, make sure it's in pairing mode. Check the device's manual for specific instructions on how to enable pairing mode.

- **Disconnect Other Bluetooth Devices**: Sometimes multiple Bluetooth devices connected to your Mac mini can interfere with each other. Try disconnecting any devices you're not actively using to improve connectivity.

- **Forget and Re-pair the Device**: In the Bluetooth settings, locate the device in the list of connected devices, click the "X" next to it, and then try pairing it again as if it were a new device.

- **Check Battery and Power**: Make sure your Bluetooth device is charged or has fresh batteries. Low battery levels can interfere with the device's ability to connect properly.

- **Clear Bluetooth Cache**: If you're still having trouble, clearing the Bluetooth cache might help. Open **Finder** and press **Command + Shift + G**, then enter **/Library/Preferences**. Look for files that start with **com.apple.Bluetooth**, and delete them. Afterward, restart your Mac mini and try reconnecting the device.

3. External Display Not Showing

If you've connected an external monitor to your Mac mini but nothing is displaying, it's time to troubleshoot the connection. Sometimes the issue is as simple as a loose cable, while other times it may involve settings adjustments or even hardware issues.

Possible Causes:

- Loose or faulty HDMI or Thunderbolt cable.

- Incorrect display settings.

- Monitor compatibility issues.

- Software or system bugs.

How to Fix It:

- **Check the Cable and Port**: Ensure the HDMI or Thunderbolt cable is securely connected to both the Mac mini and the monitor. If the cable is damaged or old, try replacing it with a new one.

- **Change the Display Input**: If your monitor has multiple inputs (e.g., HDMI 1, HDMI 2), make sure the correct input source is selected on the monitor's settings menu.

- **Adjust Display Settings**: Go to **System Preferences > Displays** and click **Detect Displays**. If the Mac mini is not automatically detecting your external monitor, this button will force it to look for connected displays. You can also adjust the resolution and arrangement of the monitors here.

- **Restart Your Mac mini**: Sometimes a restart is all it takes to solve display issues. Restart your Mac mini and check if the external monitor now works.

- **Try a Different Monitor**: If possible, connect the Mac mini to a different monitor to rule out the possibility of a faulty monitor.

4. Audio Not Playing Through Bluetooth or External Speakers

One of the more common problems is when audio from your Mac mini is not playing through external Bluetooth speakers or wired speakers, even though the speakers are connected.

Possible Causes:

- Audio output settings are misconfigured.

- The Bluetooth device is not properly paired or connected.

- Audio drivers or software glitches.

How to Fix It:

- **Check Audio Output Settings**: Go to **System Preferences > Sound > Output** and ensure that the correct device is selected as the audio output. For Bluetooth speakers or external speakers, make sure they are selected in the list of output devices.

- **Disconnect and Reconnect Bluetooth Speakers**: If you're using Bluetooth speakers, try disconnecting and reconnecting them. Go to

System Preferences > **Bluetooth**, select the device, and click **Disconnect**, then reconnect the speakers to the Mac mini.

- **Test with Wired Speakers**: If you're using Bluetooth speakers, try connecting wired speakers or headphones to the Mac mini's headphone jack to see if the issue is with the Bluetooth connection or the Mac mini itself.

- **Restart Core Audio**: Sometimes, restarting the Core Audio process can help resolve audio issues. Open the **Activity Monitor** (found in **Applications** > **Utilities**), search for **coreaudiod**, and click **Quit**. This will force the system to restart the audio services.

- **Update macOS and Audio Drivers**: Make sure your macOS is fully updated. Sometimes, audio issues are caused by outdated drivers or bugs that Apple addresses in system updates.

5. Keyboard and Mouse Not Responding

If your keyboard or mouse (whether wired or wireless) stops responding, it can severely disrupt your workflow. The fix is usually quick and easy.

Possible Causes:

- Connection issues (e.g., USB or Bluetooth).

- Dead batteries in wireless devices.

- Software glitches or OS bugs.

How to Fix It:

- **Check Power**: If you're using wireless devices, check the batteries. Replace them if necessary. For wired devices, check that the cable is securely plugged in and undamaged.

- **Reboot Your Mac mini**: A simple reboot can often fix temporary software glitches affecting peripheral devices like a keyboard or mouse.

- **Check Bluetooth Connection**: If your keyboard or mouse is Bluetooth-enabled, ensure they're properly paired with your Mac mini. Go to **System Preferences > Bluetooth** to verify the connection and re-pair if necessary.

- **Try Different Ports**: If you're using a USB keyboard or mouse, try switching to another USB port to rule out a malfunctioning port.

Final Tips for Peripheral Connectivity Troubleshooting

- **Always Update**: Regularly check for software and macOS updates, as these often address connectivity issues with peripherals.

- **Use Compatible Devices**: Ensure that your peripherals are compatible with macOS and the Mac mini. Some older devices may not work seamlessly with newer macOS versions without updated drivers.

- **Be Patient**: Peripheral connectivity problems can sometimes take time to resolve, so be patient as you go through the troubleshooting

APPLE M4 PRO MAC MINI USER GUIDE

steps. Start with the easiest solution first and work your way up to more complex fixes.

APPLE M4 PRO MAC MINI USER GUIDE

SECURITY AND PRIVACY

Setting Up Strong User Authentication

When it comes to securing your Mac mini M4 Pro, strong user authentication is your first line of defense. By setting up effective methods such as passwords, Touch ID, and even two-factor authentication (2FA), you can protect your sensitive data, ensure your privacy, and keep intruders at bay. Let's walk through setting up the strongest user authentication methods, step-by-step, to make sure your Mac mini stays secure.

1. Why Strong User Authentication Matters

Before diving into the setup, let's briefly discuss why strong authentication is so important. In the digital age, your computer is a treasure trove of sensitive information—photos, emails, passwords, and personal files. Without proper security, it's like leaving your front door wide open. Strong authentication methods help ensure that only you (or someone you trust) can access your Mac mini, safeguarding everything from your financial information to your creative work.

2. Setting Up a Strong Password

A strong password is your basic, but essential, line of defense. While it's tempting to use something simple for convenience, it's important to choose a password that is both difficult to guess and easy for you to remember. Here's how you can set up a strong password for your Mac mini:

Step-by-Step Guide to Creating a Strong Password

1. **Go to System Settings**:

   Click on the **Apple Menu** at the top-left corner of the screen, then select **System Settings**.

2. **Navigate to Users & Groups**:

   In the System Settings window, click on **Users & Groups** (this may be listed as "Account" on earlier versions of macOS). This is where you can manage your account and password settings.

3. **Select Your User Account**:

   You'll see a list of accounts on your Mac mini. Click on your **user account** (the one you use to log in) to open the settings for that account.

4. **Set or Change Password**:

   If you don't have a password set yet, click **Add Password** (or **Change Password** if you're updating it). macOS will prompt you to enter your current password if one is already set.

5. **Create a Strong Password**:

   Choose a password that's at least 12 characters long. Mix uppercase and lowercase letters, numbers, and symbols (e.g., !, @, #, $, etc.) to make it more secure. Avoid using easily guessable information, such as your name or birthday.

For instance, instead of using "John1234," go for something like **"R7z@lB1q9!Fm"**.

6. **Enable Password Hints (Optional)**:

   If you're worried about forgetting your password, macOS allows you to set a password hint, which can help you remember it without revealing too much. However, make sure the hint is vague and doesn't directly suggest your password.

7. **Confirm and Save**:

   After typing in your new password, confirm it by typing it again. Once confirmed, click **Change Password** or **Save** to complete the process.

3. Enabling Touch ID for Faster Login

Touch ID provides a convenient and secure way to unlock your Mac mini without typing your password each time. This feature uses the unique fingerprints stored in your Mac mini's Touch ID sensor to verify your identity.

Step-by-Step Guide to Setting Up Touch ID

1. **Open System Settings**:

   As before, click on the **Apple Menu** and go to **System Settings**.

2. **Go to Touch ID Settings**:

   Scroll down and select **Touch ID & Password** under the **Users & Groups** section.

APPLE M4 PRO MAC MINI USER GUIDE

3. **Add Fingerprint**:

   Here, you'll see an option to **Add Fingerprint**. You'll be prompted to place your finger on the Touch ID sensor (usually located at the top-right corner of your Mac mini keyboard or Magic Keyboard). Gently lift and place your finger multiple times until the sensor has fully registered your print.

4. **Set Up for Authentication**:

   Once your fingerprint is added, you can enable Touch ID for various features, such as unlocking your Mac mini, making purchases with Apple Pay, and authorizing app installations. Just check the boxes for each option you want Touch ID to be used for.

5. **Test It Out**:

   Once set up, you can test the Touch ID functionality by locking your Mac (click on the Apple logo > **Lock Screen**) and then using your fingerprint to unlock it.

4. Two-Factor Authentication (2FA) for Extra Security

While a strong password and Touch ID are fantastic, two-factor authentication (2FA) adds an extra layer of protection. 2FA ensures that even if someone manages to get your password, they won't be able to log into your account without the second verification step (usually a code sent to your trusted device).

Step-by-Step Guide to Enabling Two-Factor Authentication for Apple ID

1. **Open System Settings**:

   Go to **Apple Menu > System Settings**, and then click **Apple ID**.

2. **Access Security Settings**:

   In your Apple ID settings, click on **Password & Security**.

3. **Turn On Two-Factor Authentication**:

   If 2FA isn't enabled yet, you'll see an option to **Turn On Two-Factor Authentication**. Click this, and follow the on-screen prompts.

4. **Verify with Your Trusted Device**:

   You'll be asked to confirm your identity by sending a verification code to one of your trusted devices (like your iPhone or iPad). Enter the code once you receive it.

5. **Backup Method**:

   Apple will also ask you to provide a **recovery key** or phone number to help you recover your account if you lose access to your devices. This is an important step, as it ensures you won't be locked out of your Apple ID if something goes wrong.

6. **Confirm and Finish**:

   Once completed, your Apple ID is now protected by two-factor authentication. You'll receive a verification code each time you log into your account from a new device or browser.

APPLE M4 PRO MAC MINI USER GUIDE

5. Enabling "Require Password" for Additional Security

For further security, you can set your Mac mini to require a password after a specific time interval. This feature ensures that if you leave your Mac unattended, it will automatically lock and require a password to regain access.

Step-by-Step Guide to Enabling "Require Password"

1. **Go to System Settings**:
   Click on the **Apple Menu** and go to **System Settings**.

2. **Navigate to Security Settings**:
   Scroll down and select **Security & Privacy**, then click on **General**.

3. **Enable Require Password**:
   In the **General** section, check the box that says **Require password immediately after sleep or screen saver begins**. You can also adjust the time interval to suit your preferences (e.g., "5 minutes," "15 minutes").

4. **Save Your Settings**:
   Once enabled, your Mac will require the password to log in again after the set time, ensuring that no one can access it in your absence.

6. Additional Tips for Strong Authentication

- **Use Password Managers**: Instead of relying on memory for complex passwords, use a password manager to securely store and generate strong passwords.

- **Enable Automatic Locking**: Set your Mac to automatically lock after a few minutes of inactivity by going to **System Settings > Lock Screen**.

- **Avoid Public Wi-Fi for Sensitive Activities**: When working with sensitive information, avoid public Wi-Fi networks. Use a VPN if you must connect to a public network.

- **Regularly Update Your Password**: It's a good habit to update your password every few months to maintain security.

Managing Privacy and App Permissions in macOS Sequoia

Privacy is a major concern in today's digital world, and macOS Sequoia is designed with that in mind. Apple has long been at the forefront of data privacy, offering users greater control over what personal information they share and how it's used. One of the key features of macOS Sequoia is its ability to manage app permissions. With just a few simple steps, you can control how apps interact with your Mac mini M4 Pro, and what they have access to, such as your camera, microphone, and location data. Let's break down exactly how you can configure and control these settings for optimal privacy.

APPLE M4 PRO MAC MINI USER GUIDE

1. Understanding App Permissions on macOS Sequoia

App permissions are a way for macOS to ensure that apps don't access data or features on your Mac without your knowledge or consent. You might have noticed that when you install a new app or when an app updates, macOS often prompts you to grant or deny permissions for features like your camera, microphone, or location. This ensures that you remain in control of your private information and decide which apps can access it.

Here's a quick overview of what these permissions control:

- **Camera**: Controls which apps can use your Mac's built-in camera.

- **Microphone**: Manages which apps are allowed to access your Mac's microphone.

- **Location Services**: Allows apps to use your Mac's location (for things like maps, weather apps, and certain services that need your geographical position).

- **Other Sensitive Data**: This includes access to things like your contacts, photos, calendar, and more.

It's important to know that macOS Sequoia gives you the flexibility to revoke or change these permissions at any time, so you can maintain control over your privacy at all times.

2. Configuring Privacy Settings in System Preferences

To get started with managing your app permissions, open the **System Preferences** app on your Mac mini. This is where you can control most of the privacy settings on your device. Follow these steps to navigate to the privacy settings:

1. **Click on the Apple menu** in the top-left corner of your screen.

2. **Select "System Preferences"** from the drop-down menu.

3. **Click on "Security & Privacy"**.

This will open up a panel where you can configure privacy and security settings. In the **Privacy** tab, you'll see a list of categories related to app permissions, such as **Location Services**, **Camera**, **Microphone**, and more.

3. Managing Camera Permissions

The camera is a sensitive piece of hardware, and macOS Sequoia allows you to control which apps can access it. Here's how you can manage camera permissions:

1. **Go to System Preferences > Security & Privacy > Privacy**.

2. In the left-hand column, scroll down and select **Camera**.

3. On the right side, you'll see a list of apps that have requested access to your camera.

4. **Check or uncheck the box** next to each app to allow or deny camera access.

For example, apps like Zoom or FaceTime will ask for permission to access your camera to enable video calling. If you want to stop an app from using your camera, simply uncheck its box.

APPLE M4 PRO MAC MINI USER GUIDE

Tip: It's always a good idea to review these permissions regularly, especially for apps you don't use often, to ensure that no apps are accessing your camera without your knowledge.

4. Managing Microphone Permissions

The microphone is another privacy-sensitive feature. Some apps, such as voice assistants, video conferencing tools, or dictation software, require microphone access to function properly. Here's how to control which apps can use your microphone:

1. **Go to System Preferences > Security & Privacy > Privacy**.

2. Click on **Microphone** in the left-hand column.

3. You'll see a list of apps that have requested microphone access.

4. **Check or uncheck the box** next to each app to allow or deny access to the microphone.

For instance, if you use a voice recognition app like Siri, or an app like Skype, it will need microphone access. If you don't want a particular app to use your microphone, simply untick its box.

Tip: Just like with camera permissions, regularly reviewing which apps have access to your microphone ensures you're in control of your personal information.

5. Managing Location Services

Location Services is another powerful feature that can be both useful and privacy-sensitive. Many apps, like Maps, Weather, and social media platforms, use your location to provide relevant services. However, you might not always want apps to know where you are. To manage location settings:

1. **Go to System Preferences > Security & Privacy > Privacy**.

2. Select **Location Services** in the left-hand column.

3. You'll see a list of apps that have requested access to your location.

4. **Check or uncheck the box** next to each app to allow or deny location access.

By default, some apps like Safari or Google Maps may use your location to provide personalized results or directions. You can also enable **"Share My Location"** for devices signed into your Apple ID if you want to share your location across your Apple devices.

Tip: If you're concerned about privacy, you can disable **Location Services** entirely, or just disable it for apps that don't need it. It's a good idea to review these settings if you use location-based apps occasionally but don't want them tracking your whereabouts all the time.

6. Controlling Access to Other Sensitive Data

macOS Sequoia also gives you the ability to control which apps can access other sensitive data, such as your contacts, calendar, photos, and more. To manage these permissions:

1. **Go to System Preferences > Security & Privacy > Privacy**.

2. Scroll through the list of categories on the left, including **Contacts**, **Calendar**, **Photos**, and **Reminders**.

3. Select the category you want to manage.

4. On the right, you'll see a list of apps that have requested access to this data.

5. **Check or uncheck the box** to grant or deny access to each app.

For example, you might want a social media app to access your contacts, but you may not want a random weather app to access your calendar. By reviewing these settings regularly, you ensure that apps are only accessing the information you want them to.

Tip: Consider the permissions you grant to apps before installing them. Many apps only need certain permissions for specific functions (such as using your contacts for syncing or calendar access for scheduling), so make sure you're aware of which data is being used and why.

7. Best Practices for Privacy Management

To ensure your Mac mini remains secure and your personal data is protected, here are a few privacy best practices to follow:

- **Regularly review your app permissions**: Take the time every few months to review which apps have access to your camera, microphone, location, and other sensitive data. Revoke permissions for apps you no longer use.

- **Limit location sharing**: Only enable location services for apps that genuinely need it, such as navigation apps, and disable it for others.

- **Use app-specific permissions**: Some apps only require access to specific features (like the camera or microphone) to function. Only grant those permissions when necessary.

- **Keep your software updated**: Apple frequently releases updates to enhance both security and privacy. Make sure to enable automatic updates so your system is always protected against the latest threats.

- **Be cautious with third-party apps**: When downloading third-party apps, always read the privacy policy to understand what data the app will access. If the app asks for unnecessary permissions, consider whether it's worth installing.

Keeping Your Mac mini Secure with macOS Updates

Updating your Mac mini is one of the most important steps you can take to ensure its security. macOS updates aren't just about bringing new features and performance improvements — they're crucial for protecting your device from emerging security threats, vulnerabilities, and bugs. Regular updates help protect your sensitive data, personal information, and improve the overall stability of your Mac mini.

In this section, we'll walk you through how to keep your Mac mini secure by managing macOS updates. From automatic updates to manually checking for updates, we'll cover everything you need to know about how to stay ahead of potential threats and keep your Mac mini in top condition.

Why Updating macOS Matters

Each time Apple releases a new update for macOS, it often includes important security patches designed to fix vulnerabilities that could otherwise be exploited by hackers or malware. While it's easy to assume that your Mac mini is invulnerable due to its reputation for being secure, no system is entirely immune to risks. Cyber threats evolve constantly, and new methods of attack are developed every day.

Security updates often address a range of issues, including:

- **Fixing security holes** that could allow unauthorized access to your system or personal information.

- **Updating software** like Safari, Mail, and system apps to protect against exploits.

- **Improving system performance** by resolving bugs that could otherwise impact stability or introduce security flaws.

- **Patching known vulnerabilities** in macOS that could potentially be used as backdoors by hackers.

By keeping your macOS updated, you are essentially closing off these potential entry points for malicious attacks and ensuring that your system stays as secure as possible.

Benefits of Automatic Updates

One of the best ways to stay secure is by setting your Mac mini to automatically update macOS whenever a new version is released. Here's why enabling automatic updates is a smart move:

1. Protection Without the Effort

With automatic updates, you don't have to remember to manually check for updates or worry about missing an important security patch. Once enabled, macOS will automatically download and install updates in the background while you're not using your Mac mini. This ensures that your system is always running the latest security software without requiring any action from you.

2. Timely Security Patches

Apple regularly releases security updates, and waiting too long to install them could expose your Mac mini to security risks. Automatic updates ensure that these patches are installed as soon as they're available, reducing the risk of your Mac mini being targeted by cybercriminals.

3. Fewer Disruptions

When your Mac mini is set to automatically install updates, you won't be interrupted by reminders or prompts to update your system. Updates happen seamlessly and don't interfere with your workflow, as they typically install when the system is idle or after you restart.

4. Staying Current with the Latest Features

While security is the primary reason for updating, macOS updates also bring new features, improvements, and bug fixes that enhance your Mac mini experience. Automatic updates ensure you're always running the latest version of macOS, allowing you to take advantage of new functionalities as soon as they're available.

How to Enable Automatic Updates on macOS

Now that you understand why automatic updates are essential, let's walk through how to enable them on your Mac mini. Follow these simple steps:

1. **Open System Settings**

   Click on the **Apple menu** (□) in the top-left corner of your screen, then select **System Settings** (or **System Preferences** on older versions of macOS).

2. **Go to Software Update**

In the System Settings window, scroll down and click on **General**, then choose **Software Update**.

3. **Enable Automatic Updates**

Here, you will see the option **Automatically keep my Mac up to date**. Check this box to enable automatic updates.

4. **Advanced Settings (Optional)**

If you want more control over how your updates are handled, click on the **Advanced** button (in the same Software Update window). This will allow you to:

- o Automatically download updates when available.

- o Install system data files and security updates automatically.

- o Install app updates from the App Store automatically.

After you've made your selection, your Mac mini will automatically download and install updates in the background. If a restart is required for the update to take effect, your Mac will prompt you to do so at your earliest convenience.

Managing Updates Manually

While automatic updates are the easiest and most reliable option, there may be times when you want to manually check for updates. For example, you might want to review the details of an update before installing it, or you may want to install updates on your own schedule.

To manually check for updates, follow these steps:

1. **Open System Settings**

   Click on the **Apple menu** (□), then select **System Settings** (or **System Preferences** on older macOS versions).

2. **Go to Software Update**

   Click on **General**, then select **Software Update**.

3. **Check for Updates**

   Your Mac mini will automatically check for any available updates. If an update is available, it will show up here. If not, you'll see a message that says "Your Mac is up to date."

4. **Install Available Updates**

   If there's an update available, simply click the **Update Now** button to begin the installation. You may be prompted to restart your Mac mini once the update is complete.

When to Manually Check for Updates

While automatic updates should cover most of your needs, it's still a good idea to periodically check for updates manually to ensure your Mac mini is fully up to date. Here are some situations where a manual check may be particularly helpful:

- **After major software releases**: Apple frequently releases large updates with new features and system improvements. Checking for updates shortly after a major macOS release ensures that your system is running the latest version and takes advantage of new functionalities.

- **If you encounter a security warning**: In the event that a major security vulnerability is discovered, Apple will likely release a security update. It's good practice to check for updates if you hear about a vulnerability that could affect your Mac mini.

- **If your Mac mini is acting slow or buggy**: Sometimes, issues arise that might be fixed with a software update. Checking for updates can help resolve these issues.

Troubleshooting macOS Updates

In rare cases, you might encounter issues while updating your Mac mini. Here are a few common problems and solutions:

1. Update Won't Install

- **Solution**: Ensure your Mac mini is connected to the internet and has enough storage space for the update. Try restarting your Mac and then manually checking for updates again. If the issue persists, visit the Apple Support website for more troubleshooting steps.

APPLE M4 PRO MAC MINI USER GUIDE

2. Slow Download or Installation

- **Solution**: If the update is taking longer than expected, it could be due to network congestion or server issues. Try waiting a bit and then attempt the update again. Ensure that your Wi-Fi connection is stable, or consider using an Ethernet cable for a faster connection.

3. Update Stuck on Restart

- **Solution**: If your Mac mini is stuck during the update process, force restart your Mac by holding down the power button until it turns off, then turn it back on. This may help resolve the issue, but if it doesn't, try reinstalling macOS via Recovery Mode.

Staying Ahead of Security Threats

Updating your Mac mini regularly is a powerful way to stay ahead of security threats. By ensuring that your system is running the latest software, you're proactively defending your device against the ever-evolving landscape of cyber threats. It's an easy step, but it makes a world of difference in protecting your sensitive information and keeping your Mac mini running smoothly.

With automatic updates enabled, you don't have to worry about staying on top of every update yourself. However, don't forget to check occasionally to make sure everything is working as expected. And remember, the more consistently you update, the safer and more reliable your Mac mini will be.

In conclusion, keeping your Mac mini secure with regular macOS updates is simple but effective. With a bit of effort to set up automatic updates, or by

APPLE M4 PRO MAC MINI USER GUIDE

manually checking for updates on occasion, you'll ensure that your Mac mini stays protected against the latest security threats while benefiting from new features and improvements. So go ahead, enable those updates, and enjoy peace of mind knowing your Mac mini is in top shape!

Using FileVault for Data Protection

In today's digital age, security is one of the most important factors to consider when using your Mac mini M4 Pro. Whether you're working with sensitive personal data, business documents, or creative projects, it's essential to make sure that your information is safe from unauthorized access. One of the most powerful tools built into macOS for safeguarding your data is **FileVault**.

FileVault is Apple's built-in disk encryption tool that protects your data by encrypting the entire hard drive. When enabled, it ensures that all the files on your Mac mini M4 Pro are scrambled into unreadable formats without the correct password. The only way to decrypt and access your files is by entering your login password or recovery key.

If you're serious about keeping your files secure—whether it's to protect personal information or confidential work documents—FileVault is the best line of defense against unauthorized access. In this section, I'll walk you through the process of enabling FileVault, explain how it works, and give you some helpful tips on maintaining your encrypted data.

What is FileVault?

Before we dive into how to set it up, let's take a moment to understand what FileVault actually does.

FileVault uses **Full Disk Encryption (FDE)**, which means that everything on your Mac mini's internal hard drive, including system files, documents, and applications, is encrypted. This encryption prevents anyone from accessing your data without your login password. Even if someone removes your hard drive from your Mac and tries to access the data externally, it will remain encrypted and protected.

Think of FileVault as a lock on your entire Mac's data. If anyone tries to break into your system, they won't be able to read any of your files without the right key (your password or recovery key). This feature is especially important if you carry your Mac mini to work or travel, as it ensures that your data is secure in case your device is lost or stolen.

Why Should You Enable FileVault?

1. **Protection from Unauthorized Access**: The primary reason to use FileVault is to prevent unauthorized access to your sensitive information. If someone tries to boot up your Mac mini without the correct password, they won't be able to access your files, even if they try to remove the drive and connect it to another computer.

2. **Encryption Is Automatic**: Once enabled, FileVault works seamlessly in the background. You don't have to worry about manually

encrypting individual files—everything gets automatically encrypted as you go about your usual work.

3. **Secure Your Files on a Lost or Stolen Mac**: If your Mac mini is lost or stolen, FileVault ensures that even if someone manages to bypass your password (which is highly unlikely), they won't be able to read your data. This is critical if your Mac contains sensitive business or personal information.

4. **Complies with Privacy Regulations**: If you work in industries like healthcare, finance, or law, protecting sensitive client or patient data is often a legal requirement. Enabling FileVault is a simple step toward complying with privacy regulations like HIPAA or GDPR.

How to Enable FileVault on Your Mac mini M4 Pro

Let's get started with the step-by-step process of setting up FileVault. It's a straightforward process that only takes a few minutes. Follow these steps carefully, and you'll have your data encrypted in no time.

1. **Open System Preferences**

   o Click on the **Apple menu** in the top-left corner of your screen.

   o Select **System Preferences** from the drop-down menu.

2. **Go to Security & Privacy**

   o In the System Preferences window, click on **Security & Privacy**.

3. **Unlock to Make Changes**

   o To make any changes, you'll need to unlock the settings. To do this, click on the **lock icon** in the bottom-left corner of the window.

   o Enter your Mac's administrator password to unlock the settings.

4. **Enable FileVault**

   o Now that the settings are unlocked, navigate to the **FileVault** tab.

   o You'll see a message explaining what FileVault does and how it encrypts your data. To enable FileVault, click on the **Turn On FileVault...** button.

5. **Choose How to Unlock Your Mac**

   o You'll be asked to choose how you want to unlock your Mac. There are two options:

      ▪ **Use your iCloud account**: This option allows you to unlock your Mac using your iCloud account password if you forget your login password.

      ▪ **Create a recovery key**: If you don't want to use your iCloud account, you can create a recovery key, which is a series of letters and numbers that can be used to unlock your Mac if you forget your password.

Important: Make sure to **write down your recovery key** or store it in a safe place. Without it, you won't be able to unlock your Mac if you forget your password. Apple cannot help you recover the key, so it's crucial to keep it safe.

6. **Start Encryption**

   o After selecting your preferred option (iCloud or recovery key), click **Continue**.

   o Now, your Mac will begin the encryption process. This may take a while, depending on how much data is on your Mac and its storage capacity. You can continue using your Mac while the encryption happens in the background, but it may slow things down slightly during the process.

7. **Restart Your Mac**

   o Once FileVault encryption is enabled, your Mac will ask you to restart to finalize the process.

   o After the restart, you'll be prompted to log in with your password, and your Mac will now be fully encrypted.

How Does FileVault Work?

Once FileVault is enabled, your Mac mini will automatically encrypt all the data on your hard drive. This happens when the system is powered off or restarted. Every time you boot up your Mac, macOS checks for the correct password (or recovery key) before allowing access to the encrypted files.

Here's the process in simpler terms:

- **Encryption**: When FileVault is enabled, macOS uses AES (Advanced Encryption Standard) to encrypt everything on your Mac mini's internal drive.

- **Password Protection**: Each time you log in, macOS asks for your password, which is the key that unlocks the encrypted data. If the password is incorrect, macOS will prevent access to your files.

- **Automatic Encryption**: FileVault works seamlessly in the background, encrypting all files, system files, and applications. As long as the Mac is powered off, your data is protected.

- **Decryption on Login**: When you log in with your password, the Mac mini automatically decrypts your files so that you can access them as usual.

What to Do If You Forget Your Password or Recovery Key

While it's rare that you'd forget your password, it's important to know what to do if you do. Here's how to regain access to your encrypted data:

1. **Use iCloud to Reset**: If you've set up iCloud to unlock your Mac, simply click on the **Forgot Password** link after entering an incorrect password. You'll be prompted to use your Apple ID credentials to reset the password.

2. **Use the Recovery Key**: If you didn't set up iCloud, you can use the **recovery key** to unlock your Mac. At login, enter the recovery key

exactly as you wrote it down, and this will decrypt your files and allow you to reset your password.

3. **Contact Apple Support**: If you've lost both your password and recovery key, unfortunately, there's no way to recover the data. Contact Apple Support for further assistance, but they won't be able to decrypt the drive for you.

How to Turn Off FileVault

If you decide that you no longer want FileVault encryption, you can disable it at any time. Keep in mind that turning off FileVault means your data will no longer be encrypted, and anyone with physical access to your Mac can access your files.

To turn off FileVault:

1. Go to **System Preferences** > **Security & Privacy** > **FileVault**.

2. Click the **Turn Off FileVault** button.

3. You'll be prompted to enter your password to confirm the action.

4. FileVault will then begin decrypting the files on your Mac, which can take some time depending on how much data you have.

APPLE M4 PRO MAC MINI USER GUIDE

Recovering Your Mac mini: Time Machine and Recovery Mode

When it comes to safeguarding your data and ensuring your Mac mini stays healthy, **recovery** is an essential aspect of system maintenance. Life happens, and sometimes, your Mac might crash, encounter a system issue, or experience data corruption. But don't panic! Apple provides two powerful tools to get you back on track: **Time Machine** and **macOS Recovery Mode**.

In this section, we'll guide you through the process of backing up your Mac mini using **Time Machine**, Apple's built-in backup tool, and show you how to use **macOS Recovery** for system recovery if things go awry.

Backing Up Your Mac mini with Time Machine

Backing up your data is one of the most important things you can do to ensure that your files and settings are safe. Time Machine is a free, user-friendly tool that comes pre-installed on your Mac mini. It works automatically in the background, creating backups of your files, applications, and system settings. This way, if something goes wrong—whether it's a system crash, a hard drive failure, or even just a human error—you can restore everything to the way it was.

Here's how to use **Time Machine** for backups:

Step 1: Connect an External Storage Drive

Before you can start using Time Machine, you'll need an external hard drive, SSD, or a network-attached storage (NAS) device. Time Machine will use this device as a "backup disk."

- **Important**: The drive needs to be formatted correctly to work with Time Machine. If the drive is new or you're repurposing an old one, it's a good idea to format it using **Disk Utility** to ensure compatibility with macOS.

- Once you connect the external drive to your Mac mini, you may see a prompt asking if you want to use the disk for Time Machine backups. If you do, click **Use as Backup Disk**. If not, go to **System Preferences > Time Machine** to manually select the backup disk.

Step 2: Set Up Time Machine

Once the external storage drive is connected and recognized by your Mac mini, follow these steps:

1. Open **System Preferences** from the Apple menu at the top-left of your screen.

2. Click on **Time Machine**.

3. In the Time Machine window, click **Select Backup Disk**.

4. Choose your external hard drive or NAS device, then click **Use Disk**.

5. Time Machine will ask if you want to encrypt your backups for added security. This is highly recommended if your backup disk contains sensitive information.

APPLE M4 PRO MAC MINI USER GUIDE

Step 3: Start Backing Up

Time Machine automatically backs up your system once an hour while your Mac mini is plugged in and turned on. It does this quietly in the background, so you don't need to worry about starting the backup manually.

- The first backup can take longer because Time Machine will back up your entire system. Future backups, however, will only include files that have changed or been added, so they'll be much faster.

You can check the status of the backup at any time by clicking the Time Machine icon in the menu bar at the top-right of your screen.

Step 4: Restore Files from Time Machine

If you accidentally delete a file or want to recover something from a previous version, Time Machine allows you to go back in time and restore specific files.

Here's how to restore from Time Machine:

1. **Open the folder** that contained the file you want to recover.

2. Click the **Time Machine icon** in the menu bar and select **Enter Time Machine**.

3. Use the timeline on the right side of the screen to scroll back in time. You'll see snapshots of your files from different dates.

4. Once you've found the file or folder you want to restore, select it and click **Restore**.

APPLE M4 PRO MAC MINI USER GUIDE

You can also use Time Machine to restore your entire system in case of a major failure. This is where the backup really shines: you can completely restore your Mac mini to a previous state, complete with all your settings, applications, and files.

Using macOS Recovery for System Recovery

While Time Machine is your go-to for restoring files or even your entire system, sometimes you might run into problems that require more than just recovering data. For instance, if your system crashes, becomes unresponsive, or you can't boot into macOS, **macOS Recovery** is a tool that can help you fix or reinstall macOS.

Here's how to use **macOS Recovery Mode**:

Step 1: Enter macOS Recovery

To enter Recovery Mode, follow these steps:

1. **Shut down your Mac mini**.

2. **Turn it back on** and immediately press and hold **Command + R** on your keyboard. Hold it until you see the Apple logo or a spinning globe, which indicates that your Mac is starting in Recovery Mode.

Once you're in Recovery Mode, you'll see a macOS Utilities window with several options for troubleshooting.

Step 2: Use Disk Utility to Repair Your Disk

If your Mac mini is having issues with files, or if you're unable to start macOS, you can use **Disk Utility** to check for disk errors and repair them.

1. In the **macOS Utilities** window, select **Disk Utility** and click **Continue**.

2. Select your Mac's startup disk (usually named **Macintosh HD**) in the left sidebar.

3. Click the **First Aid** button at the top of the window to check the disk for errors and repair them.

4. If Disk Utility finds issues with your disk, it will attempt to fix them automatically.

Step 3: Reinstall macOS

If your system files are corrupted and repairing the disk doesn't help, you may need to reinstall macOS. Don't worry—this will not erase your personal files, but it will reinstall the operating system.

1. In the **macOS Utilities** window, select **Reinstall macOS**.

2. Click **Continue** and follow the on-screen instructions. Your Mac will download the latest version of macOS from the internet, so make sure you're connected to Wi-Fi.

3. Once the installation is complete, your Mac will restart, and macOS will be fresh and ready to go.

Step 4: Restore from a Time Machine Backup (If Needed)

If you want to restore your Mac mini to a previous state from a Time Machine backup, macOS Recovery can help with that, too:

1. In the **macOS Utilities** window, select **Restore from Time Machine Backup**.

2. Choose the backup disk (the one you set up for Time Machine) and click **Continue**.

3. Select the backup you want to restore from, and follow the on-screen instructions. You'll be able to restore your Mac mini exactly as it was at that time, including all files, apps, and system settings.

Step 5: Reset NVRAM or PRAM

If you're having issues with your Mac's settings, like display or sound problems, you can reset the **NVRAM** (non-volatile random-access memory) or **PRAM** (parameter random-access memory). This is a quick fix for many hardware-related issues.

1. Shut down your Mac mini.

2. Turn it back on and immediately press and hold **Option + Command + P + R** for about 20 seconds.

3. Your Mac will restart during this process. After it boots up again, check if the issue is resolved.

Conclusion

Both **Time Machine** and **macOS Recovery** are essential tools for keeping your Mac mini running smoothly and ensuring your data is protected. Time Machine offers a reliable, automatic way to back up your files, while macOS Recovery provides powerful tools for repairing or reinstalling macOS when things go wrong.

By using Time Machine, you can restore everything from a single file to your entire system, while Recovery Mode allows you to fix and reinstall macOS when you're dealing with a system failure. These tools give you peace of mind, knowing that no matter what happens to your Mac mini, you have a safety net to fall back on.

Remember, regular backups are key to keeping your data safe and your system running at its best. So, take a few moments to set up Time Machine, and keep your Mac mini in tip-top shape!

MAINTENANCE AND TROUBLESHOOTING

Routine System Maintenance (Cleaning, Updates, etc.)

Keeping your Apple M4 Pro Mac mini in top-notch condition is essential to ensuring it performs at its best for years to come. Routine maintenance doesn't just mean updating software or cleaning the physical device, but also taking proactive steps to ensure the system runs efficiently. This section will walk you through the key tasks to keep your Mac mini running smoothly, including cleaning tips, checking for software updates, and performing system checks.

1. Regularly Check for Software Updates

One of the easiest and most important maintenance tasks is ensuring your Mac mini is up-to-date with the latest software updates. These updates are crucial because they provide new features, fix bugs, and—most importantly—improve the overall security of your device.

How to Check for Updates:

1. **Open System Preferences:** Click on the Apple menu (☐) at the top left corner of the screen and select "System Preferences."

2. **Go to Software Update:** In the System Preferences window, click on "Software Update." Your Mac mini will automatically check for any available updates. If there is an update, it will be listed here.

3. **Install Updates:** If there is an update available, click the "Update Now" button. You may be prompted to enter your password. Your Mac will download and install the update, which may take some time depending on the size of the update. It's a good idea to leave your Mac mini connected to power during this process, especially for larger updates.

4. **Enable Automatic Updates:** If you want to make your life easier, you can enable automatic updates. This will ensure your Mac mini updates itself when new software is available, reducing the need for manual checks. Simply check the box that says "Automatically keep my Mac up to date" on the Software Update page.

Why It Matters:

Updating regularly ensures your system stays secure, stable, and as fast as possible. Apple often releases updates that include optimizations for the M4 Pro chip, helping it to run more efficiently and resolve any minor performance hiccups.

2. Clean Your Mac mini Physically

Over time, dust, dirt, and grime can accumulate on your Mac mini, affecting both its appearance and performance. While the M4 Pro Mac mini has a sleek, compact design, it's important to maintain the physical cleanliness of the device to keep it operating optimally.

Cleaning the Exterior:

1. **Turn off and unplug your Mac mini**: Before cleaning, ensure that your Mac mini is turned off, unplugged, and disconnected from all peripherals.

2. **Use a Soft Microfiber Cloth**: Grab a microfiber cloth—avoid paper towels or rough materials, as they can scratch the surface. Gently wipe down the outer surface of the Mac mini. A microfiber cloth will easily remove dust and fingerprints without leaving streaks behind.

3. **Clean the Ports Carefully**: The ports on the Mac mini, including the Thunderbolt and USB-C ports, can accumulate dirt and dust. To clean these areas, use a can of compressed air to gently blow out any debris. Make sure not to use any liquid directly in or around the ports.

4. **Wipe the Vent Areas**: The Mac mini has ventilation areas to allow heat to escape. Over time, these vents can collect dust, which can impact cooling. Use compressed air to blow any dust from these vents, ensuring that air can flow freely.

Why It Matters:

Keeping your Mac mini clean not only makes it look good but also ensures

APPLE M4 PRO MAC MINI USER GUIDE

that it stays cool and doesn't overheat. Dust build-up can lead to poor airflow, causing your Mac mini to get hotter than normal, which could impact performance and even cause system failures in extreme cases.

3. Clean Your Keyboard and Peripherals

If you're using a separate keyboard and mouse with your Mac mini, they too require regular maintenance to stay in top shape.

1. **Wipe Down the Keyboard and Mouse:** Use a soft, damp cloth (not wet) to clean the surfaces of your keyboard, mouse, and any other peripherals you might be using. Ensure there is no excess moisture near electrical components.

2. **Clean Between Keys:** For more thorough cleaning, especially if your keys have accumulated crumbs or dust, you can gently use a small brush or a vacuum cleaner with a soft nozzle attachment to clean between the keys. Just be careful not to damage the keys or apply too much pressure.

Why It Matters:

Regular cleaning helps extend the lifespan of your peripherals and keeps them working properly. Sticky or dirty keys can affect your typing efficiency, and grime can even cause malfunctions over time.

4. Run Disk Utility and Check for Disk Errors

Another key maintenance task is using macOS's built-in Disk Utility tool to check for any disk errors that may be affecting your Mac mini's performance.

This is particularly helpful if you notice your Mac is running slower than usual or if it's having trouble reading or writing files.

How to Use Disk Utility:

1. **Open Disk Utility**: Go to the Finder, select "Applications," then open "Utilities." From there, open "Disk Utility."

2. **Select Your Mac mini's Disk**: In the left-hand sidebar, select your Mac mini's hard drive (typically labeled as "Macintosh HD").

3. **Run First Aid**: Click on the "First Aid" button at the top of the Disk Utility window, and then click "Run." This will check the disk for errors and attempt to repair any issues it finds.

Why It Matters:

Running First Aid on a regular basis helps maintain the health of your hard drive, preventing data corruption and system slowdowns. It's a good practice to run it every few months to ensure everything is in order.

5. Free Up Space and Manage Storage

A cluttered storage drive can affect your Mac mini's performance, especially if it's near full capacity. Managing your storage effectively can help keep your system running smoothly and prevent any slowdowns caused by lack of space.

How to Manage Your Storage:

1. **Check Storage Usage**: Go to the Apple Menu (), select "About This Mac," and then click on the "Storage" tab. This will show you how

much space is being used and what types of files are taking up space (e.g., apps, documents, photos).

2. **Clear Unnecessary Files**: Look for any files you no longer need. This might include old downloads, cached files, or large files that you no longer use. You can use Finder to manually delete them or use a cleanup tool to help you identify unnecessary files.

3. **Optimize Storage**: macOS has a built-in tool called "Optimize Storage" that can help you reduce clutter. It will automatically store older documents and files in iCloud, freeing up local storage. To activate this, go to "System Preferences," click "Apple ID," and select "iCloud" from the sidebar.

Why It Matters:

Freeing up storage can improve your Mac mini's speed, particularly for tasks that require a lot of space like video editing or running virtual machines. Too many files on your drive can slow down your system, and keeping your storage managed ensures that you can keep using your Mac mini without issues.

6. Backup Your Data Regularly

Backing up your data is a critical aspect of maintenance. Without backups, you risk losing important documents, photos, or projects if something goes wrong with your Mac mini.

How to Back Up with Time Machine:

1. **Connect an External Hard Drive**: Plug in an external hard drive with enough storage to hold your backups.

2. **Set Up Time Machine**: Go to "System Preferences" and click "Time Machine." Select "Select Backup Disk" and choose your external hard drive. Time Machine will automatically begin backing up your files.

3. **Let Time Machine Do Its Work**: Once set up, Time Machine will back up your files every hour, and you can recover data at any time by entering the Time Machine interface.

Why It Matters:

Backing up your data ensures that, in the event of an issue, your files are safe. Whether your Mac mini experiences a hardware failure or software issue, having a backup means you can restore everything quickly without losing important information.

Monitoring System Health and Performance

Maintaining the health and performance of your Mac mini M4 Pro is essential for ensuring it runs smoothly over time. Whether you're using it for casual browsing, professional tasks, or intensive workloads like video editing or 3D rendering, keeping tabs on your system's health is crucial. Thankfully, macOS provides a suite of built-in tools that make it easier to monitor your

Mac mini's performance and ensure that everything is running at its best. In this section, we'll guide you through some of the most powerful tools available on macOS, including **Activity Monitor**, **Disk Utility**, and **Console**.

1. Activity Monitor: Your Mac's Health Dashboard

Activity Monitor is essentially your Mac mini's health dashboard. It gives you real-time insights into how your system is performing, showing you the processes that are using your Mac's resources, such as CPU, memory, disk usage, and network activity.

Opening Activity Monitor

To open Activity Monitor:

1. **Go to the Applications Folder** → **Utilities** → **Activity Monitor**.

2. Alternatively, you can **use Spotlight** by pressing **Command + Space**, typing "Activity Monitor", and hitting **Enter**.

Once opened, Activity Monitor presents a wealth of information in an easy-to-understand format, but it can be overwhelming if you don't know what you're looking for. Let's break it down.

Activity Monitor's Four Main Tabs

1. **CPU Tab**:
    This tab shows how much of your Mac mini's CPU resources are being used by each application. The "System" and "User" categories break down usage based on system processes and user applications, respectively. If you notice a process using a significant percentage of

APPLE M4 PRO MAC MINI USER GUIDE

CPU power, it might indicate that the app is consuming more resources than expected.

- o **What to look for**: High CPU usage, especially by apps that should not require a lot of power, could be a sign of inefficient coding, bugs, or even malware.

- o **Action**: If an app is using too much CPU power, try quitting and restarting it, or check if an update is available.

2. **Memory Tab**:

   This tab shows how your Mac mini is using its available memory (RAM). If your system's memory usage is high, your Mac mini may slow down, especially if it's running multiple apps at once.

   - o **What to look for**: A red "Memory Pressure" bar indicates that your Mac mini is running low on memory, which can lead to sluggish performance.

   - o **Action**: Close any unused applications or browser tabs. If this continues, you may want to upgrade your Mac mini's RAM or optimize your system to use memory more efficiently.

3. **Disk Tab**:

   Here, you'll see how much of your Mac's disk space is being used by different applications and processes. High disk usage can cause performance issues, particularly if your storage is near full capacity.

   - o **What to look for**: Large, unnecessary files or applications taking up a lot of disk space.

APPLE M4 PRO MAC MINI USER GUIDE

- o **Action**: If your disk usage is high, consider cleaning up unnecessary files, deleting old apps, or moving large files to an external drive.

4. **Network Tab**:

This tab gives you insights into your Mac mini's internet activity, showing how much data each application is sending and receiving over the network.

- o **What to look for**: A high network usage, especially when you're not actively using network-heavy apps like streaming services or large downloads.

- o **Action**: Identify the processes causing excessive data usage and consider quitting or adjusting them.

Using Activity Monitor for Troubleshooting

If your Mac mini is running slowly, Activity Monitor is your first stop for troubleshooting. By identifying resource-hungry apps, you can take action by quitting them or performing other troubleshooting steps.

- • **Force Quit**: If an app is unresponsive and draining resources, select it in the Activity Monitor and click the **X** button at the top-left corner. You can then choose to **Force Quit** the app.

2. Disk Utility: Keep Your Disk Healthy

Disk Utility is the macOS tool for managing disks and file systems. It allows you to check the health of your hard drive or SSD, perform repairs, and format drives if necessary. It's essential for ensuring that your Mac mini's storage is running optimally.

Opening Disk Utility

To open Disk Utility:

1. **Go to Applications → Utilities → Disk Utility**.

2. You can also search for it via **Spotlight** (Command + Space, then type "Disk Utility").

Checking Disk Health

The most important feature of Disk Utility is its ability to check the health of your Mac mini's storage. It's always a good idea to run these checks regularly to prevent unexpected issues, especially with SSDs which can wear out over time.

- **First   Aid**:
  This is the primary tool for checking and repairing disk errors. To run First Aid:

  1. Select your drive in the Disk Utility sidebar.

  2. Click the **First Aid** button at the top of the window.

  3. Wait for the process to complete, and Disk Utility will notify you if it found and repaired any issues.

When to Use First Aid

- If your Mac mini is acting sluggish or failing to open certain files or apps, running First Aid can help resolve any disk corruption or filesystem errors.

- If Disk Utility reports that it can't repair the drive, it's time to consider backing up your data and replacing the drive, as the hardware may be failing.

3. Console: Access to System Logs and Debugging

Console is a lesser-known but incredibly powerful tool that allows you to access system logs, which are text records of system and application events. While it might sound technical, Console is extremely helpful for troubleshooting, especially when you're experiencing unusual behavior on your Mac mini.

Opening Console

To open Console:

1. **Go to Applications → Utilities → Console**.

2. Alternatively, use **Spotlight** by pressing **Command + Space** and typing "Console".

What Console Shows

Console displays logs for all system events, including warnings, errors, and notifications generated by both macOS and the applications you run. It provides deep insights into what's happening behind the scenes on your Mac mini.

- **System Logs**:

  These logs include macOS-specific events, errors, and performance details. If something isn't working as expected, such as an app crash, Console can show you what caused it.

- **Application Logs**:

  If a specific app is misbehaving, the Console will show logs generated by that app, which might help you pinpoint the exact issue.

Using Console for Troubleshooting

If you encounter problems like frequent crashes or sluggish performance:

1. Open Console and look for any error messages or warnings that appear at the time of the issue.

2. Search for specific app names or error codes to narrow down the source of the problem.

3. You can also filter logs by different categories (e.g., **Errors**, **Faults**) to focus on critical issues.

How to Interpret Logs

Console logs can be quite technical. However, here's a simple approach to reading them:

- Look for entries marked as **Error** or **Fault** — these indicate something went wrong.

- Look for the time when the issue occurred and check the logs around that time for clues.

- If you find a recurring issue, try searching online for solutions using the error code or log message.

Maintaining Performance Over Time

As you continue using your Mac mini M4 Pro, keeping an eye on system performance should become part of your regular routine. Here are a few additional tips to help maintain your Mac mini's health:

1. **Clear Cache and Unnecessary Files**:
   Over time, cache files and temporary data can accumulate and take up storage. You can use built-in macOS tools like **Storage Management** (found under **About This Mac → Storage**) to review and clean up old files. Consider using third-party tools like **CleanMyMac** if you want a more thorough cleanup.

2. **Free Up Disk Space**:
   If you notice your disk space running low, it can slow down your Mac mini's performance. Regularly delete unused files, uninstall apps you no longer need, or move files to external storage.

3. **Keep Your System Updated**:
   Apple regularly releases updates that improve system performance and fix bugs. Make sure you're running the latest version of macOS

APPLE M4 PRO MAC MINI USER GUIDE

and that all your apps are up to date. You can enable automatic updates in the **System Preferences** under **Software Update**.

4. **Reboot Regularly**:

While macOS handles memory well, a reboot once in a while can help clear out temporary processes and free up resources. If your Mac mini feels sluggish after long periods of use, a quick restart can make a significant difference.

Common Issues and Quick Fixes

Even the most powerful and user-friendly devices like the Apple M4 Pro Mac mini can sometimes encounter hiccups. But don't worry—most of these problems are easy to fix, and you don't have to be a tech expert to resolve them. In this section, we'll walk you through some of the most common issues Mac mini users experience and provide simple, step-by-step solutions.

1. Slow Performance

If your Mac mini is feeling sluggish, it can be frustrating, especially when you're working on important tasks. Here's how to get things running smoothly again.

Causes:

- **Too many apps running**: If you have a lot of apps open, your system can become overwhelmed, causing slowdowns.

- **Low storage**: When your storage is almost full, your Mac mini has less space to work with, which can lead to slow performance.

- **Background processes**: Sometimes, apps running in the background use up resources without you even knowing it.

Quick Fixes:

- **Close Unnecessary Apps**: Go through your open apps and close the ones you're not using. You can do this easily by right-clicking on the app in your Dock and selecting "Quit."

- **Clear Storage**: Check your storage by going to **Apple Menu > About This Mac > Storage**. If you're running low, delete unnecessary files or move them to an external drive. You can also enable **Optimize Storage** in macOS, which will help manage your files automatically.

- **Check Activity Monitor**: Open **Activity Monitor** (Applications > Utilities > Activity Monitor) to see if any apps or processes are consuming too many resources. If you notice anything unusual, try quitting the process.

- **Restart Your Mac mini**: Sometimes, a simple restart is all your Mac mini needs to clear temporary files and refresh its system.

2. Wi-Fi Connectivity Issues

Wi-Fi problems can be frustrating, especially when you're trying to work online. If your Mac mini is having trouble connecting to or maintaining a Wi-Fi connection, here's what you can do.

Causes:

- **Weak Wi-Fi signal**: Your Wi-Fi router might be too far from your Mac mini or there might be interference from other devices.

- **Network settings issues**: Sometimes, your Mac mini's Wi-Fi settings might be causing problems.

- **Software bugs**: Occasionally, bugs in macOS or outdated software can cause connectivity problems.

Quick Fixes:

- **Restart Your Router**: Unplug your Wi-Fi router for about 30 seconds, then plug it back in. This can help reset the network and clear up any issues.

- **Forget and Reconnect to the Network**: Go to **System Preferences > Network > Wi-Fi**, click **Advanced**, then remove the saved networks by clicking the minus button. Reconnect to your Wi-Fi network by selecting it and entering the password again.

- **Use the Wi-Fi Diagnostic Tool**: macOS has a built-in Wi-Fi diagnostic tool. Hold down the **Option** key and click the Wi-Fi icon in the menu bar. Select **Open Wireless Diagnostics** and follow the on-screen instructions.

- **Update macOS**: Make sure your macOS is up to date. Sometimes, Wi-Fi issues are resolved in software updates.

3. No Sound or Audio Issues

If you're having trouble with your Mac mini's sound—whether it's no sound at all, or distorted audio—there are a few common fixes you can try.

Causes:

- **Muted or low volume settings**: It's easy to accidentally mute or lower the volume.

- **Audio output device issue**: Your Mac mini might be set to the wrong audio output (e.g., it's trying to send audio to Bluetooth headphones that aren't connected).

- **Software issues**: A software update or app glitch can sometimes cause audio problems.

Quick Fixes:

- **Check Volume Settings**: Ensure that your Mac mini's volume is turned up. Click the **Volume** icon in the menu bar to adjust it.

- **Check Output Device**: Go to **System Preferences > Sound > Output** and ensure the correct audio device is selected (e.g., built-in speakers, Bluetooth speakers, or headphones).

- **Restart Your Mac mini**: Sometimes, audio issues can be solved with a restart to reset the system and refresh the sound settings.

- **Reset NVRAM**: NVRAM (non-volatile random access memory) stores sound settings, so resetting it can help fix audio issues. To reset NVRAM, restart your Mac mini and immediately press and hold **Option + Command + P + R** until you hear the startup sound again.

4. External Devices Not Recognized

Whether it's an external hard drive, printer, or mouse, it can be annoying when peripherals aren't recognized. Here's how to troubleshoot the issue.

Causes:

- **Loose or faulty cables**: Sometimes the problem is as simple as a loose cable or a damaged port.

- **Outdated drivers**: Your peripheral might require updated drivers for macOS.

- **Power issues**: Some devices, especially high-powered ones like printers or external hard drives, may require more power than your Mac mini can supply.

Quick Fixes:

- **Check the Cable and Connection**: Make sure the cable connecting the device is securely plugged in. If you're using USB-C or Thunderbolt, make sure the cable is compatible with your Mac mini.

- **Try a Different Port**: Plug your device into another port to rule out a faulty port.

- **Restart Your Mac mini**: A restart can help your Mac mini recognize newly connected devices.

- **Update Device Drivers**: Check the manufacturer's website for any driver updates. Sometimes, updating the drivers can help macOS recognize the device.

- **Power Cycle the Device**: If it's an external drive or printer, unplug it from the power source for about 30 seconds, then reconnect it.

5. Apps Running Slowly or Freezing

If you've noticed that apps are freezing or running much slower than usual, it's important to troubleshoot the issue before it gets worse.

Causes:

- **Too many apps running**: Having too many applications open at once can slow down your Mac mini.

- **Corrupted app data**: Sometimes, an app's data files or settings can get corrupted, causing the app to freeze.

- **Outdated app versions**: Apps that aren't updated for the latest macOS version may not perform optimally.

Quick Fixes:

- **Force Quit the App**: If an app is frozen, you can force it to quit by pressing **Command + Option + Esc** and selecting the app you want to close.

- **Close Unnecessary Apps**: Go to **Apple Menu > Force Quit** and close apps you don't need.

- **Clear Cache and App Data**: Some apps store large caches that can slow them down. Try clearing cache files or reinstalling the app.

- **Update the App**: Make sure the app is updated to the latest version by going to the Mac App Store or visiting the app's official website.

- **Check for macOS Updates**: Sometimes, app performance issues are related to bugs in macOS itself. Go to **System Preferences > Software Update** to check if any updates are available.

6. Screen Flickering or Display Issues

Screen flickering can be distracting and make it hard to use your Mac mini. Let's look at the common causes and how to fix them.

Causes:

- **Resolution mismatch**: Sometimes, a resolution setting might not be compatible with your monitor.

- **Faulty cable or connection**: If you're using an external display, the cable or port might be the issue.

- **Graphics driver issues**: Problems with the GPU can lead to visual glitches.

Quick Fixes:

- **Check Display Settings**: Go to **System Preferences > Displays** and ensure that your monitor is set to its native resolution.

- **Update macOS and Graphics Drivers**: Check for any macOS updates that might include fixes for display or graphics issues.

- **Check the Cable and Connections**: Inspect the cables and make sure they're securely connected. Try using a different cable or port if possible.

- **Test with a Different Display**: If the flickering persists, try connecting your Mac mini to a different monitor to see if the issue is related to your display.

7. Overheating or Fan Noise

If your Mac mini seems unusually hot or the fans are constantly running loudly, it's a sign that the system might be working too hard.

Causes:

- **High system load**: Running resource-intensive applications like video editing software can push the system to its limits.

- **Dust buildup**: Over time, dust can accumulate inside the Mac mini, blocking airflow and causing it to overheat.

Quick Fixes:

- **Close Resource-Hungry Apps**: Check your **Activity Monitor** to see which apps are using the most CPU and close them if they aren't necessary.

- **Ensure Proper Ventilation**: Make sure your Mac mini is in a well-ventilated area. Avoid placing it on soft surfaces like beds or couches, which can block airflow.

- **Clean the Mac mini**: Over time, dust can accumulate inside the Mac mini, causing it to overheat. You can gently clean the exterior using a soft cloth and, if comfortable, use compressed air to blow out the dust from the vents.

Using macOS Recovery for System Restores

Sometimes, things go wrong with our computers, no matter how much we rely on them. Whether it's a software issue, a corrupted file, or even a system crash, it's important to know how to fix things when they go awry. Fortunately, Apple's macOS has a built-in tool called **macOS Recovery**, which can help you restore your system or reinstall macOS if something goes wrong. Think of it as your Mac mini's safety net, ready to catch you if you fall.

APPLE M4 PRO MAC MINI USER GUIDE

In this section, I'll walk you through how to use **macOS Recovery** to restore your system or reinstall macOS. Even if you're not super tech-savvy, don't worry—I'll keep the instructions clear and easy to follow, with plenty of tips along the way. So, let's dive in and make sure your Mac mini is back on track, no matter what's happened.

What is macOS Recovery?

Before we get started, let's quickly talk about what macOS Recovery is and why it's such an important tool. macOS Recovery is a built-in feature in every Mac, including your Mac mini M4 Pro. It's essentially a small operating system that runs separately from your main macOS. It's packed with powerful tools to help you:

- Restore your Mac to factory settings

- Reinstall macOS if something's gone wrong

- Repair your disk if you're having issues with corrupted files

- Get help with troubleshooting if you run into problems

In short, macOS Recovery is your Mac's emergency kit. Whether you need to restore your system, fix a problem, or just start fresh, it's there for you.

How to Enter macOS Recovery

Let's start with the basics—how to get into macOS Recovery in the first place. It's actually pretty simple, but you'll need to make sure you're following the steps carefully. Here's how to do it:

1. **Shut   Down   Your   Mac   mini**
   If your Mac mini is currently on, the first thing you need to do is turn it off. Go ahead and shut it down like you normally would. Just click the Apple logo at the top-left of the screen and choose "Shut Down."

2. **Turn On Your Mac mini and Enter Recovery Mode**
   Now that your Mac is off, you'll need to power it back on while holding down a special key combination. This part is crucial:

   o **For Intel-based Macs**: Press and hold **Command (⌘) + R** as soon as you press the power button to turn on your Mac. Keep holding it until you see the Apple logo or a spinning globe.

   o **For M1/M2-based Macs (which applies to your M4 Pro Mac mini)**: Press and hold the **power button** until you see the startup options window. Then, select **Options** and click **Continue** to enter macOS Recovery.

3. **Wait   for   the   macOS   Utilities   Window**
   After you follow the steps above, you'll be greeted by the **macOS Utilities** window. This is the heart of the recovery process, where you'll have several options to troubleshoot and repair your system.

Restoring Your Mac mini to Factory Settings

If you've been having major issues with your Mac mini, or if you want to start fresh for any reason (maybe you're selling it or giving it away), restoring it to factory settings is an option you can use. This will erase all your data, settings, and apps, so be sure to back up anything important before proceeding!

Here's how to restore your Mac mini to factory settings using macOS Recovery:

1. **Select "Disk Utility"**

   From the macOS Utilities window, click on **Disk Utility**. This will open a tool that allows you to manage your hard drive and storage.

2. **Erase Your Mac's Disk**

   In Disk Utility, you'll see a list of drives. Click on your **Macintosh HD** or whatever your main hard drive is called. Once selected, click **Erase** at the top of the window. This will wipe everything from your disk and prepare it for a fresh install of macOS.

   - **Choose a Name**: You can leave the name as "Macintosh HD" or choose a new one if you prefer.

   - **Format**: Make sure the format is set to **APFS** (for macOS High Sierra and later) or **Mac OS Extended (Journaled)** if you're using an older version of macOS.

3. **Confirm Erasure**

   Once you click **Erase**, the process will begin, and your Mac mini's hard drive will be wiped clean. This may take a few minutes, depending on the size of your disk. When it's done, you'll have a blank slate, ready to install macOS again.

4. **Reinstall macOS**

   After erasing your disk, exit Disk Utility and go back to the macOS Utilities window. Select **Reinstall macOS** and click **Continue**. This will start the process of reinstalling macOS on your freshly erased hard drive.

5. **Follow the On-Screen Instructions**

   The installer will guide you through the steps to install macOS. You may be prompted to select the hard drive you want to install macOS on (it should be your newly erased disk). Follow the on-screen instructions to complete the installation.

Reinstalling macOS

If your Mac mini is running slow or you're experiencing issues with the operating system, but you don't want to wipe everything out completely, reinstalling macOS is a great option. Here's how to do it:

1. **Select "Reinstall macOS"**

   From the macOS Utilities window, click **Reinstall macOS**. This option will allow you to reinstall macOS without erasing your data, apps, or settings (though it's always a good idea to back up just in case!).

2. **Choose the Disk**

   The installer will ask you where to install macOS. Select the disk where your macOS is currently installed (it should be called **Macintosh HD** unless you renamed it).

3. **Let the Installation Begin**

   Click **Install** and follow the on-screen instructions. Your Mac mini will download the latest version of macOS from the internet, so make sure you have a stable internet connection. The installation process may take a while, so be patient.

4. **Complete the Setup**

   Once the installation is complete, your Mac mini will restart, and you'll be prompted to set up macOS as if it were a brand-new computer. This includes signing in with your Apple ID, choosing your region, and setting up other preferences.

Using Disk Utility to Repair Your Disk

In some cases, you may not need to erase everything. If you're having issues with files or your disk seems corrupted, you can use **Disk Utility** to repair it. Here's how:

1. **Launch Disk Utility**

   From the macOS Utilities window, select **Disk Utility** and click **Continue**.

2. **Select the Disk to Repair**

   In the sidebar, click on the disk you want to repair. This is usually your **Macintosh HD**.

3. **Click "First Aid"**

   In the Disk Utility toolbar, click **First Aid**, then click **Run**. This will check your disk for errors and try to fix any issues it finds. If

APPLE M4 PRO MAC MINI USER GUIDE

everything goes well, you'll see a message saying that the disk was successfully repaired.

4. **Check for Errors**

   If Disk Utility finds any problems it can't fix, you may need to erase your disk or reinstall macOS. But don't worry—using **First Aid** can often solve minor issues without requiring a complete restore.

What to Do if macOS Recovery Doesn't Work

Sometimes, no matter how hard you try, things just don't go as planned. If macOS Recovery won't launch, or if you're stuck in an infinite loop of reboots, there are a few things you can try:

1. **Check Your Internet Connection**

   Make sure you're connected to a stable internet connection. For M1/M2-based Macs (like your M4 Pro Mac mini), macOS Recovery may require an internet connection to reinstall macOS.

2. **Try Internet Recovery**

   If the regular Recovery Mode isn't working, try booting into **Internet Recovery** by holding **Option + Command + R** when turning on your Mac. This will load macOS Recovery from Apple's servers, even if your local recovery partition is damaged.

3. **Contact Apple Support**

   If nothing works and you're still stuck, it's time to reach out to Apple Support. They can help you troubleshoot further or guide you through additional steps.

Wrapping Up

Using macOS Recovery can feel a bit intimidating, but with the right instructions, it's actually a straightforward process that can help restore or reinstall macOS, fix errors, and get your system running smoothly again. Just remember to back up your data whenever you can, and don't hesitate to use macOS Recovery if you run into any issues.

With this tool in your back pocket, you'll have the peace of mind knowing that you can restore your Mac mini or reinstall macOS anytime, no matter what happens.

Getting Apple Support and Warranty Information

At some point, every Mac mini user may need a little extra help or guidance, whether it's for a technical issue, a question about performance, or advice on how to make the most of your Mac mini M4 Pro. When that time comes, it's good to know where to turn. Apple offers excellent customer support and straightforward ways to check your warranty status, ensuring you can get the assistance you need when you need it.

How to Contact Apple Support for Help

Apple Support is here to assist you, and getting help is easier than you might think. Whether you prefer speaking to someone over the phone, chatting online, or using the Apple Support app, Apple has a variety of ways for you to reach out.

1. Apple Support Website

The first step in getting help is to visit the official Apple Support website. Here, you'll find a treasure trove of resources, including:

- **Support Articles**: Apple's comprehensive library of troubleshooting guides and step-by-step solutions for common issues (e.g., problems with Wi-Fi, screen resolution, software glitches).

- **Contact Options**: You can choose to chat with a live representative, schedule a call, or even request a callback if you're too busy to wait on hold.

To access Apple Support:

1. Go to https://support.apple.com.

2. Select the category that best fits your issue, such as *Mac*, *Mac mini*, or *macOS*.

3. Browse the suggested solutions or, if you still need help, click on the *Contact Support* button to choose your preferred method of communication.

2. Apple Support App

If you prefer using your phone, the Apple Support app is another great option. This free app offers support through live chat, phone calls, and even offers the ability to book appointments with Apple technicians at your nearest Apple Store or authorized service provider.

Steps to use the Apple Support app:

1. Download the Apple Support app from the **App Store** (it's free!).

2. Open the app and log in with your Apple ID.

3. Select your Mac mini M4 Pro or another Apple device from the list of products.

4. Browse available help articles or tap *Get Support* to talk to an Apple representative or schedule a service.

3. Phone Support

Sometimes, a conversation with an expert over the phone can be the fastest way to resolve an issue. You can contact Apple Support via phone by calling Apple's customer service number. In many regions, the general contact number is 1-800-MY-APPLE (1-800-692-7753), but it can vary by location. You may need to wait a few minutes to speak with a representative, but they'll be able to guide you through any technical issues or questions.

If you're outside of the United States, visit Apple's country-specific support page to find the correct phone number for your region.

4. Apple Stores and Authorized Service Providers

If you live near an Apple Store or an Apple-authorized service provider, you can always visit in person. The Apple Genius Bar offers hands-on support for technical issues, hardware repairs, and in-depth questions. Here's how to make an appointment:

1. Visit the Apple Support website or the Apple Support app.

2. Select *Genius Bar* as your preferred method of support.

3. Choose a nearby Apple Store and select a time that works for you.

4. You'll receive a confirmation email with your appointment details.

You can also check the availability of Apple-authorized service providers on the Apple website to find local businesses that are certified to offer Apple repairs and support.

5. Social Media and Online Communities

Apple also has a strong presence on social media platforms like Twitter (@AppleSupport). You can tweet your issue or direct message Apple Support for quick help. While this may not always be the most detailed form of support, it's great for receiving general assistance or quickly resolving simple issues.

If you want to connect with other Mac mini users, Apple's **Support Communities** is an excellent place to ask questions, get advice, or find helpful troubleshooting tips from fellow users. It's a great option for those who prefer to learn from others' experiences.

How to Check Your Mac mini M4 Pro's Warranty Status

Now that you know how to get help, it's important to also keep track of your Mac mini's warranty status. Whether you're troubleshooting an issue or considering an upgrade, knowing your warranty status ensures you don't miss out on valuable support or repair options.

1. Checking Warranty Status via the Apple Website

Apple makes it very simple to check the warranty status of your Mac mini M4 Pro with just a few clicks. Here's how:

1. Go to the Apple Check Coverage website: https://checkcoverage.apple.com.

2. Enter your Mac mini's **serial number**. You can find the serial number by:

   o Clicking the **Apple logo** in the top-left corner of your screen.

   o Selecting **About This Mac**.

   o The serial number will be listed under the *Overview* tab.

3. Once you've entered the serial number, click **Continue**.

Apple will show you:

- **Warranty Status**: Whether your device is covered under Apple's standard warranty.

- **AppleCare Coverage**: If you purchased AppleCare+ (Apple's extended warranty and support plan), this will show whether it's still active.

- **Repair and Service Options**: Information on what's covered under your warranty and whether your device is eligible for repair.

2. Check via the Apple Support App

Alternatively, you can use the **Apple Support app** to check your warranty status directly on your iPhone or iPad.

1. Open the **Apple Support** app.

2. Tap on **Products**.

3. Choose your Mac mini M4 Pro from the list of devices.

4. Tap on **Warranty** to view your device's warranty details, including the expiration date and eligibility for AppleCare coverage.

3. What's Covered Under Your Warranty?

Apple's standard warranty provides coverage for repairs and defects caused by manufacturing issues, including:

- Hardware repairs for defective components.

- Battery service (if it's below 80% of its original capacity).

- Software support via macOS updates and troubleshooting.

AppleCare+ extends the coverage to include:

- Coverage for accidental damage (with a service fee).

- Additional technical support for up to three years.

- Priority access to Apple's support team.

If your device is out of warranty, repairs or service might incur additional charges, but it's still worth contacting Apple to see if they can help.

4. What If My Warranty Has Expired?

Even if your warranty has expired, Apple Support can still provide assistance. Depending on the issue, they may offer out-of-warranty repairs or direct you to Apple-authorized service providers for third-party repair options. However, keep in mind that any out-of-warranty service will come with a fee.

Why Knowing Your Warranty Matters

Your warranty status is more than just a piece of information—it ensures you can get help when you need it. If you run into problems with your Mac mini M4 Pro, whether it's a faulty hard drive, malfunctioning ports, or even software glitches, being aware of your warranty can save you money. AppleCare+ offers extended protection, making it a good idea to consider if you plan on keeping your Mac mini for several years.

Also, knowing when your warranty expires gives you a clear timeline to act if something goes wrong. If you're experiencing issues close to the expiration date, you'll want to reach out to Apple Support sooner rather than later.

TIPS, TRICKS, AND SHORTCUTS

Essential macOS Keyboard Shortcuts

One of the simplest ways to boost your productivity on your Apple M4 Pro Mac mini is by mastering macOS keyboard shortcuts. These little combinations of keys are your secret weapon for speeding up everyday tasks, navigating macOS more efficiently, and reducing the need for repetitive mouse clicks. The best part? You don't need to be a tech wizard to use them—just a little practice, and you'll find yourself zipping around macOS in no time.

Whether you're working on a professional project, editing photos or videos, or simply managing your files, keyboard shortcuts save you time and effort. In this section, we'll break down the essential macOS shortcuts that you'll want to get comfortable with right away.

1. Basic Navigation Shortcuts

These shortcuts are your gateway to navigating macOS with ease. They'll help you quickly switch between apps, manage windows, and get around the system like a pro.

- **Command + Tab**: Switch between open apps. This one's a game-changer for multitaskers. Just press **Command +**

APPLE M4 PRO MAC MINI USER GUIDE

Tab, and macOS will display a list of your open apps. Keep holding **Command** and tap **Tab** to cycle through them. It's faster than using the mouse to click between open windows, especially when you have several apps running.

- **Command + Space**: Open Spotlight Search. Spotlight is like a supercharged search engine built right into your Mac. Press **Command + Space**, and you can search for files, apps, documents, emails, and even make quick web searches. It's a powerful tool that cuts down on hunting for files and launches apps faster than navigating through the Finder.

- **Control + Arrow Keys**: Switch between desktop spaces. If you're a fan of working with multiple desktops (spaces), these shortcuts make it a breeze to flip between them. Press **Control + Left Arrow** to move to the previous space and **Control + Right Arrow** to move to the next one. This is especially useful for keeping different projects organized on separate desktops.

2. Window Management Shortcuts

Managing windows is often one of the most tedious parts of working on a computer. Thankfully, macOS provides shortcuts that help you stay organized and get things done faster.

- **Command + M**: Minimize the active window. Need to clear up some space on your screen without closing an app? Simply press **Command + M**, and the active window will minimize to the Dock. If you've got multiple windows open for the same app, use this shortcut to quickly hide them without closing anything.

- **Command + W**: Close the current window. Closing a window is easy with **Command + W**. This shortcut works in almost every app, so you can quickly shut down a document, a tab in Safari, or a Finder window.

- **Command + Option + M**: Minimize all windows of the active app. Instead of minimizing each window one by one, **Command + Option + M** minimizes *all* open windows of the active app at once. It's a neat and quick way to clear your screen.

- **F3 or Mission Control**: View all open windows in one go. Pressing **F3** (or using a trackpad gesture of swiping up with three fingers) activates Mission Control, where you can see all open windows and easily switch between them. It's ideal for organizing your workspace when you've got many windows open at once.

3. Text Editing Shortcuts

If you do a lot of writing, coding, or text editing on your Mac mini, these shortcuts are essential for speeding up your work. They'll help you format, navigate, and manipulate text with precision.

- **Command + C**: Copy. The classic shortcut that everyone knows—**Command + C** copies the selected text or item to the clipboard.

- **Command**   +   **V**:   Paste. After copying something, use **Command** + **V** to paste it wherever your cursor is. This is the bread and butter of text editing and file management.

- **Command**   +   **X**:   Cut. Want to move a piece of text or a file to a new location? Use **Command** + **X** to cut it from its current spot, and then **Command** + **V** to paste it elsewhere.

- **Command**   +   **Z**:   Undo. Made a mistake? **Command** + **Z** undoes your last action. This works across most apps, from text editors to graphic design software.

- **Command** + **Shift** + **Z**: Redo. If you undo something by accident, **Command** + **Shift** + **Z** redoes the last action. This gives you a second chance to get things right.

- **Command** + **A**: Select all. If you need to select everything in a document, file folder, or webpage, use **Command** + **A**. It's a huge time-saver when working with large amounts of text or files.

- **Command**   +   **F**:   Find. Need to search for a specific word or phrase within a document or webpage? Use **Command** + **F** to bring up the search function.

- **Option** + **Left/Right Arrow**: Jump between words. When navigating through text, use **Option** + **Left Arrow** to jump the cursor back one word, and **Option + Right Arrow** to move forward. This is much faster than using the arrow keys to move letter by letter.

- **Command + Delete**: Delete the entire line. Instead of holding down the backspace key, use **Command + Delete** to delete the entire line of text quickly. It's incredibly efficient when you need to clear out a section of text.

4. File and Finder Shortcuts

Working with files on the Mac mini can be much faster when you use these Finder-specific shortcuts. From opening files to managing your system, these shortcuts make file management a breeze.

- **Command + N**: New Finder window. Press **Command + N** to open a new Finder window. This allows you to quickly browse your files, folders, and connected drives without needing to click through menus.

- **Command + Shift + N**: New folder. **Command + Shift + N** creates a new folder in the current Finder window. It's a quick way to organize files when you're dealing with lots of documents or media.

- **Command + I**: Get Info. Want to know the details of a file, such as its size, creation date, or permissions? Select the file and press **Command + I** to open the Info window. This is a great way to check file properties without opening the file itself.

APPLE M4 PRO MAC MINI USER GUIDE

- **Command + Shift + G**: Go to Folder. If you know the exact path to a folder, **Command + Shift + G** opens a prompt where you can type the path directly. It's perfect for accessing system files or specific directories without navigating through multiple layers of Finder.

- **Command + Option + Space**: Open Spotlight in Finder. This shortcut opens Spotlight search directly within Finder, letting you search your files and folders quickly.

5. System and Accessibility Shortcuts

For system management and accessibility, these shortcuts will save you time and make navigating macOS even more efficient.

- **Command + Option + Esc**: Force Quit apps. Sometimes apps freeze or stop responding. **Command + Option + Esc** opens the Force Quit window, where you can select and close the unresponsive app.

- **Command + Shift + 4**: Take a screenshot (select area). Need to capture part of your screen? **Command + Shift + 4** turns your cursor into a crosshair, letting you drag and select the area to screenshot. The image is saved to your desktop.

- **Command + Shift + 5**: Screenshot options. **Command + Shift + 5** opens the screenshot toolbar, giving you more options, such as recording your screen or taking a screenshot of the entire window.

- **Command + Option + F5**: Enable VoiceOver. VoiceOver is a built-in screen reader that can be turned on with **Command + Option + F5**. It's invaluable for users with visual impairments.

- **Control + Option + Command + 8**: Invert screen colors. This shortcut inverts the colors on your screen, which may be helpful for users with certain visual needs or for reducing eye strain.

Wrapping Up

Mastering these macOS keyboard shortcuts will drastically speed up your workflow, making you a more efficient Mac mini user. Whether you're managing files, editing text, or navigating the system, these shortcuts save time and reduce the need for repetitive clicking. With a little practice, they'll become second nature, and you'll wonder how you ever worked without them.

The more you use these shortcuts, the smoother your daily tasks will become, freeing up your time for more important and creative endeavors. Keep experimenting with them, and soon enough, you'll be a macOS keyboard shortcut pro!

Hidden macOS Features You Should Know About

Apple's macOS is filled with hidden gems—features that may not be immediately obvious but can make your workflow a whole lot smoother once you discover them. These aren't just fun tricks; they're powerful tools that can save you time, boost productivity, and make your Mac experience a lot more enjoyable. Let's dive into some of these under-the-radar features that you should absolutely be using on your Mac mini M4 Pro.

1. Spotlight Search: Beyond Basic Searches

Spotlight is one of those macOS features that most users only scratch the surface of. Sure, you know it's the search bar that appears when you hit Command + Space, but did you know it's so much more than just a search tool? Spotlight is a power-packed assistant that can help you do everything from performing calculations to finding documents, apps, and even converting units—all without leaving your desktop.

How to Use Spotlight Like a Pro

- **Search Your Files**: Of course, the most basic use of Spotlight is searching for apps, documents, and folders. But it gets smarter over time—spotlight indexes everything on your Mac so you can find what you need in seconds.

- **Perform Calculations**: Just type a math problem directly into the search bar. Need to know how many cups are in 3 liters? Type "3 liters in cups," and Spotlight will do the math for you. No need to open a calculator app!

- **Unit and Currency Conversion**: Type something like "5 USD in EUR" or "10 miles in km," and Spotlight will give you an instant conversion. It's perfect for when you need to quickly convert currencies, units, or even temperature!

- **Spotlight Web Search**: Spotlight also lets you search the web directly. If you're looking for something online, type your search query into Spotlight, hit Return, and it will take you straight to the results page in Safari.

- **Look Up Definitions**: Highlight a word and hit Command + Shift + D to instantly pull up its dictionary definition. Whether it's a technical term or something you just don't quite understand, Spotlight can serve as your personal dictionary.

Pro Tip: You can even use Spotlight to find and launch system preferences, making it easier to jump straight to settings without having to dig through multiple menus.

2. Automator: Automate Your Everyday Tasks

If you find yourself performing the same repetitive tasks over and over again, Automator is about to become your best friend. This built-in macOS app allows you to create custom workflows that automate tedious tasks, saving you tons of time in the long run.

How to Create a Simple Automator Workflow

- **Automate File Organization**: Want to sort files by type, date, or name? With Automator, you can create a workflow that organizes your files automatically whenever they're added to a specific folder. For example, you can have Automator sort images into subfolders based on the date or move PDFs to a particular directory.

- **Batch Rename Files**: Have a bunch of files that need to be renamed with a specific pattern? Automator can do this in a flash. Simply create a workflow, drag the files you want to rename, and specify how they should be renamed.

- **Send Automated Emails**: Need to send the same email to a group of people? You can set up an Automator workflow that drafts and sends the email automatically. Perfect for sending reminders or weekly reports!

- **Resize Images in Bulk**: If you work with images often, Automator can resize them all at once. You can set it to automatically shrink your image files when you drag them into the workflow, ensuring they're the right size without manual intervention.

Pro Tip: Automator also lets you create "Services" that integrate directly into your right-click menu, making it even easier to execute your workflows with a single click.

3. Clipboard Manager: Never Lose Your Copy Again

How many times have you copied something, only to realize you've overwritten it by copying something else? With the Clipboard Manager, you can finally kiss those frustrating moments goodbye. This feature gives you access to your clipboard history, letting you view and paste previously copied items.

How to Use Clipboard Manager

- **Accessing Clipboard History**: By default, macOS doesn't save a history of what you've copied, but using the Clipboard Manager (or third-party apps like Paste), you can view a history of your clipboard activity. No more frustration when you need to paste something you copied earlier!

- **Pin Important Items**: You can "pin" frequently used snippets or text so they're always available for pasting. This is perfect for things like email templates, addresses, or other bits of text you need to use often.

- **Sync Across Devices**: With iCloud, your clipboard history can even sync across your Mac and iPhone, making it incredibly easy to copy something on one device and paste it onto another.

Pro Tip: Look for third-party clipboard manager apps like Paste or CopyClip for even more advanced clipboard management options.

4. Preview: A Hidden Powerhouse for PDF and Image Editing

Preview is an app that most Mac users overlook, but it's actually packed with powerful features that can save you time, especially if you work with PDFs and images regularly. Not only can you view images and documents, but Preview also lets you annotate, edit, and even merge files without the need for expensive software.

How to Get the Most Out of Preview

- **Annotate PDFs**: Whether you need to highlight text, add notes, or draw shapes, Preview allows you to easily annotate PDFs. This can be a lifesaver when reviewing documents or adding feedback.

- **Merge PDFs**: Need to combine multiple PDFs into one? Simply open them all in Preview, then drag and drop pages from one PDF to another. It's that easy.

- **Convert Image Formats**: Preview also lets you convert image files from one format to another. For example, you can open a PNG and export it as a JPEG, or vice versa. It's quick and painless!

- **Image Editing**: Resize, crop, rotate, or adjust the color of images directly in Preview. You can even add text or shapes to images, which is especially handy if you need to mark up screenshots or design simple graphics.

Pro Tip: Preview also has the ability to fill out and sign PDF forms. You can create your signature directly in the app and use it on any document that needs a signature.

5. Night Shift: Protect Your Eyes While Working Late

If you tend to work late into the night (guilty!), you've probably experienced eye strain or difficulty falling asleep afterward. That's because the blue light emitted by your screen can interfere with your sleep cycle. Enter **Night Shift**, a feature that reduces blue light and adjusts your display to warmer tones in the evening.

How to Enable Night Shift

- **Schedule Night Shift**: You can set Night Shift to turn on automatically at sunset and off at sunrise, or you can manually adjust the color temperature of your display. Head to **System Preferences > Displays > Night Shift**, and you can fine-tune the settings to suit your preferences.

- **Quick Toggle**: If you want to quickly toggle Night Shift on or off, you can add it to your menu bar for easy access. Just go to **System Preferences > Displays** and check the box to show Night Shift in the menu bar.

Pro Tip: If you find yourself still struggling with eye strain, consider using macOS's True Tone feature as well. This automatically adjusts the display based on ambient lighting to make your screen easier on the eyes.

6. Siri Shortcuts: Automate Tasks with Voice Commands

Siri has always been a useful assistant, but with **Siri Shortcuts**, you can now take it to the next level. Siri Shortcuts allow you to create custom voice commands for everyday tasks, from opening apps to sending texts, all with a simple voice prompt.

How to Set Up Siri Shortcuts

- **Create a Shortcut**: Open the **Shortcuts app** on your Mac, and you can start creating personalized shortcuts. Want Siri to open a specific app, adjust your system settings, or send a message to a friend? You can automate all that and more.

- **Run Multiple Actions**: Siri Shortcuts lets you chain multiple actions together into one shortcut. For example, you can create a shortcut that opens your favorite music app, adjusts the volume, and sets the mood lighting for you with a single command.

Pro Tip: You can even integrate Siri Shortcuts with Automator to run more complex workflows using just your voice.

Increasing Productivity with Multitasking on macOS M4 Pro

In today's fast-paced world, managing multiple tasks simultaneously is a crucial skill, especially if you're juggling work, personal projects, or even just managing different apps and windows. Thankfully, macOS offers several powerful multitasking features that make it easy to stay organized and productive, whether you're working on a creative project, analyzing data, or simply navigating through your daily tasks.

Let's dive into how you can maximize your productivity using macOS multitasking features, including **Split View**, **Mission Control**, and **Virtual Desktops**.

1. Split View: Organize Your Workspace Efficiently

Split View is one of macOS's most useful multitasking features. It allows you to view two applications side by side in full-screen mode, effectively doubling your screen real estate without the need to constantly switch between apps or windows. This is particularly useful when you need to compare documents, reference research while writing, or multitask between different apps without distractions.

How to Use Split View

1. **Activate Split View**:

    o Open the two apps or windows you want to use.

    o Hover your mouse over the green full-screen button in the upper-left corner of one of the windows.

    o Click and hold the green button until you see the window resize slightly.

    o Drag that window to the left or right side of the screen. The other app will automatically fill the other side.

2. **Adjust Split View**:

   o Once Split View is active, you can adjust the width of the windows by dragging the divider between the two apps.

   o You can easily swap the positions of the two apps by dragging one window to the opposite side.

3. **Exiting Split View**:

   o To exit Split View, simply click the green button again, and both apps will return to their regular size on the desktop. You can also swipe up using three fingers on your trackpad to return to the normal desktop view.

Tips for Using Split View Effectively:

- **Maximize Focus**: By using Split View, you reduce distractions because both apps are isolated in their own space. This is ideal for reading and writing or comparing two documents.

- **Ideal Pairings**: Split View works best when pairing apps that require constant attention, like email and calendar apps, or a web browser and a text editor.

- **App Shortcuts**: Use the keyboard shortcut Command + Tab to quickly switch between apps while in Split View for even faster multitasking.

2. Mission Control: Get a Bird's Eye View of Your Workspace

Mission Control offers a comprehensive overview of everything happening on your Mac. Whether you're managing multiple apps, documents, or browsing several tabs in Safari, Mission Control allows you to see all your open windows in one place. It's like a control center for your desktop that helps you stay organized.

How to Use Mission Control

1. **Access Mission Control**:

   o Swipe up on your trackpad with three fingers or press the **Mission Control** key (F3 on most Macs) to open Mission Control. This will show you all your open windows, apps, and desktops.

2. **Organize Windows**:

   o Mission Control allows you to quickly see which apps are open and where they are. You can drag and drop windows into different positions to organize them however you like.

   o You can also drag windows into **virtual desktops** (we'll talk more about that in a moment) or switch to a different desktop view without losing track of your workflow.

3. **Add New Spaces**:

   o At the top of the Mission Control screen, you'll see an option to add a new "Space." Spaces are essentially additional virtual

APPLE M4 PRO MAC MINI USER GUIDE

desktops where you can group apps and windows related to specific tasks.

- o To create a new Space, click the + button in the top-right corner of Mission Control. Once you've added a new Space, you can easily drag apps or windows into it for organization.

Tips for Using Mission Control Effectively:

- **Easily Switch Between Apps**: Mission Control allows you to quickly jump between different windows and apps, saving time and reducing the need to minimize and maximize individual windows.

- **Keep Your Desktop Clean**: Instead of having a cluttered desktop with dozens of windows, use Mission Control to tidy up your workspace by grouping apps by task. For example, all your research can go on one desktop, while your writing tools can go on another.

- **Focus on What Matters**: Use Mission Control to focus on specific tasks by creating a clean desktop with only the apps you need open. This minimizes distractions and helps you stay focused.

3. Virtual Desktops: Create Custom Workspaces

Virtual Desktops (also known as Spaces) let you set up multiple desktops on your Mac mini, each with its own set of apps and windows. This feature is especially useful when you want to separate work tasks from personal browsing or creative projects. You can switch between these desktops without having to minimize or close apps, making it easier to keep track of everything.

APPLE M4 PRO MAC MINI USER GUIDE

How to Use Virtual Desktops

1. **Add a New Virtual Desktop**:

   o Open **Mission Control** (swipe up with three fingers or press F3).

   o At the top of the Mission Control screen, you'll see a + sign in the right corner. Click it to add a new virtual desktop.

2. **Switch Between Desktops**:

   o You can easily switch between desktops by swiping left or right with three fingers on the trackpad. You can also use the Control + left/right arrow keyboard shortcut to switch between desktops.

   o If you have a full-screen app or Split View active, macOS will assign those apps to a new desktop automatically.

3. **Move Apps Between Desktops**:

   o While in Mission Control, drag and drop open windows or apps from one desktop to another. This lets you customize your workspace according to what you're working on at the time.

Tips for Using Virtual Desktops Effectively:

- **Separate Tasks by Desktops**: Use different desktops to organize your tasks. For instance, keep your work and personal apps on separate desktops, or use one desktop for research and another for writing or coding.

- **Quick Navigation**: You can swipe between your virtual desktops in an instant, making it easy to switch tasks without losing track of your progress.

- **Dedicated Spaces for Specific Projects**: If you're working on several projects at once, create a dedicated desktop for each. This helps you stay organized and ensures that each project has the space it needs.

4. Combining Split View, Mission Control, and Virtual Desktops

To truly optimize your productivity, combine these multitasking features. Here's how you can use them together for maximum efficiency:

A Workflow Example:

- **Step 1**: Use **Mission Control** to organize your workspace into multiple desktops. For example, create one desktop for email, another for research, and a third for writing.

- **Step 2**: Once you've set up your desktops, use **Split View** to maximize screen real estate within each desktop. For instance, you could have a browser and a note-taking app open side by side on your research desktop.

- **Step 3**: If you need to jump between desktops, use the **three-finger swipe** or **keyboard shortcut** to switch quickly without disrupting your workflow.

Managing Battery Life (for Portable Setups)

While the Apple M4 Pro Mac mini is primarily a desktop computer, you may be using it in more flexible, portable setups, perhaps with a mobile power source or external battery for situations like on-the-go video production, remote work, or testing in different environments. Although the Mac mini isn't designed with an internal battery like laptops, there are still ways to optimize the power consumption, particularly if you're running it in environments where power efficiency is key.

In this section, we'll go over practical steps to ensure your Mac mini stays energy-efficient, even if you're running it away from a fixed power supply, or simply looking to conserve energy while at home or the office.

1. Optimize Power Settings for Mac mini M4 Pro

The first thing you'll want to do is head into **System Preferences** and adjust your energy settings for the most efficient use of battery (or power source) if you're using a portable setup. Even though the Mac mini doesn't have a built-in battery, optimizing its power use when plugged into an external power source can still make a big difference in overall energy consumption.

Step-by-Step: Adjusting Energy Preferences

- Open **System Preferences** on your Mac mini.

- Click on **Battery**.

APPLE M4 PRO MAC MINI USER GUIDE

- You'll see options for **Battery** and **Power Adapter** (if using an external power source). Under the **Battery** section, make sure to enable **Low Power Mode** if it's available. This mode helps decrease the performance of the processor to save battery life.

- Under the **Power Adapter** section, uncheck options that keep your Mac mini running at full power when not in use (e.g., **"Prevent computer from sleeping automatically when the display is off"**).

By enabling **Low Power Mode** and modifying settings like **Display Sleep** (set to turn off the display after a few minutes of inactivity), your Mac mini will consume less energy, especially when not actively in use.

2. Screen Brightness and Display Settings

If you're using an external display in your portable setup, managing its brightness can make a big difference in power usage.

Practical Tips:

- **Lower Screen Brightness**: One of the most effective ways to save power is by reducing the brightness of your screen. Adjust the brightness through the **Display** preferences, or use the physical brightness buttons if your monitor supports it.

- **Auto-Brightness**: Many external monitors come with an auto-brightness feature that adjusts based on ambient lighting. Enabling this setting can help reduce the amount of power your display uses by dimming the screen when not needed.

- **Energy-Efficient Display Mode**: If your external monitor has an **Energy Saving** or **Eco Mode**, turn it on. This mode reduces the brightness and optimizes the screen for minimal power consumption.

3. Disable Unnecessary Background Apps and Processes

Your Mac mini's performance might be great, but sometimes it can work harder than necessary if you've got a bunch of background apps running. The more active processes, the more power is consumed, even if you don't realize it.

Steps to Reduce Background Activity:

- **Activity Monitor**: Open **Activity Monitor** from **Applications** > **Utilities** to check which apps are using the most CPU power. If you see apps running that you aren't actively using, quit them. Just right-click and select **Quit Process** or **Force Quit** to free up resources.

- **Manage Startup Items**: Some apps start automatically when your Mac mini boots up. You can disable these by going to **System Preferences** > **Users & Groups**, then click on **Login Items**. Remove unnecessary items that don't need to launch at startup.

- **Close Unused Tabs/Apps**: If you use apps like web browsers, be mindful of how many tabs are open. Browsers (especially with lots of tabs) can drain power quickly. Close tabs you don't need and reduce the number of apps running in the background.

4. Turn Off Unused Peripherals

When using your Mac mini in a portable setup, the peripherals connected to it can also draw power. If you're running on an external battery or limited power source, it's essential to minimize energy wastage.

Tips for Peripheral Management:

- **Disconnect Unnecessary Devices**: USB drives, printers, cameras, or external hard drives that aren't actively in use should be unplugged. These devices continue to draw power from your Mac mini, even if you're not using them.

- **Disable Bluetooth**: If you don't need to connect Bluetooth devices (like headphones, mouse, or keyboard), turn Bluetooth off. To do this, click the Bluetooth icon in the menu bar and choose **Turn Bluetooth Off**.

- **Disable Wi-Fi When Not Needed**: If you don't need an internet connection, disable Wi-Fi. While it's often necessary for work, turning it off when you're not actively using it can save power.

5. Sleep Mode and Energy Saving Features

Taking advantage of your Mac mini's **sleep mode** can help conserve power during idle times. Even though the Mac mini M4 Pro doesn't have a built-in battery, you can still use sleep settings to prevent the system from running at full power when it's not in use.

Configuring Sleep Mode:

- Go to **System Preferences** > **Battery** > **Battery**.

- Set your Mac mini to sleep after a certain period of inactivity (e.g., 10-15 minutes).

- You can also adjust the display sleep time separately under the **Display** tab to make sure the screen turns off when it's not being used.

Using Hot Corners:

If you often step away from your setup, **Hot Corners** is a useful feature to make your Mac mini sleep automatically when you move the mouse to a specific corner of the screen. To set this up:

- Go to **System Preferences** > **Desktop & Screen Saver** > **Screen Saver** > **Hot Corners**.

- Choose a corner to activate the sleep feature when the cursor touches it.

6. Software Updates and Maintenance

Though it's essential to keep your software up to date, constant updates can use more power, especially if the Mac mini is working harder to download and install them. Manage your update settings to minimize disruptions and avoid using unnecessary power.

Managing Updates for Battery Efficiency:

- **Update Preferences**: Under **System Preferences** > **Software Update**, ensure **Automatically keep my Mac up to date** is checked. This way, updates can be installed when the Mac mini is plugged into a power source, avoiding any battery drain during updates.

- **App Updates**: Consider using the **App Store** to keep apps up-to-date and schedule the updates during the night or when your Mac mini is plugged into a power source.

7. Using External Battery Packs (If Applicable)

If you are using an external battery pack to power your Mac mini for portable work, you'll want to ensure you're using it efficiently.

External Battery Tips:

- **Choose the Right Power Bank**: For Mac mini, you'll need a high-capacity battery with sufficient wattage (at least 100W or more). Power banks designed for laptops with high power delivery (PD) support are best for this.

- **Charge While Not in Use**: If you're planning on using an external power source, make sure to charge it fully while the Mac mini is idle, and then use it as needed. This helps preserve the battery pack's life and ensures it's ready when you need it.

8. Power Consumption Monitoring Tools

To track and fine-tune your energy usage, you can use third-party apps or built-in macOS tools to monitor your Mac mini's power consumption.

Tools for Power Monitoring:

- **iStat Menus**: This is a comprehensive system monitoring tool that gives you detailed stats on CPU, RAM, battery (for laptops), network, and power consumption. It can be handy for checking which processes are using the most power.

- **Activity Monitor**: As mentioned earlier, Activity Monitor is great for checking CPU usage, which can give you insights into how much power your system is consuming when running different processes.

9. Long-Term Battery Health Tips (For Portable Setup Usage)

Though the Mac mini doesn't come with an internal battery, if you are relying on an external power source, keeping that power source in good condition is key.

Maintaining Power Source Health:

- **Avoid Overcharging**: Don't leave your battery pack plugged in all the time. Like any rechargeable battery, it's good to allow it to discharge a bit between charges to preserve battery health.

- **Keep Your Battery Cool**: Extreme temperatures can affect the performance of your power bank. Keep it cool to prolong its lifespan.

- **Use Only Certified Power Accessories**: Always use high-quality, certified cables and power adapters to ensure efficient charging and avoid any power issues.

Quick Tips for Efficient Workflow on the Mac mini M4 Pro

The Apple M4 Pro Mac mini is a powerhouse, and when it's optimized for efficiency, it can become an essential tool in streamlining your workflow. Whether you're a creative professional, a software developer, or a busy professional juggling multiple tasks, the Mac mini's performance and customization options are here to make your life easier. Below are some practical tips for getting the most out of your Mac mini, along with a few third-party app recommendations and customizations that can elevate your productivity.

1. Master Keyboard Shortcuts for Speed

One of the quickest ways to speed up your work on the Mac mini is by mastering keyboard shortcuts. These tiny but powerful combos can help you navigate macOS Sequoia faster than you ever imagined. Here's a collection of shortcuts you should start using right away:

- **Command + Spacebar**: Open Spotlight Search – Your all-in-one search bar to quickly find files, apps, and even search the web.

- **Command + Tab**: Switch between open apps – No need to drag your mouse to the dock or the taskbar; this shortcut lets you jump between apps with ease.

- **Command + Option + Esc**: Force Quit apps – If an app becomes unresponsive, this is the fastest way to close it without rebooting the system.

- **Command + Shift + 4**: Screenshot – Capture any part of the screen. Add the **Control** key to save directly to the clipboard.

- **Control + D**: Duplicate files – Quickly duplicate files and folders in Finder.

By incorporating these shortcuts into your daily routine, you'll be able to complete repetitive tasks like switching apps, searching, and taking screenshots with much more speed and ease.

2. Use Mission Control to Manage Multiple Windows

Mission Control is one of the Mac's most underrated features when it comes to organizing your workspace. If you're juggling a lot of tasks or working across multiple projects, Mission Control can make navigating through open windows a breeze.

- **How to use Mission Control**: Swipe up with three fingers on your trackpad (or press **F3** on your keyboard). This will give you a bird's eye view of all your open windows. You can drag windows into new desktops or even create multiple virtual desktops for different tasks.

- **Create Desktops for Different Workflows**: You can set up dedicated desktops for different tasks. For example, have one desktop for writing, another for research, and another for design work. Switch between them with a simple swipe.

Mission Control helps you keep your digital workspace organized and accessible without feeling overwhelmed by open apps and files. This approach reduces distractions and improves focus by creating a clean, segmented workspace.

3. Optimize Your Dock for Quick Access

The Dock is a great place to store your most-used apps, but there are ways to make it even more efficient. Here's how you can tweak it to fit your workflow needs:

- **Add Folders to the Dock**: Drag folders into your Dock for quick access to frequently used files and folders. You can organize these into different categories, like "Work" or "Personal," and easily access them without searching through Finder.

- **Remove Unnecessary Apps**: If you don't use an app often, remove it from the Dock. A clutter-free Dock will allow you to focus on what matters most.

- **Use Stack Views**: If you want to keep a tidy desktop, use stacks in the Dock to group apps or folders. You can set it to "fan" view, "grid," or "list" for easier navigation.

Customizing your Dock can save you time and minimize the friction that comes with constantly opening apps and files. Make it work for you by only including what you truly need.

4. Automate Routine Tasks with Automator

The Automator app on macOS is a hidden gem that allows you to automate repetitive tasks. With Automator, you can set up workflows for everything from renaming files in bulk to resizing images, and even automating email responses. By using Automator, you can eliminate the need to manually repeat the same steps over and over again.

- **Create Custom Workflows**: Let's say you need to batch rename a set of images. With Automator, you can create a workflow that automatically renames all the files according to a naming convention you choose, all in one go.

- **Automate File Management**: Set up a workflow to automatically move files into specific folders after downloading or when a new file is added. This reduces the time spent on file organization.

You can access Automator via **Applications > Automator**. Don't worry if you're not a developer – Automator provides an easy drag-and-drop interface to create workflows, making it incredibly user-friendly.

APPLE M4 PRO MAC MINI USER GUIDE

5. Use Split View for Multi-Tasking

When you need to have two apps open side-by-side for easy multitasking, Split View is your best friend. This feature allows you to use two apps in a full-screen mode, without distractions.

- **How to Use Split View**: Hover your mouse over the green window maximize button in the upper-left corner of any app window. From there, select **Tile Window to Left of Screen** or **Tile Window to Right of Screen**. Then, select the second app to fill the other half of your screen.

- **Productivity Tip**: Split View is perfect when you need to compare documents, write notes while researching, or even drag-and-drop files between apps. The screen remains clean and free from the chaos of multiple windows.

Split View enhances focus by preventing you from jumping between apps. It's a small feature that saves a lot of time when you're trying to get multiple tasks done quickly.

6. Streamline Email Management with Clean Email Apps

If your email inbox is overwhelming, it's time to take control. Third-party apps can help manage your email and reduce clutter, allowing you to spend more time on actual work and less time sifting through spam or unnecessary threads.

- **Third-Party App Recommendation**: **CleanMyMac X** offers a feature to clean up your email inbox by unsubscribing from unwanted newsletters and organizing your inbox. It can help declutter by automatically identifying important emails and sorting them.

- **Another Option**: **Mailbutler** integrates with Apple Mail and provides tools like snooze, scheduled emails, and follow-up reminders, which can improve your email management efficiency.

By using a third-party app for email management, you can reduce the mental load of handling multiple threads and keep your inbox focused only on important communications.

7. Take Advantage of Third-Party Productivity Apps

The Mac mini M4 Pro is a beast when it comes to handling third-party apps, and there are some excellent tools that can make your workflow even more efficient. Here are a few that will make your life easier:

- **Trello**: For organizing tasks and projects. Trello's intuitive, board-based system is perfect for keeping track of multiple tasks or managing collaborative projects. It syncs across devices, so you're always in the loop.

- **Notion**: An all-in-one workspace for notes, tasks, wikis, and databases. Notion is incredibly flexible, allowing you to customize it to fit your workflow. Whether you're managing personal projects or collaborating with a team, Notion keeps everything organized in one place.

- **Fantastical**: An advanced calendar app that integrates with iCloud, Google, and other services. It has powerful features like natural

APPLE M4 PRO MAC MINI USER GUIDE

language processing, which allows you to input calendar events in a conversational way (e.g., "Meeting with John tomorrow at 3 PM").

8. Customize Trackpad and Mouse Settings for Precision

The Mac mini offers a ton of trackpad and mouse customization options that can improve your productivity. Adjusting the trackpad or mouse settings can enhance the precision of your interactions, saving you time and making you feel more in control.

- **Customize Trackpad Gestures**: In **System Preferences > Trackpad**, you can tweak gestures for more precise control. For example, set up three-finger swipes for switching between full-screen apps or four-finger pinches to bring up Mission Control. These small adjustments can speed up navigation.

- **Set Mouse Tracking Speed**: If you use a mouse, adjusting the tracking speed can make your movement smoother and more responsive, which reduces the time spent on click-and-drag tasks.

9. Use Cloud Storage for Effortless File Access

Keeping all your documents and files in cloud storage is not only safer, but it also makes it easier to access your files from anywhere and collaborate with others in real-time.

- **iCloud Drive**: For macOS users, iCloud Drive is the default cloud storage solution. Ensure iCloud is synced across all your devices to access files on the go.

- **Google Drive/Dropbox**: If you use Google Workspace or need more storage, services like Google Drive and Dropbox are also excellent for storing large files or collaborating on documents with others.

Syncing your documents to the cloud means you'll never lose them, and you'll always have access to them wherever you are.

FAQS

1. What should I do if my Mac mini won't turn on?

Answer:

First, make sure that your Mac mini is properly plugged into a power outlet. If it's plugged in, check the power cable for any visible damage. Hold down the power button for 10 seconds to perform a hard reset. If the Mac mini still doesn't power up, try connecting it to a different power source or outlet. If these steps don't work, it might be time to contact Apple Support for further troubleshooting.

2. How do I reset my Mac mini if it's frozen or unresponsive?

Answer:

If your Mac mini is unresponsive, try force quitting any apps that are stuck by pressing Cmd + Option + Esc. If that doesn't help, you can try restarting the computer by holding the power button for about 10 seconds until it shuts down. After that, turn it back on. If the problem persists, you can boot into macOS Recovery by restarting the Mac and holding Cmd + R during startup to reinstall macOS or troubleshoot with the Disk Utility.

3. Can I upgrade the RAM or storage on my Mac mini M4 Pro?

Answer:

Unfortunately, the RAM and storage in the Mac mini M4 Pro are soldered onto the motherboard, meaning they can't be upgraded after purchase. To ensure you get the best configuration for your needs, it's important to select the right amount of RAM and storage at the time of purchase. Apple offers various storage options ranging from 512GB to 8TB, and you can choose up to 64GB of unified memory.

---

4. How do I connect multiple monitors to my Mac mini M4 Pro?

Answer:

The Mac mini M4 Pro supports up to three 6K displays. To connect multiple monitors, simply plug your displays into the Thunderbolt 4 ports on the back of the Mac mini using the appropriate cables (USB-C to DisplayPort, USB-C to HDMI, etc.). Once connected, go to the **Apple Menu > System Preferences > Displays**, and you'll be able to arrange and configure the display settings for each monitor. You can adjust the resolution and arrangement of the monitors in the display settings.

5. Why is my Mac mini running slow, and how can I speed it up?

Answer:

If your Mac mini is running slow, there are a few things you can try:

- **Close unused apps**: Too many open apps can consume your system's resources. Try closing apps that you're not currently using.

- **Clear up storage space**: Use **Apple Menu > About This Mac > Storage** to check your disk usage. If your disk is almost full, deleting unnecessary files can improve performance.

- **Optimize startup items**: Go to **System Preferences > Users & Groups > Login Items** and remove unnecessary items that slow down startup.

- **Reset PRAM**: If the above steps don't work, reset your PRAM by restarting the Mac and holding down Option + Cmd + P + R during startup.

---

6. How do I connect my Bluetooth keyboard and mouse to my Mac mini?

Answer:

To connect a Bluetooth keyboard and mouse, make sure they are in pairing mode. Then, go to **Apple Menu > System Preferences > Bluetooth**, and you should see the devices listed there. Click **Connect** for each device, and you're all set! If you're having trouble, try turning off Bluetooth and then turning it back on. Also, ensure that your devices are within range of the Mac mini.

7. How can I improve the battery life on my Mac mini M4 Pro?

Answer:

The Mac mini M4 Pro doesn't have a battery since it's a desktop device. However, if you're using an external UPS (Uninterruptible Power Supply) to protect it from power surges, make sure that it's not overloaded and is providing consistent power. Also, ensure your energy preferences are set to reduce unnecessary power usage—go to **System Preferences > Battery** and adjust settings to save energy when the system is idle.

8. How can I back up my data on the Mac mini M4 Pro?

Answer:

You can use **Time Machine**, which is a built-in backup feature on macOS. To set it up, go to **Apple Menu > System Preferences > Time Machine**, and select an external drive as your backup disk. Time Machine will automatically back up your files every hour, and you can restore previous versions of documents if needed. If you prefer cloud backups, consider using iCloud Drive or third-party cloud services like Google Drive or Dropbox.

9. What do I do if my Mac mini is not recognizing external devices?

Answer:

If your Mac mini isn't recognizing external devices like printers, storage drives, or monitors, here are a few steps you can take:

1. Check the physical connections to ensure everything is plugged in correctly.

2. Test the devices with other computers to see if the issue is with the Mac mini or the device itself.

3. Restart your Mac mini and reconnect the devices.

4. Go to **System Preferences > Security & Privacy > Privacy** to make sure the device has the necessary permissions.

5. If using Thunderbolt or USB-C devices, make sure you're using certified cables and that the ports on both the device and Mac mini are clean and free of debris.

---

10. How do I reinstall macOS if something goes wrong?

Answer:

To reinstall macOS, restart your Mac mini and hold **Cmd + R** during startup to enter macOS Recovery. Once in Recovery Mode, choose **Reinstall macOS** from the utilities menu. Follow the on-screen instructions to reinstall the operating system. This will reinstall macOS without erasing your files, but it's always a good idea to back up your data before proceeding.

11. How can I update my Mac mini M4 Pro to the latest version of macOS?

Answer:

To ensure your Mac mini is running the latest version of macOS, go to **Apple Menu > System Preferences > Software Update**. If an update is available, you'll see an option to install it. You can also choose to have macOS update automatically by enabling the **Automatically keep my Mac up to date** option in the Software Update settings.

12. Can I use my Mac mini with a Windows PC monitor?

Answer:

Yes, you can use a Windows PC monitor with your Mac mini as long as it has compatible input ports (HDMI, DisplayPort, etc.). You may need a suitable adapter (USB-C to HDMI or USB-C to DisplayPort) depending on your monitor's input. Once connected, you can adjust the display settings via **System Preferences > Displays** to ensure the best resolution and performance.

13. How do I transfer data from my old Mac to the Mac mini M4 Pro?

Answer:

To transfer data from your old Mac, you can use **Migration Assistant**:

1. On your old Mac, open **Migration Assistant** (Applications > Utilities).

2. Select **To another Mac** and follow the on-screen instructions.

3. On your Mac mini, open Migration Assistant and select **From a Mac, Time Machine backup, or startup disk**.

4. Choose your old Mac from the list of available devices, and select the data you want to transfer. The process can take a while depending on the amount of data, so make sure both Macs are connected to the same network.

---

14. Why is my Mac mini running hot, and how can I cool it down?

Answer:

Mac minis are designed to stay cool, but if it's running hot, it could be due to heavy workloads or environmental factors:

1. Ensure the Mac mini is placed in a well-ventilated area to prevent overheating.

2. Check if any processes are consuming too much CPU using **Activity Monitor** (Applications > Utilities).

3. Try closing unnecessary apps or restart the Mac mini to free up system resources.

4. If you're running intensive tasks (like video rendering or 3D modeling), consider using an external cooling pad or fan.

If the issue persists, it may be worth checking with Apple Support for hardware inspection.

---

15. How can I use my Mac mini with a TV instead of a traditional monitor?

Answer:

You can connect your Mac mini to a TV using the HDMI port. Here's how:

1. Connect an HDMI cable from your Mac mini to the TV.

2. Make sure the TV is set to the correct HDMI input.

3. Once connected, go to **System Preferences > Displays**, and you can adjust the display settings like resolution and arrangement to suit your needs.

4. You may also want to adjust the sound settings in **System Preferences > Sound** to output audio through the TV.

16. How do I use macOS Sequoia on a dual boot with Windows?

Answer:

You can set up dual boot on your Mac mini with **Boot Camp** to run Windows alongside macOS Sequoia:

1. Go to **Applications > Utilities** and open **Boot Camp Assistant**.

2. Follow the on-screen instructions to create a partition for Windows.

3. Install Windows from an ISO file, following the prompts in Boot Camp Assistant.

4. After installation, you'll have the option to choose between macOS and Windows when you restart your Mac mini.

Note that dual booting requires a valid Windows license, and you may need to install additional drivers for compatibility.

---

17. How do I use Siri on my Mac mini M4 Pro?

Answer:

To use Siri, ensure your Mac mini has a microphone (built-in or external). Here's how to activate Siri:

1. Go to **System Preferences > Siri**.

2. Check the box next to **Enable Ask Siri**.

3. Optionally, select a shortcut for Siri or use the keyboard shortcut (Cmd + Space) to activate Siri.

4. You can ask Siri to open apps, search the web, set reminders, control smart home devices, and much more.

If Siri is not responding, ensure that your internet connection is working, as Siri requires it to process requests.

---

18. Can I use a Mac mini with external speakers or sound systems?

Answer:

Yes, the Mac mini M4 Pro supports external audio systems via its audio output ports. You can connect speakers or sound systems through the following options:

1. **Headphone Jack (3.5mm)**: Connect external speakers or headphones directly to the headphone jack.

2. **Bluetooth**: Pair Bluetooth speakers or headphones by going to **System Preferences > Bluetooth** and selecting your device.

3. **USB or HDMI Audio**: If your speakers support USB or HDMI audio input, you can use the respective ports to connect.

To manage audio output, go to **System Preferences > Sound** and select your desired output device.

19. How do I restore my Mac mini from a Time Machine backup?

Answer:

Restoring your Mac mini from a Time Machine backup is easy:

1. Restart your Mac mini and hold Cmd + R during startup to enter **macOS Recovery**.

2. Select **Restore from Time Machine Backup** and click **Continue**.

3. Choose the Time Machine backup disk and select the date and time of the backup you want to restore from.

4. Follow the on-screen prompts to complete the restoration process.

Ensure that your Time Machine backup disk is connected to the Mac mini during the restoration.

---

20. Can I use my Mac mini M4 Pro with a gaming console like Xbox or PlayStation?

Answer:

While the Mac mini M4 Pro is not designed to directly connect with gaming consoles like Xbox or PlayStation, you can stream games from your console to the Mac mini:

1. For Xbox, you can use the **Xbox app for macOS** (available from the Microsoft Store) to stream your Xbox console games to your Mac.

2. For PlayStation, you can use **PS Remote Play** on macOS to stream games from your PlayStation console.

Alternatively, you can connect the Mac mini to a TV or monitor via HDMI and use a game controller to play games on the Mac mini.

---

21. How do I update my apps on the Mac mini?

Answer:

To keep your apps up to date on the Mac mini:

1. Open the **App Store** from the Dock or **Applications** folder.

2. Click the **Updates** tab at the top of the App Store window.

3. If there are updates available for any of your installed apps, click **Update All** or select individual updates.

You can also set apps to update automatically by going to **System Preferences > App Store** and checking **Automatically check for updates**.

---

22. How can I improve the security of my Mac mini M4 Pro?

Answer:

To enhance the security of your Mac mini:

1. **Enable FileVault**: Go to **System Preferences > Security & Privacy > FileVault** to encrypt your hard drive and protect your data.

2. **Use a Strong Password**: Set a strong password in **System Preferences > Users & Groups**.

3. **Enable Two-Factor Authentication**: Use Apple's two-factor authentication for your Apple ID to add an extra layer of security.

4. **Set Up a Firewall**: Go to **System Preferences > Security & Privacy > Firewall** to enable the firewall to block unauthorized connections.

5. **Keep Software Up to Date**: Regularly update macOS and apps to ensure security patches are applied.

---

23. How do I set up an external SSD with my Mac mini M4 Pro?

Answer:

Setting up an external SSD is easy:

1. Plug the external SSD into one of the Thunderbolt or USB-C ports on your Mac mini.

2. If the drive is new, macOS will prompt you to format it. Use **Disk Utility** to format the SSD (choose **APFS** or **Mac OS Extended** depending on your needs).

3. After formatting, you can use the SSD for storage, Time Machine backups, or installing apps.

Make sure to safely eject the SSD by dragging it to the Trash or using **Finder** before unplugging it.

---

24. Can I use my Mac mini for video editing or 3D rendering?

Answer:

Absolutely! The Mac mini M4 Pro, with its powerful M4 Pro chip and 20-core GPU, is well-suited for video editing and 3D rendering. You can run professional software like **Final Cut Pro**, **Adobe Premiere Pro**, or **Blender** with ease. The GPU acceleration and powerful processor will make handling high-definition videos and 3D graphics fast and efficient.

For the best experience, ensure your system is optimized (e.g., freeing up storage space and closing unnecessary apps) to handle demanding tasks.

Final Thoughts: These FAQs cover a range of common concerns that Mac mini M4 Pro users might encounter. The answers are designed to be simple and approachable for readers of all technical levels, ensuring that the guide feels helpful and humanized. With this section, readers should feel more confident troubleshooting and understanding their Mac mini setup.

ADDITIONAL RESOURCES

Recommended Software and Apps for Mac mini M4 Pro

The **Mac mini M4 Pro** is an incredibly powerful machine, capable of handling everything from professional video editing to intense software development. But to make the most out of your Mac mini, you'll need the right software. Below, I've curated a list of **essential apps** across different use cases—productivity, creative work, software development, and system utilities—to help you get the most out of your Mac mini M4 Pro.

1. Productivity Tools

For getting work done efficiently, your Mac mini needs reliable productivity tools. These apps will help you manage time, tasks, and communications effortlessly.

Microsoft Office 365

One of the top productivity suites in the world, **Microsoft Office 365** offers powerful tools like Word, Excel, PowerPoint, and Outlook. Whether you're writing reports, crunching numbers, or creating presentations, these tools provide everything you need. The cloud integration allows you to access files from anywhere, and if you're working within a team, real-time collaboration is a breeze.

- **Key Features**: Document editing, spreadsheets, presentations, email management, and cloud storage via OneDrive.

- **Ideal For**: Business professionals, students, and anyone looking for comprehensive productivity tools.

Notion

If you're someone who thrives on organizing ideas, projects, and tasks, **Notion** is the perfect tool. This all-in-one workspace allows you to take notes, manage tasks, track projects, and create databases—all within a sleek, easy-to-use interface. The best part? It's highly customizable to fit your workflow.

- **Key Features**: Note-taking, task management, knowledge base, and customizable templates.

- **Ideal For**: Students, project managers, and anyone who needs a flexible, powerful organizational tool.

Trello

For team collaboration and project management, **Trello** is a simple but powerful app. It uses a card-and-board system that makes it easy to track tasks and progress. You can assign tasks, set due dates, and attach files, all while keeping your team up to speed.

- **Key Features**: Visual project management, task assignment, due dates, file sharing.

APPLE M4 PRO MAC MINI USER GUIDE

- **Ideal For**: Teams, freelancers, and anyone managing collaborative projects.

Slack

Communication is key when working remotely or with teams. **Slack** offers a platform for instant messaging, file sharing, and channel-based collaboration. It integrates with a wide variety of apps, so you can bring everything into one place.

- **Key Features**: Real-time messaging, file sharing, integration with external tools, channel-based collaboration.
- **Ideal For**: Remote teams, businesses, and freelancers.

2. Creative Software

The **Mac mini M4 Pro** is an excellent machine for creatives, thanks to its powerful M4 Pro chip, which is ideal for tasks like video editing, photo manipulation, and graphic design. Here are some must-have apps for all things creative.

Adobe Creative Cloud

If you're serious about graphic design, video editing, or photography, **Adobe Creative Cloud** is a must-have suite of tools. With apps like **Photoshop**, **Illustrator**, **Premiere Pro**, and **After Effects**, you have access to everything you need to produce high-quality content.

- **Key Features**: Image editing, video editing, motion graphics, photo manipulation, cloud storage.

- **Ideal For**: Graphic designers, video editors, photographers, and content creators.

Final Cut Pro

As a **Mac mini M4 Pro** user, you're going to love **Final Cut Pro** for video editing. It's a professional-grade video editing software with a sleek, intuitive interface and advanced features like magnetic timeline and multi-camera editing. Plus, it's optimized to run smoothly on the Mac mini's powerful M4 Pro chip.

- **Key Features**: Professional video editing, multi-camera editing, advanced color grading, optimized for macOS.

- **Ideal For**: Professional video editors, filmmakers, content creators.

Affinity Designer

If you're looking for a more affordable, yet powerful alternative to Adobe Illustrator, **Affinity Designer** is a great choice. It's perfect for vector graphics, whether you're designing logos, illustrations, or UI/UX elements.

- **Key Features**: Vector design tools, pixel-perfect drawing, multi-platform support, seamless switching between vector and raster.

- **Ideal For**: Graphic designers, illustrators, and UI/UX designers.

DaVinci Resolve

DaVinci Resolve is a free (and paid) professional video editing software known for its powerful color grading tools and high-end editing capabilities.

If you're serious about producing cinematic-quality videos, DaVinci Resolve is the app to use.

- **Key Features**: Video editing, color correction, visual effects, audio post-production, optimized for powerful hardware like the Mac mini.

- **Ideal For**: Professional video editors, colorists, and filmmakers.

3. Development Environments

The **Mac mini M4 Pro** is a fantastic choice for developers, whether you're building websites, apps, or working with data. The performance of the M4 Pro chip, combined with macOS's Unix-based system, makes it a perfect environment for development.

Xcode

If you're developing for the Apple ecosystem (iOS, macOS, watchOS, or tvOS), **Xcode** is the integrated development environment (IDE) you need. It includes everything from a code editor to an iOS simulator, and it's fully optimized for the Mac mini's M4 Pro chip, so you can expect fast performance during code compiling and testing.

- **Key Features**: Swift programming, iOS and macOS app development, simulator, debugging tools.

- **Ideal For**: iOS/macOS developers, app creators.

Visual Studio Code

For web and software developers, **Visual Studio Code** (VS Code) is a lightweight yet powerful code editor. With an extensive library of extensions, VS Code supports almost any language you can think of, including JavaScript, Python, Ruby, and more. It also integrates well with Git and other version control systems.

- **Key Features**: Syntax highlighting, Git integration, customizable themes and extensions, debugging.

- **Ideal For**: Web developers, Python programmers, software engineers.

Docker

If you're working with containerization, **Docker** is a tool that simplifies deploying, testing, and managing applications in containers. It allows developers to build software in isolated environments, making it easier to manage dependencies and avoid conflicts.

- **Key Features**: Containerization, deployment automation, version control, multi-platform support.

- **Ideal For**: DevOps engineers, backend developers, and anyone building scalable software applications.

Homebrew

For developers who love command-line tools, **Homebrew** is the essential package manager for macOS. It allows you to easily install, manage, and update software libraries directly from the terminal. Homebrew is especially

APPLE M4 PRO MAC MINI USER GUIDE

useful for managing development environments like Node.js, Python, or Ruby.

- **Key Features**: Command-line installation, package management, easy-to-use.

- **Ideal For**: Developers, especially those working with multiple programming languages and tools.

4. System Utilities

To ensure your Mac mini M4 Pro is running at peak performance, system utilities are essential. These apps help you monitor system health, optimize storage, and keep everything running smoothly.

CleanMyMac X

CleanMyMac X is one of the best tools for keeping your Mac mini in top shape. It helps clean out system junk, cache files, and outdated apps. It also monitors your system's health and offers recommendations for boosting performance, whether that's freeing up disk space or optimizing memory usage.

- **Key Features**: System cleanup, performance monitoring, privacy protection, malware removal.

- **Ideal For**: Anyone looking to keep their system clean and optimized.

Disk Drill

For data recovery and disk management, **Disk Drill** is a powerful tool that can recover lost files and manage disk space. If you've accidentally deleted important files or need to perform disk diagnostics, this app is invaluable.

- **Key Features**: Data recovery, disk management, file scanning, partition repair.

- **Ideal For**: Those looking to recover lost data or optimize storage.

Magnet

Mac users love **Magnet** for window management. It allows you to quickly organize and snap your windows into different positions on your screen, making multitasking much easier. Whether you're working on multiple documents or monitoring different apps, this app will keep things organized.

- **Key Features**: Window snapping, multiple workspace management, customizable keyboard shortcuts.

- **Ideal For**: Power users, multitaskers, anyone with a dual or multi-monitor setup.

iStat Menus

If you want to closely monitor your Mac mini's system health, **iStat Menus** is a must-have tool. It provides real-time information on CPU usage, memory, disk activity, temperature, and more. This allows you to quickly spot any performance bottlenecks and ensure your system is running smoothly.

APPLE M4 PRO MAC MINI USER GUIDE

- **Key Features**: System monitoring, CPU and memory stats, real-time data display.

- **Ideal For**: Power users, developers, and anyone needing detailed system insights.

Getting the Most from Apple Services (iCloud, Apple Music, Apple TV+, and iMessage)

Apple offers a suite of interconnected services that help users maximize the value of their Apple devices, including the Mac mini M4 Pro. Whether you're looking to store your data securely in the cloud, enjoy seamless entertainment, or communicate with others, Apple services make it easy to integrate all aspects of your digital life. In this section, we'll guide you through how to set up and get the most out of Apple's services, such as iCloud, Apple Music, Apple TV+, and iMessage.

1. iCloud: Keeping Your Data in Sync Across All Your Devices

iCloud is Apple's cloud storage and cloud computing service, designed to keep your data synchronized across all your Apple devices. It stores your photos, files, apps, and more in the cloud, so you can access them wherever you go. The beauty of iCloud lies in its seamless integration across your devices, including the Mac mini, iPhone, iPad, and even Windows PCs.

Setting Up iCloud

To get started with iCloud on your Mac mini M4 Pro:

1. **Sign In to iCloud**: Click on the **Apple menu** (☐) in the top-left corner and select **System Preferences**. Then click **Apple ID**. If you're not signed in, enter your Apple ID and password to sign in. If you don't have an Apple ID yet, you can create one right from this screen.

2. **iCloud Settings**: Once logged in, you'll see a list of iCloud services. You can select which services to enable, including **iCloud Drive**, **Photos**, **Mail**, **Contacts**, **Calendars**, **Notes**, **Safari**, and more. Choose what fits your needs, and everything will sync across all your Apple devices.

3. **iCloud Drive**: This feature allows you to store documents, app data, and other important files in the cloud, making them accessible from any device. To enable iCloud Drive, simply check the box next to **iCloud Drive** in the Apple ID settings. You can also manage iCloud storage here and buy additional space if needed.

Benefits of iCloud

- **Automatic Backup**: iCloud automatically backs up your Mac mini, iPhone, and iPad, so you never have to worry about losing your data.

- **Cross-Device Sync**: Whether you're working on a document on your Mac mini or taking a photo on your iPhone, iCloud ensures everything is synced across your devices in real-time.

- **Find My**: If your device gets lost, iCloud's **Find My** feature can help you track it. This also works with Apple AirTags for tracking physical items like keys or bags.

- **Shared Folders**: You can share files and folders with others via iCloud Drive, making it perfect for collaboration and sharing important documents or photos.

2. Apple Music: Access to Millions of Songs, Playlists, and More

Apple Music is one of the leading music streaming services, offering access to a vast library of songs, curated playlists, exclusive content, and radio stations. It integrates seamlessly with the Mac mini, iPhone, and other Apple devices, allowing you to enjoy music wherever you go.

Setting Up Apple Music

1. **Sign In**: Open the **Music** app on your Mac mini. If you already have an Apple ID, sign in with it to access your account. If not, you can sign up for Apple Music directly through the app or website.

2. **Choose Your Plan**: Apple Music offers several subscription plans:

   o **Individual Plan**: Access to all features for one person.

   o **Family Plan**: Share your Apple Music subscription with up to six family members.

   o **Student Plan**: A discounted plan for students.

3. **Creating Playlists and Exploring Music**: After signing in, you can explore the library, create personalized playlists, and discover curated recommendations. You can also follow your favorite artists, so you're always updated with their latest releases.

4. **Offline Listening**: With Apple Music, you can download your favorite albums and playlists for offline listening, ensuring you have your music even when you're not connected to the internet.

Benefits of Apple Music

- **Huge Library**: Apple Music offers over 75 million songs, making it one of the largest music libraries available. You can find just about anything, from new hits to classic albums.

- **Curated Playlists**: Whether you're into pop, rock, classical, or niche genres, Apple Music provides curated playlists designed to match your mood or activity. Playlists like **"New Music Mix"**, **"Favorites Mix"**, and **"Chill Mix"** are updated weekly to keep your music fresh.

- **Live Radio and Podcasts**: Apple Music also offers live radio stations, including **Beats 1**, where you can listen to exclusive shows from famous DJs and artists. The podcast library is extensive, so you can stay up to date with the latest shows.

- **Music Sharing**: With the Family Plan, you can share your playlists, albums, and music with your family members, allowing everyone to enjoy their favorite tunes on their own devices.

3. Apple TV+: Streaming High-Quality Original Content

Apple TV+ is Apple's premium video streaming service, offering exclusive, original content that you can't find anywhere else. From award-winning series and movies to thought-provoking documentaries, Apple TV+ provides a new and exciting way to enjoy entertainment on your Mac mini M4 Pro.

Setting Up Apple TV+

1. **Sign In**: Open the **TV** app on your Mac mini, and sign in with your Apple ID. If you don't have a subscription to Apple TV+, you can sign up directly from the app or website.

2. **Choose Your Plan**: Apple TV+ offers a **monthly subscription**. If you've recently purchased a new Apple device (like the Mac mini M4 Pro), you may be eligible for a **free trial** that lasts up to three months.

3. **Explore Content**: Once signed in, you can browse the Apple TV+ library, which includes a wide variety of shows, movies, and documentaries. Apple's original content includes exclusive series like **Ted Lasso**, **The Morning Show**, and **Greyhound**. You can also download movies and shows to watch offline.

Benefits of Apple TV+

- **Exclusive Content**: Apple TV+ is home to award-winning original content from some of Hollywood's top talent. The service continually adds new movies and shows, ensuring there's always something fresh to watch.

- **4K HDR Streaming**: Enjoy your favorite shows and movies in **4K resolution** with **HDR** for stunning visual quality, making it a great choice for viewers who want high-quality streaming.

- **Share with Family**: With a Family Plan, you can share your Apple TV+ subscription with up to six family members, giving everyone access to the content they want.

- **Offline Viewing**: Download your favorite shows and movies to watch offline when you're on the go.

4. iMessage: Easy and Secure Messaging Across Devices

iMessage is Apple's messaging platform, allowing you to send text messages, photos, videos, and more, all encrypted for security. iMessage works seamlessly across your Mac mini M4 Pro, iPhone, iPad, and even Apple Watch, ensuring you stay connected with friends, family, and colleagues.

Setting Up iMessage

1. **Sign In with Apple ID**: Open the **Messages** app on your Mac mini. If you're not already signed in, enter your Apple ID and password to start using iMessage.

2. **Sync Across Devices**: After signing in, your messages will sync across all devices that are signed in with the same Apple ID. You can send and receive messages from your iPhone, iPad, and Mac mini without any issues.

3. **Send Messages**: To send a message, simply click on the **New Message** button in the Messages app, enter the recipient's name or phone number, and start typing. You can also send media, such as images and videos, directly from your Mac mini.

Benefits of iMessage

- **Rich Messaging**: iMessage allows you to send text, photos, videos, voice messages, and even documents. You can also send **memojis**, stickers, and other fun media to personalize your conversations.

- **End-to-End Encryption**: Apple ensures your messages are private with end-to-end encryption, meaning only you and the recipient can read your messages.

- **Cross-Device Sync**: iMessage seamlessly syncs your messages across all Apple devices. Whether you start a conversation on your iPhone or Mac mini, you can continue it seamlessly on any other Apple device.

- **Group Chats**: iMessage supports group chats, so you can stay in touch with family, friends, or coworkers easily. You can share photos, videos, and locations, all within a single conversation.

CONCLUSION

Final Thoughts on Your Mac mini M4 Pro Experience

As you reach the end of this guide, it's time to reflect on what the **Apple Mac mini M4 Pro** can truly offer you. Whether you're a creative professional, a software developer, or just someone who wants a reliable and powerful machine for everyday tasks, this desktop has the potential to be a game-changer. The **M4 Pro** chip, combined with its compact and sleek design, makes it more than just a computer – it becomes a tool that can enhance your productivity, elevate your creative projects, and seamlessly integrate into your workflow.

Transforming Your Workflow

The first thing you'll likely notice when using the Mac mini M4 Pro is how quickly it adapts to your needs. Thanks to its powerful M4 Pro chip and optimized macOS Sequoia, you'll experience incredibly fast processing speeds and smooth multitasking. Imagine jumping between tasks with ease, whether you're editing a 4K video, compiling code, or running multiple virtual machines. The **14-core CPU** ensures that even the most intensive processes won't slow you down, allowing you to be more efficient and accomplish more in less time.

The **unified memory** system also plays a big role in ensuring that your Mac mini feels responsive and quick. Instead of dealing with lag or slowdowns, everything you do—from opening applications to working with large files—will feel seamless. Your Mac mini can handle multiple apps open at once, effortlessly switching between projects, so you're always in the flow.

With the Mac mini M4 Pro, you're no longer tied down by slow performance or cumbersome hardware. It's the kind of computer that frees you up to do more, without worrying about whether your machine can keep up. Whether you're a designer, engineer, or entrepreneur, this device can help you break free from limitations and focus on what truly matters—your work.

Enhancing Your Productivity

What truly sets the **Mac mini M4 Pro** apart is its ability to seamlessly enhance your productivity. From the moment you turn it on, the machine is designed to help you stay focused and get things done quickly. With its robust multi-core performance, you'll be able to complete tasks faster, and even when you're working on demanding projects, you won't experience significant delays.

The intuitive design of **macOS Sequoia** also ensures that everything you need is just a few clicks away. Whether you're organizing files in Finder, setting up your ideal workspace with multiple displays, or using Siri to complete tasks hands-free, the Mac mini integrates smoothly into your workflow. It's a device that works the way you do, and that's what helps you get more done.

In addition, the Mac mini M4 Pro offers an impressive selection of connectivity options. From **Thunderbolt 5 ports** to **HDMI**, you can easily connect your favorite peripherals, displays, and other devices, all without any hassle. Whether you're a photographer, video editor, or software developer, you'll find that this device is equipped with the ports and capabilities needed to expand your workspace and maximize your workflow.

Another aspect that enhances productivity is its energy efficiency. The Mac mini consumes less power than traditional desktop computers, allowing you to work for longer periods without worrying about overheating or high energy bills. Plus, its compact form factor means you can keep your workspace neat and organized, no matter how many devices you need to connect.

Meeting Your Professional and Creative Needs

When it comes to meeting professional and creative needs, the **Mac mini M4 Pro** is ready to rise to the challenge. For creatives, it's a powerhouse capable of handling heavy-duty tasks like **3D rendering, video editing, and digital art creation**. The 20-core GPU is a game-changer, ensuring that your projects are rendered in high definition with incredible speed. You won't be waiting for hours to finish rendering your latest video or animation; instead, the Mac mini's incredible GPU performance ensures that you can focus on the creative process rather than the technical limitations of your hardware.

For professionals in fields like **software development**, the Mac mini M4 Pro offers unmatched performance for compiling code, running multiple virtual machines, and testing software in real-time. With its multiple Thunderbolt 5 ports, you can connect to fast storage devices, external GPUs, and multiple monitors for an expansive and efficient development environment.

If you're someone who works with large datasets, whether for **data analysis, machine learning**, or **AI development**, the Mac mini M4 Pro provides ample resources to handle even the most demanding workloads. With the power of the M4 Pro chip, data processing becomes faster and smoother, allowing you to run multiple simulations or work on high-performance applications without worrying about performance bottlenecks.

For **entrepreneurs** or anyone with a busy digital life, the Mac mini M4 Pro helps streamline everything. Its **fast boot times** and **reliable performance** ensure that you're always ready to tackle the day. From keeping track of your calendar and emails to managing your business apps and documents, the Mac mini M4 Pro makes managing multiple tasks feel effortless.

Making the Most of Your Mac mini M4 Pro

With this guide, you now have everything you need to make the most out of your Mac mini M4 Pro. We've covered how to set it up, optimize its performance, and configure it to meet your unique needs. Whether you're just getting started or you're already well into your journey with your new Mac mini, this guide will serve as a go-to resource to help you navigate the powerful features of the Mac mini and unlock its full potential.

Rest assured, as you continue exploring and working with your Mac mini M4 Pro, you'll find new ways to streamline your workflow and increase your productivity. The Mac mini isn't just a computer; it's a tool designed to empower you to accomplish more, express your creativity, and achieve professional success. The more you use it, the more you'll realize just how indispensable it becomes to your daily routine.

The Mac mini M4 Pro isn't just about specs and features; it's about how those features come together to help you be the best version of yourself, whether in your career, creative pursuits, or personal projects. You now have a machine that can keep up with your ambition and help you reach new heights.

So, as you continue working with your Mac mini M4 Pro, remember that you have the power to transform your work, enhance your creativity, and take your productivity to the next level. With this guide at your side, you're all set to make the most out of your Mac mini M4 Pro and achieve things you never thought possible.

Join the Mac mini Community

The Apple Mac mini M4 Pro isn't just a cutting-edge piece of hardware; it's part of a vibrant, ever-growing ecosystem of users, creators, and tech enthusiasts who share a passion for maximizing the potential of their machines. Whether you've just unboxed your Mac mini or you're a seasoned

APPLE M4 PRO MAC MINI USER GUIDE

user looking for fresh insights, there's an immense community of people who are eager to connect, share experiences, and help each other grow. Becoming part of the Mac mini community is more than just a way to troubleshoot; it's an opportunity to learn new things, get inspiration, and be a part of something bigger.

Why Should You Join the Mac mini Community?

When you join a community of like-minded individuals, you open the door to a wealth of knowledge and support that can make your experience with the Mac mini M4 Pro even better. Here's why it's worth getting involved:

1. **Access to Expertise**:

   The Mac mini community is filled with experienced users—developers, creatives, engineers, and everyday professionals—who have spent countless hours learning about the ins and outs of their machines. By joining forums and discussion groups, you can tap into their knowledge. Whether it's a technical issue or a best practice for optimizing performance, the community is full of people eager to help.

2. **Get Help with Troubleshooting**:

   Everyone runs into issues at some point. Whether your Mac mini isn't performing as expected, you're having trouble with macOS features, or you just need advice on how to set up an app or connect peripherals, the community is a great place to find solutions. Experienced users and Apple experts often share tips, tricks, and solutions that can save you hours of frustration. Chances are, if you're having an issue, someone else has already dealt with it—and they'll be happy to guide you toward the solution.

3. **Discover New Tips, Tricks, and Workflows**: One of the best things about being in a community is the constant exchange of ideas. You can discover new shortcuts, software recommendations, and workflows that can help you use your Mac mini in ways you never thought of. Whether you're into video editing, gaming, music production, or software development, the community members will likely have suggestions that can improve your efficiency and creativity.

4. **Stay Updated on macOS Changes and Upgrades**: Apple frequently rolls out updates to macOS, and staying on top of the latest changes can help you get the most out of your Mac mini. Being part of the Mac mini community means you're always in the loop. When a new feature is released or a major update hits, community members are quick to discuss its impact, share their experiences, and offer advice on how to best utilize these changes.

5. **Build Your Network**:
The Mac mini community isn't just about troubleshooting and tips—it's also about building relationships. You can connect with people who share your professional interests or creative passions, whether you're a content creator, developer, designer, or business professional. Networking with others in the community can lead to

collaborations, new job opportunities, or simply forging friendships with people who share your interests.

6. **Inspiration   from   Fellow   Users**: Seeing how others use their Mac mini M4 Pro can be a huge source of inspiration. From unique setups to innovative projects, the Mac mini community is full of people pushing the limits of what the Mac mini can do. Whether it's someone developing a groundbreaking app, creating stunning digital art, or editing a feature film, their work can inspire you to explore new possibilities with your own Mac mini.

7. **Share   Your   Own   Experience**: The community is not just about receiving help; it's also about contributing. By sharing your experiences, whether it's solving a tricky problem, showing off your latest project, or simply offering advice, you can help others in the community. Sharing your journey—your successes and challenges—can be incredibly rewarding. Plus, it's a great way to build a reputation as a helpful, engaged member of the community.

Where Can You Join the Mac mini Community?

Now that we've covered why you should join the community, let's explore where you can connect with fellow Mac mini M4 Pro users. Whether you prefer online forums, social media groups, or dedicated Apple platforms, there are plenty of ways to get involved.

1. **Apple's Official Support Communities**

   Apple's own support forums are a great place to start. Here, you can engage with other Mac mini users, ask questions, and find troubleshooting guides for common issues. Apple support specialists occasionally participate in the discussions, offering official answers and insights into solving problems.

   Where to find it: Apple Support Communities

2. **Reddit**

   If you're a fan of forums, Reddit has some fantastic communities where you can join discussions with Mac mini users. Subreddits like r/macmini and r/apple are filled with discussions about everything from setup tips to troubleshooting. The best part? You can ask specific questions and get responses from users all over the world, some of whom have expertise in specialized areas like app development or video production.

   Where to find it: r/macmini | r/apple

3. **Facebook Groups**

   Facebook has several groups dedicated to Mac users, including those specifically for the Mac mini. These groups are often quite active, with members posting about their setups, sharing advice, and offering recommendations for software and hardware. It's also a place to find user reviews of new updates or peripherals, as people often post their experiences with different setups.

APPLE M4 PRO MAC MINI USER GUIDE

Where to find it: Search for "Mac mini groups" on Facebook to find relevant communities.

4. **Discord Servers**

   For those who prefer real-time chat, Discord has several Mac mini-focused servers where users gather to discuss their Macs. These are great places to interact with people instantly, ask quick questions, and participate in live chats about the latest macOS updates, hardware modifications, or creative workflows.

   Where to find it: Search for Mac-related Discord communities or look for invites in forums like Reddit.

5. **Mac   User   Blogs   and   YouTube   Channels**

   Another excellent way to engage with the community is by following influential Mac mini users through blogs and YouTube channels. Many content creators offer reviews, tutorials, and tips for getting the most out of your Mac mini. You can often engage with the creators by commenting on their posts or videos, and you may find yourself interacting with other viewers who share similar interests.

A FINAL NOTE OF THANKS

Dear Reader,

Thank you for choosing this guide to help you unlock the full potential of your Apple M4 Pro Mac mini! We hope that the step-by-step instructions, tips, and troubleshooting advice have empowered you to make the most of your device and transform the way you work, create, and connect.

Your experience matters, and we would love to hear your thoughts on this guide. Your feedback is incredibly valuable not only to us but to future readers who are looking for a reliable resource to help them navigate their Mac mini journey. If you found this guide helpful, please take a moment to leave a feedback

Your feedback helps others discover this book and ensures that we can continue providing high-quality, user-friendly content. Whether it's a compliment or constructive feedback, every word you share helps us grow and improve.

Thank you once again for your trust and support. We hope your Mac mini M4 Pro serves you well for many years to come, and that you continue to explore all the possibilities it has to offer!

www.ingramcontent.com/pod-product-compliance
Lightning Source LLC
LaVergne TN
LVHW081513050326
832903LV00025B/1476

9798281481724